KITCHEN LIGHT CHOREOGRAPHY

A COLLECTION OF LOWER-FAT RECIPES TO BENEFIT CLEVELAND BALLET

©1994, Cleveland Ballet Council.

First published in 1994 by Cleveland Ballet Council,
One Playhouse Square, Suite 330,
1375 Euclid Avenue, Cleveland, Ohio 44115

Edited and indexed by Janis L. McLaughlin
Cover and illustrations by Nancy Schwartz
The Committee gratefully acknowledges the legal advice provided by Baker & Hostetler in preparing this publication.

Library of Congress Catalog Card Number: 94-71214
ISBN 0-9609252-9-5

All rights reserved. No part of this publication may be reproduced or used in any form or by any means - graphic, electronic, or mechanical, including photocopying. recording, taping, or information storage and retrieval systems - without written permission of the publisher.

The Committee thanks the following for offering editorial assistance: Patricia Cornacchione; Karen G. Fleegler, R.N., C.C.P., I.A.A.P.; Donna Washington Gracon; Chavanne B. Hanson, M.P.H., R.D., L.D.; Mary Anne Lucas; Anah Pytte; Janet Weimann.

UNDERWRITERS

Due to the generosity of the following underwriters, all proceeds from the sale of this cookbook directly benefit the Cleveland Ballet.

ENTHUSIASTIC

"For many years we have represented Aga stoves which have been called the Rolls Royce of cooking stoves. After reviewing this carefully researched and prepared cookbook, we enthusiastically recommend it."

DANIEL COULTER **BUILDER'S KITCHENS**, AKRON

"Everyone knows there are no calories in party foods. We at Executive Caterers have been proving it for years! This cookbook skillfully demonstrates our belief that fine dining, delicious food and good nutrition can be combined to please the most discerning palate. We are proud to be part of this most special project and we offer our congratulations to those people of the Cleveland Ballet who have made this possible"

HARLAN DIAMOND **EXECUTIVES CATERERS**

DISCERNING

"I am tremendously excited about the contents of this low-fat cookbook as it complements my personal philosophy of healthy living—eat low fat, treadmill daily and, most of all, keep laughing."

MORT WEISBERG **MULTI-CARE MANAGEMENT**

EXCITED

"As Cleveland's hometown baker, we have always strived to offer our community the best. So it is with honor that we present to you — our friends and neighbors — this compilation of delicious, low-fat recipes. We're sure that each will help satisfy even the most demanding palate. Enjoy!."

NICK ORLANDO, SR.
ORLANDO BAKERY

HONOR

"It was not too long ago when the difference between eating well and eating healthily meant enduring a bland and mostly tasteless diet. Not today! After six months of dining on the recipes contained within these pages, I offer a 21 gram salute to its many contributors. Light Kitchen Choreography will add savor, flavor, and good health to your life."

PATRICK PARKER **PARKER HANNIFIN CORPORATION**

21 GRAM SALUTE!

CONTENTS

INTRODUCTION	vi
APPETIZERS	1
SOUPS	31
SALADS	49
PASTA - RICE	73
MAIN COURSES	91
VEGETABLES	163
SAUCES	203
BREADS	211
DESSERTS	225
TO DIE FOR	263
SUBSTITUTION GUIDE	276
HINTS	281
INDEX	282
SUPPORTERS	298
ACKNOWLEDGMENTS	300

CREATING **LIGHT KITCHEN CHOREOGRAPHY** WAS TRULY A LABOR OF LOVE.

WE HOPE YOU ENJOY USING THIS BOOK

AS MUCH AS WE ENJOYED PUTTING IT TOGETHER.

THE COOKBOOK COMMITTEE

Madeleine Parker, *President of the Cleveland Ballet Council*
Jane Herget and Pamela LaMantia, *Cookbook Committee Co-chairs*

Toby Alfred	Fern Felice	Kathleen Kukuca	Teresa Phillips
Diane Andrica	Pat Gaskins	Debbie Latson	Nancy Schwartz
Joyce Chevrier	Mariann Grdina	Mary Anne Lucas	Kathleen Stenson
Mary Colarik	Evelyn Greene	Janis L. McLaughlin	Tanya Tuffuor
Halle Connor	Naomi Guttmann	Peter Nguyen	Roberta Uhrich
Marsha Dobrzynski	Sue Hannebrink	Hermine Krasny Ostro	

LETTER FROM DR. CARL E. ORRINGER

Dear Friends,

When I was asked to write a letter of introduction to this visually pleasing, nutritionally accurate, gastronomically spectacular, lovingly prepared volume, I hardly knew which hat to put on my head.

As a co-author of several books, I have learned over the years that visual appeal is often what entices potential readers to make that magic transition from wary browser to trusted friend. As you explore the clearly displayed, easy to read, user-friendly format of the pages that follow, you will feel that this book is one which begs to be a regular part of your family's mealtime madness. It almost asks to have a tomato stain here or there, but promises not to mind the mess as long as you enjoy the meal.

I am most definitely concerned with nutritional accuracy. After having developed and directed preventive cardiology programs at both the University of Michigan Medical Center and University Hospitals of Cleveland, I have long felt that people who take healthy eating seriously deserve to know the nature of the fuels that they are putting into their "tanks." The careful nutrient analysis done by Nutritional Data Resources provides the assurance that the recipes you're preparing will be as healthy as you had hoped that they would be.

No cookbook is worth its weight unless the recipes really work and are tested by real people. The recipes that you will encounter are guaranteed winners. They have all, at a minimum, been triple tested by members of the Cleveland Ballet Council. I guarantee you that these people are a hungry lot, since many of them build up voracious appetites sitting in their cars waiting for their children to finish ballet lessons when the temperature outside is five below zero.

Most importantly, this book has been painstakingly prepared with the heaping cupful of love by all the contributors, and, in particular, by the cookbook committee. The hundreds of hours that were selflessly donated have evolved into a creative effort of which we can all be proud.

We all recognize the value of the Cleveland Ballet in our community. The are the essence of what makes our city's cultural heritage among the strongest in the United States. The anticipation that this book will benefit this magnificent organization makes the entire effort nothing but a pleasure for all of us who have been lucky enough to participate.

Set the table. It's time to eat!

With best regard,

Carl E. Orringer, MD

Carl E. Orringer, M.D. *Medical Director, University Hospitals Synergy, University Hospitals of Cleveland*

LETTER FROM NUTRITIONISTS

The motto at Nutritional Data Resources is "Better nutrition through better information."

People have always been interested in food and its preparation. Taste, color, texture delight the senses. There is a never-ending quest for new recipes, new ingredients, new combinations. This culinary adventure continues with a modern twist.

Today concern with nutrition is just as important as taste. People are interested in the science of nutrition as well as the art of cookery. This cookbook is designed to present a wide array of tempting gourmet recipes along with sound nutrient information. All recipes were carefully selected and tested with both aspects in mind. The emphasis is on keeping the fat content low and the quality high.

Registered, licensed dietitians at Nutritional Data Resources carefully analyzed recipes for calories, protein, fiber, carbohydrate, sodium, cholesterol and, most important, fat. These nutrients were selected because of their importance to health in several ways. Healthy eating habits help you maintain normal body weight and decrease your risk of heart disease and cancer. A low-fat diet with adequate fiber is generally accepted as the best approach to good health.

What is a low-fat diet? Most health authorities agree that 30% of calories from fat or less is a national goal. Many people find the fat content of foods on package labels expressed in grams and also percents of daily intake. Others look for fat as a percent of calories per serving. For example, the Grilled Indian Lamb prepared according to the recipe in this book is 32% fat. Using a 30% FAT MAXIMUM as a guideline, this food would be too high in fat. In reality, the important concept is 30% of DAILY CALORIC VALUE from fat. Therefore, we believe that percent per individual food may be misleading since it eliminates some foods unnecessarily. If the Grilled Indian Lamb is served with a low-fat accompaniment such as Crostini and a green salad as suggested in the hints line, the combination is well below 30%.

This cookbook will focus on the GRAMS OF FAT PER SERVING. Each person in the family will have a different "FAT BUDGET" based on individual caloric needs.

How to calculate your personal fat budget.

To watch your fat intake day by day, it is easier to track fat grams than to repeatedly calculate the percentage of calories from fat. To find your fat budget, multiply the total calories you consume by .30, then divide that answer by 9. (There are 9 calories in one gram of fat.) This gives you the maximum number of grams of fat that you should eat in a day.

For example, 1200 calories x .30 (30 calories from fat) = 360 calories from fat
     ÷ by 9 (calories in 1 gram fat)
     = 40 MAXIMUM NUMBER OF FAT GRAMS PER DAY

Look for your own fat budget in grams...

Typical daily values	30% Calories from fat	20% Calories from fat
1200 calories	40 grams	27 grams
1500 calories	50 grams	33 grams
1800 calories	60 grams	40 grams
2000 calories	67 grams	44 grams
2500 calories	83 grams	55 grams

Other nutrients are provided for your information. New labeling laws suggest the following guidelines:
 SODIUM should be less than 2,400 mg per day
 CHOLESTEROL should be less than 300 mg per day
 DIETARY FIBER should be more than 25 mg per day
 Consult your physician for special dietary needs.

In computing the nutrient values, some assumptions were made to facilitate computations. They were:
 OPTIONAL ingredients were not included,
 GARNISHES were not included,
 "Salt and pepper to taste" was 1/2 teaspoon salt per 8 servings.
 (Note: 1 teaspoon salt = 2300 mg sodium),
 Veal, pork, lamb and beef are lean cuts trimmed of visible fat,
 Chicken is skinless unless otherwise specified.

Please keep in mind that variations are expected based on differences in product waste, cooking times, etc. Also, nutrient values are averages based on current information. We hope this cookbook will meet your need for "Better nutrition through better information." Please call if we can assist you with nutrient analysis software and service.

 Naomi D. Guttman, R.D., L.D.
 Roberta V. Uhrich, R.D., L.D.
 Nutritional Data Resources
 Willoughby, Ohio 44094
 (800) NDR-DIET or in Ohio (216) 951-6593

APPETIZERS

APPETIZERS

Layered Taco Dip

1/2	cup nonfat sour cream
1/4	cup nonfat mayonnaise
1/2	package taco mix
1	9 1/2-ounce can jalapeño bean dip
1	cup green onion, chopped to include white and green parts
2	medium tomatoes, chopped
1	4 1/2-ounce can chopped black olives
1	cup nonfat cheddar cheese, shredded

Combine the sour cream, mayonnaise and taco mix and mix until well blended.

On a large, flat, decorative platter, layer in the following order: bean dip, mayonnaise mixture, onion, tomatoes, olives and cheddar cheese.

Serves: 12

Scoop up this appetizer with low-fat, salt-free tortilla chips.

90 Cal., 6gm Protein, 10gm Carb., 3.2gm Fat, 417mg Sodium, 2mg Chol., 1.9gm Fiber

APPETIZERS

Middle East Chick Pea Dip

1	19-ounce can chick peas, drained
1/2	cup plain, nonfat yogurt
1/4	cup light buttermilk ranch salad dressing
1/2	teaspoon salt
1	tablespoon fresh lemon juice
2	tablespoons fine, dry, seasoned bread crumbs
1/2	teaspoon crushed red pepper
2	tablespoons pitted ripe olives, chopped
1	scallion, minced

In a food processor or blender combine chick peas, yogurt, salad dressing, salt, lemon juice, bread crumbs and red pepper. Cover and process until smooth. Stir in olives and scallion. Chill, covered, at least 1 hour.

Serves: 10

Serve with vegetable dippers or low-fat crackers.

88 Cal., 3gm Protein, 14gm Carb., 2.5gm Fat, 340mg Sodium, .3mg Chol., 1.9gm Fiber

APPETIZERS

Pesto Dip

1	cup nonfat mayonnaise
1	cup nonfat sour cream
1	10-ounce package frozen, chopped spinach, thawed and well-drained
1	ounce Parmesan cheese, grated
1/4	cup walnut pieces
1/4	cup fresh basil, chopped, or 2 teaspoons dried basil
1	clove garlic, crushed
	salt and pepper to taste
	assorted fresh vegetables

In a food processor or blender, blend all ingredients until smooth. Cover and chill.

Yield: 2½ cups
      1 tablespoon per serving

For an elegant appetizer, place 1 teaspoon of the Pesto Dip on the tip of a French endive leaf or serve with nonfat, toasted bread sticks or assorted fresh vegetables.

20 Cal., 1gm Protein, 3gm Carb., .7gm Fat, 97mg Sodium, 1mg Chol., .3gm Fiber

APPETIZERS

Red Pepper Dip

2	green onions, chopped
2	garlic cloves, minced
1	teaspoon olive oil
1	7-ounce jar roasted red peppers, drained and chopped
1/2	teaspoon salt
1/2	teaspoon thyme
1/4	teaspoon pepper
1	8-ounce package nonfat cream cheese, quartered
1	tablespoon skim milk

In a small skillet, sauté onions and garlic in oil until soft. Stir in red peppers, salt, thyme and pepper. Sauté 1 minute longer.

Place cream cheese and red pepper mixture in a food processor and blend ingredients together. Add milk and use pulse button to blend into mixture. Refrigerate.

Serves: 8

Serve this spicy dip with raw vegetables.

44 Cal., 6gm Protein, 4gm Carb., .7gm Fat, 344mg Sodium, 5mg Chol., .6gm Fiber

APPETIZERS

Seafood Dip

1	8-ounce package nonfat cream cheese, room temperature
2	tablespoons onion, finely minced
2	tablespoons beet horseradish
2	teaspoons Dijon mustard
1	tablespoon parsley, finely minced
1	teaspoon garlic, finely minced
4	tablespoons nonfat mayonnaise
2	dashes hot pepper sauce
1/4	cup dry vermouth
1	6-ounce can of shrimp or fresh shrimp, chopped
6	ounces imitation crab or fresh crab, flaked
	salt and pepper to taste
2	tablespoons slivered almonds, toasted

Place softened cream cheese in a bowl, add the onion, beet horseradish, mustard, parsley, garlic, mayonnaise, hot pepper sauce, and vermouth. Beat with an electric mixer until well blended. Stir or fold in the shrimp and crab and the salt and pepper.

Put the mixture into a small baking dish and bake in a preheated 350° oven for 35 minutes. Top with toasted almonds and return to the oven for another 3 minutes.

Serves: 12

Serve with toast points or crackers.

64 Cal., 9gm Protein, 3.4gm Carb., 1.3gm Fat, 341mg Sodium, 34mg Chol., .3gm Fiber

APPETIZERS

Spinach Dip

1	cup nonfat mayonnaise
1	pint nonfat sour cream
1	package frozen chopped spinach, defrosted and well drained
1	package dry leek soup mix
1	can water chestnuts, chopped

Combine all ingredients and chill. Serve with assorted fresh vegetables.

Serves: 10

A nonfat version of an old favorite.

111 Cal., 5gm Protein, 22gm Carb., .3gm Fat, 600mg Sodium, .2mg Chol., 1.7gm Fiber

APPETIZERS

Gravelax (Cured Salmon)

1/4	cup crushed black pepper
1/4	cup sugar
1/8	cup salt
2	whole salmon fillets
2	large bunches of dill

Sauce:

4	tablespoons Dijon mustard
1	tablespoon lemon juice
1/4	teaspoon white pepper
1/2	tablespoon sugar
1	tablespoon olive oil
1/2	cup low-fat mayonnaise
2	tablespoons dill, finely chopped

❋   ❋   ❋

Sauce:
   Mix all ingredients to make a smooth sauce.

To prepare fish:
   Combine the pepper, sugar and salt.
   Place several branches of dill in a large pan. Add one salmon fillet, skin side down. Place more dill branches to cover the salmon. Liberally sprinkle the mixed pepper, sugar and salt over the dill. Place the other salmon fillet, skin side up, in the opposite direction to the bottom one. Cover the fish with aluminum foil. Place a wooden board on top and weigh down with 3 or 4 large cans. Refrigerate 36 hours. Before serving, scrape off dill branches and as much of the spices as possible with a dull knife.
   If serving as an appetizer, place one fillet on a decorative platter with dill and lemon slices as decoration. Pre-slice into 1/8-inch slices across the fillet and then make one cut down the length of the fish.

Serves: 30

Serve with crackers, pumpernickel or toast cut diagonally into 4 pieces and a dollop of sauce.

54 Cal., 6gm Protein, 3gm Carb., 2.3gm Fat, 333mg Sodium, 13mg Chol., .3gm Fiber

APPETIZERS

Crab Cakes with Sauce Remoulade

Crab Cakes:

2	pounds lump crab meat
4	tablespoons onions, diced
4	tablespoons peppers, red, yellow and green, diced
2	tablespoons chicken broth
1	pound potatoes, boiled and mashed
4	ounces light cream cheese
1	tablespoon fresh cilantro, chopped
1	egg
	salt and pepper, cayenne pepper to taste
1	tablespoon vegetable oil

Crab Cakes:

Simmer onions and peppers in chicken broth until onions are transparent. In mixing bowl, combine all remaining ingredients except oil, mixing well. Taste for seasoning. Make 12, 4-ounce patties, each about $1/2$-inch thick.

In nonstick frying pan heat 1 tablespoon vegetable oil and cook patties 2 to 3 minutes on each side. More oil may need to be added for the second batch.

(continued)

Sauce Remoulade:

- 1 pint fat-free mayonnaise
- 6 tablespoons cornichons, finely chopped
- 2 tablespoons capers, coarsely chopped
- 2 ounces Dijon mustard
- $1/2$ tablespoon shallots, chopped
- $1/2$ teaspoon fresh tarragon
- 2 tablespoons chili sauce (optional)
- juice of $1/2$ lemon
- salt, white pepper, cayenne pepper to taste

Sauce Remoulade:

Mix all ingredients, taste for seasonings. Refrigerate until ready to use.

Note: To make sauce lighter, substitute $1/3$ of mayonnaise with low-fat yogurt.

Serves: 12

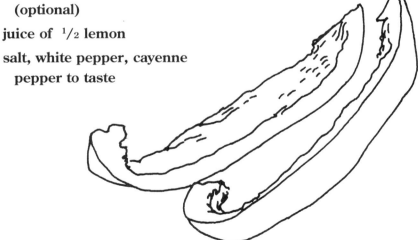

174 Cal., 15gm Protein, 16gm Carb., 5.3gm Fat, 802mg Sodium, 102mg Chol., 1.1gm Fiber

APPETIZERS

Marinated Shrimp with Herb Mayonnaise

3	pounds shrimp, shelled and deveined
3	cups dry white wine
1½	cups water
1	onion, thinly sliced
1	stalk celery, cut in half
2	carrots, cut in half
5	parsley sprigs
1	bay leaf
¼	teaspoon thyme
½	teaspoon tarragon
5	peppercorns

Vinaigrette:

3	tablespoons red wine vinegar
1	teaspoon Dijon mustard
½	teaspoon mixed dried herbs or 1 tablespoon fresh herbs (basil, tarragon, parsley)
1	garlic clove, pressed
½	cup olive oil
	salt and pepper to taste

Shrimp:

   Combine the wine, water, vegetables, herbs and pepper, bring to a boil, add the shrimp and cook for about 5 minutes until shrimp turn pink and are just done. Let shrimp cool in the broth, then drain.

   Marinate overnight in vinaigrette in refrigerator.

Vinaigrette:

   Mix everything except olive oil together until blended, add olive oil slowly to make a smooth dressing.

(continued)

Herb Mayonnaise:

2	tablespoons parsley, chopped
1	tablespoon chives, chopped
1	teaspoon tarragon, chopped
1	teaspoon chervil, chopped
2	teaspoons dill
1/2	teaspoon onion salt
1	garlic clove, pressed
1/2	cup nonfat mayonnaise
1 1/2	cups nonfat sour cream

Herb Mayonnaise:

Combine all ingredients in mixing bowl, blend well, cover and refrigerate overnight.

When ready to serve, drain shrimp and arrange on a large platter, sprinkle with chopped parsley and serve with Herb Mayonnaise.

Serves: 15

Prepare a day ahead and serve as an appetizer before a meal of Grilled Veal Chops and Mango Chutney, Oven Baked French Fries and green salad.

133 Cal., 14gm Protein, 7gm Carb., 4.8gm Fat, 224mg Sodium, 97mg Chol., .1gm Fiber

APPETIZERS

Mussels in Herbed Vegetable Broth

Court Bouillon:

2	cups clam juice (bottled variety)
2	cups dry white wine
2	carrots, cut into 1-inch pieces
1	onion, quartered
1	celery stalk, cut into 1-inch pieces
1	garlic clove
1	bouquet garni (parsley, thyme and bay leaf)
½	tablespoon salt
6	black peppercorns, crushed

Court Bouillon:
   In a large, non-aluminum sauce pot, combine all ingredients, bring to a boil, turn heat to medium and simmer gently for 30 minutes. Strain.

(continued)

Broth:

3	shallots, finely chopped
1	garlic clove, finely chopped
2	teaspoons tomato paste
1	teaspoon thyme
1	bay leaf
1	tablespoon fresh tarragon, chopped
1	tablespoon fresh basil, chopped
1	tablespoon fresh or frozen chives, chopped
	pinch of saffron threads
	salt and pepper to taste
3/4	pound potatoes, diced
1	small zucchini, diced
1	celery stalk, diced
1	large tomato, diced
3	pounds mussels, scrubbed and beard removed
1/2	cup low-fat sour cream
1	cup 1% milk

Broth:

In a large stock pot, cook shallots and garlic in 1/4 cup court bouillon over low heat until soft, about 5 minutes. Add tomato paste and 2 cups more court bouillon, whisk together and add thyme and bay leaf. Bring to a boil, lower heat, simmer gently for 10 minutes. Then add all fresh herbs, saffron and salt and pepper. Remove from heat.

In a skillet, cook all vegetables except tomato separately until just done. Add to broth, with tomato. Add any remaining court bouillon to vegetable broth, or more clam juice if broth does not seem to be sufficient. Heat broth. Add mussels, cover and steam mussels until they open, about 10 minutes.

Mix milk and low-fat sour cream together. Add to mussels, stir well.

Ladle into 4 soup plates, garnish with saffron threads or chopped parsley and serve immediately.

Serves: 4

230 Cal., 17gm Protein, 32gm Carb., 3.7gm Fat, 484mg Sodium, 33mg Chol., 3.4gm Fiber

APPETIZERS

Smoked Trout with Dill Sauce

Dill Sauce:

2	tablespoons red wine vinegar
1	tablespoon fresh dill, chopped
1 1/2	teaspoons sugar
1 1/2	teaspoons dry mustard
2	teaspoons lemon juice
2	teaspoons green onions, minced
1/8	teaspoon ground red pepper
	dash hot pepper sauce
	salt and pepper to taste
1/3	cup nonfat yogurt
10	slices firm white bread
1	tablespoon olive oil
1-2	garlic cloves, minced
1	cup smoked trout, flaked and boned

Garnish:

lemon slices

dill sprigs

Dill Sauce:
Combine vinegar, dill, sugar, mustard, lemon juice, onion, pepper, pepper sauce, salt and pepper and yogurt in blender. Process until smooth.

Trim crust from bread and cut bread into decorative shapes with a cookie cutter. Heat olive oil in a small saucepan and add minced garlic. Heat for 1 minute on medium-high heat, remove from heat and brush on bread. Put under broiler and brown.

To serve:
Place some smoked trout on each bread slice, top with a small dollop of dill sauce and garnish with a fresh dill sprig and lemon slices on serving platter.

Serves: 10

77 Cal., 6gm Protein, 8gm Carb., 2gm Fat, 127mg Sodium, 8mg Chol., .3gm Fiber

APPETIZERS

Tuna Tartare

1	pound fresh tuna (dark brown part removed)
2	garlic cloves, finely chopped
4	tablespoons black olives, finely chopped
4	tablespoons capers, coarsely chopped
	juice of 1 lemon
2	tablespoons fresh coriander, finely chopped
2	tablespoons parsley, finely chopped
	salt and pepper to taste
1/4	teaspoon red pepper
	few drops of hot pepper sauce (optional)

Garnish:
    chopped parsley

Grind tuna in a food processor. In a mixing bowl, combine tuna with other ingredients. Mix well. Taste for seasoning. Put on serving platter, sprinkle with chopped parsley. Serve with crackers or thin slices of black bread and lemons cut in quarters.

Serves: 10

Tuna tartare is a delightful alternative for those who love beef tartare.

74 Cal., 13gm Protein, 1gm Carb., 2gm Fat, 223mg Sodium, 32mg Chol., .4gm Fiber

APPETIZERS

Salmon Carpaccio with Frankfurt Green Sauce

Frankfurt Green Sauce:
- 2 hard-boiled eggs, finely chopped
- 12 ounces nonfat yogurt
- 1/4 cup nonfat cream cheese
- 1 tablespoon mustard
- 2-3 tablespoons each: chives, parsley (flat leafed), watercress, oregano, basil, tarragon or lemon balm, finely chopped
- 1 tablespoon fresh dill, finely chopped
- 2-3 tablespoons lemon juice
- salt and pepper to taste
- 1 tablespoon vegetable oil (optional)

Frankfurt Green Sauce:
    Place the eggs, yogurt, cream cheese and mustard in a bowl and mix well. Add the chopped herbs, lemon juice and salt and pepper.
    Blend well and refrigerate.
    If sauce is too strong in herb flavor, add more yogurt and a pinch of sugar.

(continued)

Salmon Carpaccio:

1	1-pound fresh salmon fillet
1	tablespoon each: dill, chives, parsley (flat leafed), basil and tarragon, finely chopped
2	tablespoons lemon juice
	salt and pepper to taste

Salmon Carpaccio:

Slice the salmon fillet horizontally into 2 thin slices or have the fish monger do it.

Mix all the herbs with the lemon juice and salt and pepper.

Lay the fillets slices flat, evenly spread the herbs over them. Roll each up into a tight roll and refrigerate for 2 hours, covered with plastic wrap.

Carefully slice into thin wheels, arrange 5 per plate with dill or parsley garnish and serve with Frankfurt Green Sauce.

Serves: 4

Serve with pumpernickel party rounds.

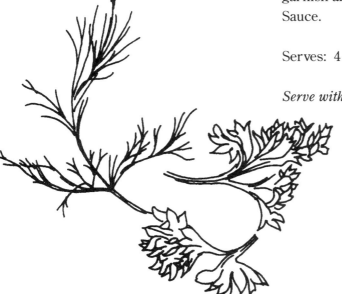

121 Cal., 15gm Protein, 6gm Carb., 4.2gm Fat, 572mg Sodium, 91mg Chol., .4gm Fiber

APPETIZERS

Steamed Whole Fish with Lime Mousseline Sauce

Court Bouillon:

1	cup clam juice
1	cup white wine
1	cup water
2	carrots, scraped, cut in 1-inch pieces
1	onion, peeled, quartered
1	celery stalk, cut in 1-inch pieces
1	garlic clove, crushed
1	bouquet garni (parsley, thyme, bay leaf)
$1/2$	tablespoon salt
6	black peppercorns
2	whole Canadian whitefish, 2 - 3 pounds each, gutted, but left intact

Garnish:

lemon slices and parsley

To prepare fish:

Put all the ingredients for Court Bouillon in saucepan, bring to boil, transfer to a fish steamer and place over 2 burners on moderate heat. Put fish on steaming insert. Place over liquid, cover and steam until fish is done. Check at thickest part after 15 minutes. Make a small slit to the bone, flesh should be opaque; if not, continue steaming, checking every 5 minutes. Remove fish from steamer, drain and place on serving platter. Cool to room temperature. Remove skin and fins.

(continued)

Lime Mousseline:

1	**cup low-fat mayonnaise**
2	**limes, juiced**
2	**egg whites, stiffly beaten**
	salt and pepper to taste

Lime Mousseline:

In a bowl, mix low-fat mayonnaise with half the lime juice. Taste. The lime flavor should be distinct, but not overpowering. Add more if necessary. Add salt and pepper, whisk in $1/3$ of beaten egg whites, then carefully fold in remaining egg whites. Put into sauce boat. Sprinkle with a little lime zest.

To serve:

Cut the fish down the middle and divide into serving portions. Decorate the platter with lemon slices and parsley. Serve with the Lime Mousseline on the side.

Serves: 8 as a first course

An elegant first course that is also excellent for a buffet.

---

289 Cal., 45gm Protein, 7gm Carb., 7.4gm Fat, 618mg Sodium, 108mg Chol., .04gm Fiber

APPETIZERS

Onion Tart

$1^1/_2$	cups unbleached flour
1	ounce cake yeast
$^3/_4$	cup lukewarm 1% milk
3	tablespoons butter
1	teaspoon salt
$3^1/_2$	pounds onions, quartered and thinly sliced
2	eggs
$^3/_4$	cup 1% milk
1	cup plain low-fat yogurt
$^1/_2$	cup nonfat sour cream
	salt and pepper to taste
	caraway seeds (optional)

Put flour into a large bowl, make a well in the middle of the flour and crumble the yeast into it. Add $^3/_4$ cup warm milk and stir together with a little of the flour. Cover and let rise in a warm, draft-free place. Melt butter, add salt and add to the flour mixture. Beat dough vigorously and knead well. Cover again and let rise until doubled. Preheat oven to 350°.

In a little water, cook onions until transparent. Mix eggs, milk, yogurt and sour cream in a bowl, add onions.

Roll out dough on a floured surface. Place rolled dough on a large baking sheet making sure it comes up the sides. Pour onion mixture over it and distribute evenly. If desired, sprinkle caraway seeds over all. Bake 40 minutes, serve warm.

Serves: 18

109 Cal., 4gm Protein, 16gm Carb., 3.2gm Fat, 240mg Sodium, 37mg Chol., 1.2gm Fiber

APPETIZERS

Parmesan Artichoke Toast

1	baguette
1	tablespoon olive oil
1	tablespoon butter
4	cloves garlic, minced
2	tablespoons parsley, minced
1	9-ounce package frozen artichoke hearts, thawed and chopped
1/2	cup nonfat mayonnaise
1/2	cup grated light Parmesan cheese
1/4	teaspoon red pepper sauce

Slice baguette in half lengthwise. Heat olive oil and butter in a small saucepan, add garlic and parsley and heat for 2-3 minutes.

In a small bowl mix artichoke hearts, mayonnaise, Parmesan cheese and red pepper sauce. Set aside.

Lightly spread olive oil-butter mixture on baguette halves. Place under broiler and toast until lightly golden. Remove from oven and spread with artichoke-Parmesan mixture and return the baguette halves to the broiler. Broil until browned. Cut loaves into 1-inch thick slices.

Serves: 12

92 Cal., 3gm Protein, 14gm Carb., 3.1gm Fat, 225mg Sodium, 4.4mg Chol., 1gm Fiber

APPETIZERS

Seafood Strudel

4	ounces imitation crab or fresh lump crab
6	ounces fresh salmon, grilled or poached, boned and flaked
1/2	cup low-fat Swiss cheese or mozzarella cheese
3	ounces fresh mushrooms, grilled or sautéed in defatted chicken broth
1/4	cup bread crumbs
1/2	teaspoon onion powder
1/4	teaspoon hot pepper sauce
1	egg white
2	teaspoons vegetable oil
8	sheets frozen phyllo dough, thawed
2	teaspoons butter, melted

In a medium mixing bowl, combine the crab, salmon, cheese, mushrooms, bread crumbs, onion powder, hot pepper sauce and set aside.

Beat the egg white lightly with a fork, add the oil and beat a little more. Unfold phyllo and spread one of the sheets flat. Keep a damp towel on the remaining phyllo so as not to dry out. Brush with egg white-oil mixture. Top with another sheet and brush with the egg white-oil mixture, repeating until the last sheet of phyllo is coated. Put the crab filling mixture along the lengthwise edge of the phyllo dough. Roll the phyllo jelly roll style and place, seam-side down, on a baking sheet which has been sprayed with vegetable spray. Spread the top and sides of the phyllo with the melted butter. Place in a preheated 375° oven for 15 minutes or until golden brown.

Remove from oven and cool. Cut the strudel into 1/4-inch wide slices and arrange decoratively on a platter to serve.

Serves: 15

92 Cal., 6gm Protein, 11gm Carb., 2.8gm Fat, 103mg Sodium, 16mg Chol., .3gm Fiber

APPETIZERS

Oven-dried Tomatoes

12	Italian (plum) tomatoes
	extra virgin olive oil in a spray bottle
3	large garlic cloves, finely chopped
	salt and pepper to taste

Garnish:
 fresh whole basil leaves

Slice tomatoes lengthwise into $1/4$-inch slices.

Line a cookie sheet with parchment paper and place the sliced tomatoes in a single layer on the parchment paper.

Spray the tomatoes with the olive oil and sprinkle the garlic evenly over the tomatoes. Add salt and pepper.

Bake in a 250° oven for $1^{1}/_{2}$ hours. Garnish with basil.

Serves: 6

Serve with slices of Italian bread.

36 Cal., 1gm Protein, 6gm Carb., 1.5gm Fat, 194mg Sodium, 0mg Chol., 2gm Fiber

APPETIZERS

Los Frijoles Negros Fritos con Salsa de Verano
Black Bean Cakes with Summer Salsa

1	15-ounce can black beans
1	tablespoon onion, chopped
1	garlic clove, minced
¼	cup flour
¼	teaspoon salt
	dash hot cayenne pepper sauce
	vegetable spray

Garnish:

nonfat sour cream

Drain the beans, reserving liquid. Process beans with 2 tablespoons reserved liquid (or as little as needed) in a food processor or blender to make a semi-smooth mixture. Remove from food processor or blender, add other ingredients and stir. Adjust with more flour or liquid as needed to achieve the consistency of a very thick batter.

Spray a nonstick skillet with vegetable spray. Drop 2 tablespoons of batter into skillet as for pancakes. Spread batter to make 3 or 4-inch cakes. (Make the cakes no bigger than 3 or 4 inches or they will be unwieldy and difficult to turn.) Fry over medium heat until browned and the tops are no longer glossy. Carefully flip to fry other side. Away from the heat source, spray skillet with additional vegetable spray as needed and fry remaining batter. Remove when done to a heated platter. Top with sour cream and Salsa de Verano (Summer Salsa).

(continued)

Salsa de Verano:

2	**Roma or plum tomatoes, diced**
1/2	**cup red bell pepper, diced**
1/2	**cup green bell pepper, diced**
1	**tablespoon fresh parsley or cilantro, chopped**
1/4	**cup green onion, diced**
	juice of 1 fresh lime
1/4	**teaspoon salt**
dash	**hot cayenne pepper sauce**

Combine all ingredients and allow flavors to develop for at least one hour. Adjust seasonings to taste. Can be made 12 hours ahead. Keep refrigerated.

Yield: 2 cups

This sauce also goes well with scrambled eggs or broiled fish entrees.

34 Cal., 2gm Protein, 6gm Carb., .1gm Fat, 77mg Sodium, 0mg Chol., 1.2gm Fiber

APPETIZERS

Potato Rounds with Tapenade

Potato Rounds:
4	large potatoes
	salt and pepper to taste
1	tablespoon vegetable oil

Tapenade:
18	ounces black olives, pitted
4	garlic cloves
3/4	tablespoon mixed dried herbs
1	tablespoon olive oil
1/2	cup chicken broth (may use slightly more)
2	anchovy fillets (optional)

Potato Rounds:
 Peel and slice potatoes into 1/2-inch rounds. Salt and pepper the potato slices. Heat oil in a nonstick frying pan. Brown potato slices slightly on both sides and cook until done.

Tapenade:
 Place first 4 ingredients in food processor and, while motor is running, add chicken broth in a stream until a smooth thick consistency is achieved. Scrape down sides, add anchovy fillets, if desired, and run again. Set aside in a bowl.
 Serve potato rounds with a tablespoon of tapenade on each slice.

Serves: 6 - 8

Instead of potato rounds, serve tapenade with toasted baguette or Ciabatta bread slices. Excellent followed by Red Pepper Soup and Coq au Vin.

99 Cal., 1gm Protein, 11gm Carb., 6.1gm Fat, 273mg Sodium, 0mg Chol., 2gm Fiber

APPETIZERS

Potassium Froth

6	blanched almonds
1/2	banana
3	ounces water
2	ice cubes
1/2	teaspoon lemon juice
	dash of vanilla
	nutmeg to taste

Place all ingredients into a blender. Blend until frothy. Serve.

Serves: 1

Used as an appetizer before dinner at the Spa.

Mario's International Spa & Hotel

100 Cal., 2gm Protein, 15gm Carb., 4.3gm Fat, 2mg Sodium, Potassium 285mg, 0mg Chol., 1.7gm Fiber

APPETIZERS

Terrine of Chicken and Herbs

Chicken:

2	chicken breasts, skinned
2	cups white wine
2	cups water
2	shallots, cut in half
1/2	lemon, sliced
1	carrot, cut into 1-inch pieces
1	garlic clove, crushed
2	sprigs parsley
3	cloves
1	bay leaf
1/2	teaspoon thyme
	salt and pepper

Chicken:

Combine all the ingredients in saucepan. Bring to boil and simmer until chicken is cooked through, 15 - 20 minutes. Take out chicken breasts, let cool, then cut into 1/2-inch pieces. Set aside. Strain liquid into another saucepan, discarding solids.

(continued)

Terrine:

4	**carrots**
1	**egg white**
2	**envelopes unflavored gelatin**
2	**tablespoons parsley, finely chopped**
2	**tablespoons fresh coriander, finely chopped**
2	**tablespoons chives, finely chopped**
	salt and pepper

Terrine:

Cook carrots in reserved broth until tender, remove from broth and chop finely. Add the egg white to the broth and cook 5 minutes to clear the broth. Strain broth through a cheesecloth-lined fine sieve into a saucepan.

Add enough water to make 4 cups of broth. Sprinkle gelatin over broth, heat to dissolve gelatin. Add herbs, carrots, salt and pepper, mix well.

In the bottom of a loaf pan, place half of the chicken pieces, cover with 2 cups of the broth, refrigerate until almost set. Add remaining broth and chicken pieces. Refrigerate for 6 hours.

To serve:

Unmold onto platter, slice and serve.

Serves: 8

Serve with Frankfurt Green Sauce or Fresh Tomato Sauce.

67 Cal., 10gm Protein, 4gm Carb., 1.2gm Fat, 169mg Sodium, 22mg Chol., 1.2gm Fiber

APPETIZERS

Spicy Pork Tenderloin with Lime Mayonnaise

Lime Mayonnaise:
- 1 cup low-fat mayonnaise
- 2 tablespoons fresh lime juice
- 1 teaspoon lime zest

Pork Tenderloin:
- 2 large garlic cloves, minced
- 2 teaspoons paprika
- 1 teaspoon salt
- 1 teaspoon oregano
- 1 teaspoon cumin
- 1/2 teaspoon ground black pepper
- 1/4 teaspoon ground red pepper
- 2 pork tenderloins (1 1/2 pounds total)
- 2 baguettes, thinly sliced
- lime wedges and fresh cilantro for garnish

Lime Mayonnaise:
Mix ingredients for lime mayonnaise and chill for up to three days.

Pork Tenderloin:
Combine garlic, paprika, salt, oregano, cumin and peppers in a small bowl. Rub spice mixture over pork, wrap and refrigerate overnight. Thirty minutes before roasting, remove pork from refrigerator. Preheat oven to 425°. Unwrap pork, place in roasting pan and roast 20 to 25 minutes. Cool to room temperature. (Can be made ahead, wrapped and refrigerated for up to 3 days.)

Slice very thin and serve on bread with a dollop of lime mayonnaise.

Option: Brush bread with light olive oil, parsley and garlic and grill or broil it before placing pork slices on it.

Garnish with lime wedges and cilantro.

Serves: 24

187 Cal., 11gm Protein, 25gm Carb., 4.9gm Fat, 446mg Sodium, 17mg Chol., .7gm Fiber

SOUPS

Asparagus Soup

2	bunches asparagus, trimmed and cut into 1-inch pieces
5	cups water
1	tablespoon cornstarch
1	cup 1% milk
2	shallots, finely chopped
1	tablespoon white wine
	dash of nutmeg
	salt and pepper to taste

Cook asparagus in the water until done. Remove with slotted spoon, reserving cooking liquid.

Dilute cornstarch in a little water, heat milk, add cornstarch, cook, stirring over low heat until thickened.

In saucepan, cook shallots in a $1/4$ cup of cooking liquid and wine until shallots are soft, add asparagus, 4 cups cooking liquid, reduce over moderate heat to 3 cups. Add thickened milk and purée in food processor. Return to saucepan, add nutmeg, salt and pepper, heat and serve.

Serves: 4

53 Cal., 4gm Protein, 8gm Carb., .7gm Fat, 317mg Sodium, 3mg Chol., 1.2gm Fiber

SOUPS

Carrot Soup

2	cups onions, chopped
1	garlic clove, cut in half
4-5	cups chicken broth, divided
2	pounds carrots, peeled and chopped
1	cup orange juice
$1/2$	teaspoon ground ginger
	salt and pepper to taste

Put onions and garlic in a large pot with $1/2$ cup chicken broth and sauté over low heat until transparent.

Add carrots and remaining chicken broth, bring to a boil, cover, lower heat and simmer until the carrots are tender.

Strain the carrots and onions through a sieve, reserving the liquid.

Purée the solids in a food processor with a little of the liquid until very smooth.

Return purée to the pot, add the orange juice and enough of the reserved cooking liquid to bring it to the consistency desired.

Add the ground ginger and salt and pepper to taste. Reheat and serve.

Serves: 6

For a beautiful presentation, add a small dollop of Mock Crème Fraîche in the middle of each filled soup plate and sprinkle chopped chives over all.

108 Cal., 3gm Protein, 23gm Carb., .9gm Fat, 1,368mg Sodium, .8mg Chol., 5.3gm Fiber

SOUPS

Chlodnik

Cold Vegetable and Yogurt Soup

1	1-pound can beets
1	cucumber, peeled and diced
1	dill pickle, diced
½	cup radishes
1	clove garlic, crushed with ½ teaspoon salt
½	teaspoon sugar (optional)
2	tablespoons onion, chopped
1	quart nonfat plain yogurt
1	vegetable bouillon cube dissolved in beet liquid

Garnish:

4	tablespoons parsley, chopped
4	tablespoons fresh dill, chopped

Drain beets and cut in fine strips, save liquid. Combine beets, cucumber, pickle, radishes, garlic, sugar and onion with yogurt in a two-quart bowl. Stir the beet juice and bouillon into the yogurt mixture. Chill, garnish before serving.

Serves: 6

More flavorful if made a day in advance.

106 Cal., 10gm Protein, 17gm Carb., .2gm Fat, 767mg Sodium, 3mg Chol., 2gm Fiber

Corn Chowder

1	large onion, chopped
2	teaspoons canola oil
1	large white potato, or 2 medium red potatoes, cut into chunks
4	ears of fresh corn cut off the cob or 2 cups frozen corn
1	teaspoon thyme
4	cups chicken broth
	salt and pepper to taste

Garnish:

chopped chives

Sauté onion in canola oil until golden. Add the potatoes and corn to the onions and sauté for about 3-5 minutes on low heat.

Add thyme and chicken broth and simmer until potatoes are tender, about 15-20 minutes.

Cool slightly and purée in blender until smooth.

Season to taste and garnish with chopped chives.

Serves: 4

This chowder can be made creamier by using evaporated skim milk in place of the chicken broth.

218 Cal., 6gm Protein, 43gm Carb., 4.2gm Fat, 1,378mg Sodium, 1mg Chol., 6.5gm Fiber

SOUPS

Cucumber Mint Soup

4	medium cucumbers, peeled, halved, seeds removed
1	clove garlic
2	cups chicken broth
3	cups plain low-fat yogurt
1/2	teaspoon salt
1/4	teaspoon ground white pepper
1	tablespoon lemon juice
3/4	cup fresh mint leaves

Garnish:
    mint sprigs

Cut 3 1/2 cucumbers into 1-inch pieces, combine with garlic and place in food processor. Process for 30 seconds.

Add chicken broth, yogurt, salt, pepper, lemon juice and 3/4 cup of mint leaves. Process until smooth.

Chill, covered, for 3 hours or overnight.

Ladle chilled soup into bowls, garnish with remaining cucumber cut in slices and mint sprigs

Serves: 8

This chilled soup is refreshing on a warm summer day.

76 Cal., 6gm Protein, 10gm Carb., 1.7gm Fat, 539mg Sodium, 6mg Chol., 1.9gm Fiber

Italian Bread Soup

1	tablespoon olive oil
4	large cloves garlic, minced
1	small onion, finely chopped
2	stalks celery, finely chopped
2	small carrots, finely chopped
4	medium red potatoes, diced
4	medium tomatoes, finely chopped
10	cups chicken stock
4	cups spinach, finely shredded
1/4	cup Italian parsley, chopped
2	tablespoons fresh oregano, chopped
2	tablespoons fresh thyme, chopped
2	cups Great Northern beans, cooked
	salt and pepper to taste
8	slices stale Italian bread, cubed
1/4	cup Romano cheese, grated

In a large pan, heat the oil, adding the garlic, onion, celery, carrots and potatoes. Sauté on low about 10 minutes. Add the tomatoes, stock, spinach, parsley, oregano and thyme. Simmer 20 minutes, stirring occasionally. Add the beans and season with salt and pepper to taste. In a heatproof soup tureen, layer the bread and soup. Cover and refrigerate 4 hours or overnight.

When ready to serve, sprinkle top of soup with 1/4 cup Romano cheese and bake in a 350° oven for 30 minutes.

Serves: 8

Bellissimo! Best if made the day before.

247 Cal., 11gm Protein, 44gm Carb., 4.1gm Fat, 2,045mg Sodium, 3mg Chol., 6.1gm Fiber

SOUPS

Manhattan Clam Chowder

1	tablespoon olive oil
2	large carrots, peeled and finely chopped
2	large ribs celery, finely chopped
1	large onion, finely chopped
2	large potatoes, peeled and coarsely diced
2	tablespoons dry red wine
1	16-ounce can juice-packed tomatoes, coarsely chopped with liquids
2	cups chicken broth
1	tablespoon fresh parsley, chopped
1	teaspoon garlic, finely minced
$1/4$	teaspoon dried thyme, crumbled
2	10-ounce cans whole, diced or minced clams, including liquid, or 20 ounces of fresh clams steamed and chopped, reserving broth

black pepper, freshly ground (to taste)

salt (to taste)

Garnish:

fresh parsley, chopped

In a large, nonstick pot, heat the oil and sauté the carrots, celery and onions over medium heat for 5 to 6 minutes or until just softened. Add the potatoes and stir to combine.

Add the wine and allow to boil for 1 minute. Add the tomatoes, broth and seasonings and bring to a boil Cover, reduce heat, and simmer for 25 minutes.

Add the clams and continue to cook for an additional 10 minutes or until heated through.

Season to taste with salt and serve the soup hot, garnished with fresh parsley.

Serves: 6

166 Cal., 11gm Protein, 22gm Carb., 3.5gm Fat, 827mg Sodium, 23mg Chol., 3.9gm Fiber

SOUPS

Mushroom Soup

4	shallots, thinly sliced
3	garlic cloves, sliced
8	cups chicken broth, divided
2	pounds portabello mushrooms, brushed clean, stems removed and coarsely chopped
2	teaspoons fresh thyme
	salt and pepper to taste
1/2	lemon, juiced

Garnish:
low-fat sour cream
chopped parsley

In a large, nonstick frying pan, cook shallots and garlic over low heat in 1 cup of broth until transparent. Add mushrooms, thyme, salt and pepper and cook until mushrooms are done and all liquid is evaporated, about 10 minutes. Purée in food processor with 1 cup of broth until very smooth.

Put mixture in a large saucepan with lemon juice, 5 to 6 cups of broth and heat. Adjust seasoning and liquid (a little water may need to be added to achieve desired consistency). Ladle into soup bowls and serve with a dollop of low-fat sour cream in the middle and fresh, chopped parsley sprinkled over all.

Serves: 6

44 Cal., 3gm Protein, 7gm Carb., 1.1gm Fat, 1,997mg Sodium, 1mg Chol., 1gm Fiber

SOUPS

Parsnip Mushroom Soup

2 tablespoons butter
½ pound mushrooms, coarsely chopped
½ cup leeks, white only, sliced
1 pound parsnips, thickly sliced
6 cups chicken broth
  nutmeg, salt and pepper to taste

Garnish:
  nonfat sour cream or Mock Crème Fraîche
  thinly sliced mushrooms

Melt butter in medium saucepan, add mushrooms and leeks, cover with waxed paper and steam over low heat for 10 minutes.

Stir in parsnips, add broth and nutmeg, salt and pepper; let it come to a boil, lower heat, cover and simmer for 30 minutes.

Transfer to food processor, purée until smooth, reheat briefly and garnish.

Serves: 6

Serve with Fougasse.

129 Cal., 3gm Protein, 20gm Carb., 5gm Fat, 1,407mg Sodium, 11mg Chol., 4.3gm Fiber

Red Pepper Soup

2	teaspoons canola oil
1	medium onion, finely chopped
3	large sweet red peppers, seeded and finely chopped
4	cups chicken broth
1	cup vegetable juice cocktail
1	teaspoons salt
$1/4$	teaspoon black pepper

Garnish:
    chopped parsley

Heat the oil in a small skillet, add the onion and sauté for a few minutes until soft. Transfer the onion to a blender together with the chopped red peppers and a little of the broth. Blend until smooth.

Place in a medium-size pot and add the rest of the broth and the vegetable juice. Add salt and pepper, bring to a boil and simmer for 20 minutes.

Garnish with chopped parsley and serve.

Serves: 6

Serve with crusty French bread.

44 Cal., 2gm Protein, 6gm Carb., 1.8gm Fat, 521mg Sodium, .7mg Chol., 1.2gm Fiber

Spanish Black Bean Soup

1 1/2	cups dried black beans, washed and soaked in 4 cups of water overnight, then drained
4	cups water
2	cups chicken broth
1	tablespoon olive oil
2	tablespoons fresh lemon juice
1	tablespoon balsamic vinegar
1	onion, minced
1	carrot, minced
1	celery stalk with leaves, chopped
1	garlic clove, minced
2	tablespoons fresh parsley, chopped
1/2	teaspoon cayenne pepper
1	teaspoon salt (optional)
6	tablespoons sherry

Garnish:

1	thinly sliced lemon

Place drained beans in covered pot. Add 4 cups water and 2 cups broth. Bring to a boil and simmer. Add olive oil, lemon juice and balsamic vinegar. Cook 2 to 3 hours until beans are tender. Add onion, carrot, celery, garlic, parsley, cayenne, salt and sherry. Simmer an additional 30 to 45 minutes until vegetables are tender. Purée half of the mixture and combine with non-puréed half. Reheat if necessary. Garnish each bowl of soup with a lemon slice.

Serves: 4

284 Cal., 14gm Protein, 42gm Carb., 4.8gm Fat, 702mg Sodium, .5mg Chol., 18.5gm Fiber

Sopa De Frijoles Negro
Black Bean Soup

1	pound black beans
2	quarts water
2	teaspoons vegetable oil
1 1/2	cups onions, finely diced
1 1/2	cups celery, finely diced
1 1/2	cups carrots, finely diced
1	tablespoon garlic, minced
1	bay leaf
1	teaspoon dried thyme
3	tablespoons ground cumin, divided
1/2	teaspoon dried oregano
12	cups chicken broth
2	smoked ham hocks
1	teaspoon cayenne pepper
4	tablespoons fresh lime juice
	salt and pepper to taste

Garnish:
  low-fat sour cream

Soak beans overnight in water and drain.

In a large Dutch oven, heat oil and add onions, celery and carrots. Place a sheet of waxed paper cut to fit the pot on top of vegetables and sweat them until tender, stirring occasionally. Remove waxed paper and add garlic, bay leaf, thyme, 1 tablespoon cumin and oregano, and cook 5 minutes.

Add chicken broth, ham hocks and beans and bring to a boil. Reduce heat to medium-low and cook, uncovered, for 2 to 2 1/2 hours or until beans are very soft. Remove hocks and let cool. Remove bay leaf and discard. Purée 4 to 6 cups of the bean soup mixture in a food processor and return to the Dutch oven. Remove meat from the hocks and add to the soup pot. Add cayenne, remaining cumin and lime juice, and salt and pepper to taste.

Serve with a dollop of low-fat sour cream, if desired.

Serves: 12

136 Cal., 9gm Protein, 19gm Carb., 3.1gm Fat, 1,814mg Sodium, 8mg Chol., 6.9gm Fiber

SOUPS

Soup "Au Pistou"

Sauce:

1	cup fresh basil leaves, packed
4	cloves garlic, crushed
1/4	cup Parmesan cheese, grated
1	tablespoon olive oil

Soup:

2	large carrots, peeled and sliced into circles
2	large potatoes, peeled and cubed
1/2	pound dried white beans, soaked overnight in water
2	fresh tomatoes, diced
1	cup pumpkin or winter squash, peeled and diced (optional)
1/2	cup low-fat smoked ham, diced
1/2	pound green beans, cleaned and cut into 1/2-inch slices
2	medium zucchini, sliced into half circles

Process all sauce ingredients in a food processor to make a smooth paste.

Put carrots, potatoes, white beans, tomatoes, pumpkin and ham into a large soup pot. Cover with water 2 inches above ingredients and simmer about 45-60 minutes until white beans are almost tender. Add water while cooking, if necessary. Add green beans and zucchini and cook 20 minutes longer.

Add sauce to soup. Mix well and cook another 5 minutes. Let stand covered in a warm place.

Serves: 8

Best if made in the morning and eaten lukewarm in the evening.

208 Cal., 12gm Protein, 35gm Carb., 3.6gm Fat, 183mg Sodium, 7mg Chol., 6.2gm Fiber

Spicy Gazpacho with Hot Pepper Oil

Hot Pepper Oil:
- 1/8 cup crushed red pepper flakes
- 1/2 cup virgin olive oil

Spicy Gazpacho:
- 1 garlic clove, peeled
- 2 tablespoons parsley sprigs
- 2 large, ripe tomatoes, peeled, cored, and coarsely chopped (1 to 1 1/4 pounds)
- 1 medium green bell pepper, cored, seeded and coarsely chopped
- 2-3 scallions, chopped, or 1/2 medium Bermuda onion, chopped
- 1 cup radishes, ends removed, cleaned and cut in half
- 1 medium cucumber, peeled and coarsely chopped
- 2 tablespoons fresh basil, chopped, or 1/2 teaspoon dried

Hot Pepper Oil:
   Combine ingredients and bring to a boil over medium heat. Do not allow red pepper to blacken or oil to smoke. Cool. Put in container in refrigerator. Store with red pepper in oil or strain for a "less hot" oil.

(continued)

2½ cups tomato juice
1 tablespoon hot pepper oil (see recipe)
3 tablespoons red wine vinegar
½ teaspoon salt
¼ teaspoon black pepper, freshly ground
  hot pepper sauce (optional)

Garnish:

toasted bread crumbs

Spicy Gazpacho:

Mince the garlic and parsley in a food processor or blender. Add the chopped tomatoes, green pepper, scallions, radishes, cucumber and basil to the work bowl. With the motor running, add the tomato juice in a stream, processing only until the vegetables are chopped fine but not puréed. The consistency of the soup should be quite thick and coarse.

Turn into a mixing bowl and stir in any remaining tomato juice, the oil, vinegar, and seasoning to taste. Chill.

Before serving, thin with a little extra tomato juice, if desired, and garnish each portion with toasted bread crumbs.

Serves: 6

Hot pepper oil makes this one very hot - so adjust it to your own taste!
Serve with crusty French bread or nonfat bread sticks for a light lunch.

67 Cal., 2gm Protein, 10gm Carb., 2.6gm Fat, 559mg Sodium, 0mg Chol., 3gm Fiber

Squash Soup with Lemon and Basil

4	cups chicken broth
1	large onion, finely chopped
1	garlic clove, finely chopped
3	medium zucchini, shredded
3	medium summer squash, shredded
1	large carrot, shredded
4	tablespoons fresh basil, chopped
	grated rind of 1 lemon
1	tablespoon lemon juice
	salt and pepper to taste

In a large saucepan heat $1/2$ cup of chicken broth. Add onion and garlic and cook over low heat until onion is translucent. Add remaining ingredients. Cook until vegetables are tender, about 7 minutes. Taste for seasoning. Serve.

Serves: 6 - 8

This unique squash soup may also be seasoned with curry.

32Cal., 2gm Protein, 6gm Carb., .6gm Fat, 822mg Sodium, .5mg Chol., 1.5gm Fiber

SOUPS

Summer Fruit Soup

2	cups water
1/2	cup sugar
	zest of 1 lemon
	zest of 1 lime
	zest of 1 orange
1 1/2	teaspoon vanilla extract
2	sprigs fresh mint (approximately 16 leaves, lightly crushed)
2	fresh peaches, cut in half, thinly sliced
2	purple plums, cut in half, thinly sliced
3	cups assorted berries (raspberries, blackberries, strawberries, etc.)
8	mint leaves, cut in slivers

Combine the first 7 ingredients in a small saucepan. Bring to a boil, simmer 3 minutes. Remove from heat, set aside 3 hours.

Strain syrup and refrigerate until well chilled.

Add sliced peaches and plums to syrup. Chill.

Before serving add berries and mint leaves, cut in slivers.

Serves: 4

For a special dash, 1/2 cup dry white wine or champagne could be added just before serving.

180 Cal., 1gm Protein, 45gm Carb., .5gm Fat, 5mg Sodium, 0mg Chol., 5.1gm Fiber

Winter Vegetable Soup

4	cups chicken broth
4	carrots, diced
1	cup wax beans, sliced
4	ribs celery with leaves, sliced
1	large potato, diced
1	large white onion, chopped
1	clove garlic, pressed
2	tablespoons fresh dill, chopped
1/2	cup nonfat milk
1/2	cup plain nonfat yogurt
1/3	cup dry white wine
	salt and pepper to taste

In a medium stock pot, bring broth, vegetables and herbs to a boil. Lower heat, cover and simmer for 45 minutes until vegetables are semi-tender. Mash a few pieces of potato in the soup base to thicken it. Let cool. Add milk, yogurt, wine, salt and pepper and reheat. Serve hot.

Serves: 8

Serve this soup with a hearty whole wheat bread.

79 Cal., 4gm Protein, 14gm Carb., .5gm Fat, 894mg Sodium, 1mg Chol., 2.5gm Fiber

SALADS

SALADS

Black Bean, Corn and Tomato Salad

2   cans black beans,
  drained and rinsed

1   10-ounce package frozen corn
  or 2 ears fresh corn
  off the cob

2   large ripe tomatoes,
  peeled and chopped

      salt and pepper

1   small red onion, finely chopped

Mix all ingredients. Refrigerate for 20 minutes or until chilled.

Serves: 4 - 6

Also serve as a salsa with low-fat chips.

---

157 Cal., 9gm Protein, 31gm Carb., 1.1gm Fat, 378mg Sodium, 0mg Chol., 12.8gm Fiber

Black-eyed Pea Salad

Dressing:

1/8	cup olive oil
1	teaspoon Dijon mustard
2	tablespoons red wine vinegar
1	clove garlic, minced

Salad:

2	15-ounce cans black-eyed peas, drained
2	scallions, chopped
1	small red pepper, chopped
1	small green pepper, chopped
1/4	cup parsley, chopped
1/4	cup chervil, chopped (optional)

Combine dressing ingredients and set aside.

Combine salad ingredients. Pour dressing over salad ingredients. Allow to marinate for several hours at room temperature or longer in the refrigerator.

Serves: 6

Serve this salad cold or at room temperature.

197 Cal., 11gm Protein, 27gm Carb., 5.1gm Fat, 69mg Sodium, 0mg Chol., 7.9gm Fiber

Cucumber Tomato Salad

2	large cucumbers, peeled, seeded and chopped
3	tomatoes, chopped
½	red onion, diced
1	green pepper, diced
2	tablespoons olive oil
2	tablespoons lemon juice
1	large clove garlic, minced
2	tablespoons fresh basil, chopped, or 1 teaspoon dried basil
1	tablespoon fresh oregano, chopped, or ½ teaspoon dried oregano
	salt to taste (optional)
	freshly ground black pepper to taste

Combine all the vegetables in a large bowl.

Mix the remaining ingredients in a cup.

Pour the dressing over the vegetables and toss very gently.

Cover and let the salad marinate in the refrigerator for at least 1 hour. (The longer the salad marinates, the more flavor it will have.) Toss occasionally.

Taste to adjust seasonings before serving.

Serves: 8

Serve with Cajun Fish and crusty French bread.

55 Cal., 1gm Protein, 6gm Carb., 3.7gm Fat, 6.7mg Sodium, 0mg Chol., 2.1gm Fiber

SALADS

Fattoosh

2	rounds of pita bread
1	cup fresh parsley, coarsely chopped
1	green onion, chopped
1	head iceberg lettuce, coarsely chopped
4	tomatoes, cut in small wedges
1	green pepper, chopped
1	lemon, juiced
	salt and pepper to taste
	pinch of garlic powder
	pinch of sumak
1/4	cup olive oil
2	teaspoons mint, chopped

Toast the pita bread, break it into small pieces and set aside.

Place the chopped vegetables in a bowl and toss until well mixed. Add the lemon juice, salt, pepper, garlic, sumak, oil and mint.

Toss bread with the above ingredients and mix well. Serve immediately before bread gets soggy.

The sumak used in this recipe can be found in a Middle East food store, not in your backyard. Serve Fattoosh with Middle East Chick Pea Dip and Pita Bread.

Serves: 6

Nate's Deli and Restaurant

115 Cal., 4gm Protein, 15gm Carb., 5.2gm Fat, 279mg Sodium, 0mg Chol., 3.9gm Fiber

SALADS

Fresh Corn Salad

6	ears of corn, boiled or roasted, kernels cut from the cob
1	cup red onion, finely chopped
1	cup cilantro, finely chopped
2	medium tomatoes, chopped
	salt and pepper to taste

Dressing:

1/4	cup fresh lime juice
1	tablespoon olive oil
1/2	teaspoon Dijon mustard

Stir dressing ingredients together until well mixed. Combine remaining ingredients. Pour dressing over vegetables. Let marinate at room temperature at least 4 hours before serving.

Serves: 6 - 8

A good way to use leftover corn!

95 Cal., 3gm Protein, 19gm Carb., 2.6gm Fat, 157mg Sodium, 0mg Chol., 4.3gm Fiber

SALADS

Golden Raisin Coleslaw

Vinaigrette:

4	tablespoons golden raisins
3	tablespoons red wine vinegar
2	tablespoons olive oil
1/2	cup water
2	tablespoons onion, finely chopped
1	teaspoon Dijon mustard
	salt and pepper to taste

Coleslaw:

2	cups cabbage, grated
1	carrot, coarsely grated
1/2	cup golden raisins

In a small saucepan, combine the 4 tablespoons of raisins, vinegar, oil, water, onion, mustard, salt and pepper to taste and boil the mixture, stirring, for 30 seconds. In a blender, purée the vinaigrette until it is smooth.

Combine the cabbage, carrot and 1/2 cup of raisins.

Pour vinaigrette over vegetables and toss.

Serves: 6

Serve with Grilled Ginger Chicken Patties.

---

106 Cal., 1gm Protein, 20gm Carb., 3.6gm Fat, 205mg Sodium, 0mg Chol., 2.7gm Fiber

SALADS

Grilled Marinated Chicken on Oriental Salad

4	chicken breasts, about 4 ounces each, boned and skinned
1 1/2	cups bean sprouts
1	cup snow peas
1/2	cup water chestnuts
1	cup alfalfa sprouts
1	cup cherry tomatoes, halved

Marinade:

2	tablespoons garlic, crushed
3	tablespoons light soy sauce
3	tablespoons Oriental sesame oil
6	tablespoons rice vinegar
1	teaspoon freshly ground black pepper
1/2	teaspoon chili oil (optional)

Prepare marinade. Marinate chicken breasts in 3/4 of marinade for 24 hours. Remove chicken and grill over mesquite charcoal until cooked through, turning several times and basting with marinade.

While chicken is cooking, mix bean sprouts, snow peas, water chestnuts and alfalfa sprouts. Lightly toss salad with remaining 1/4 of marinade. Arrange on plates and serve chicken breasts on top of salad. Garnish with cherry tomatoes.

Serves: 4

Sesame oil gives this great flavor! Tastes great served with Crostini.

286 Cal., 28gm Protein, 16gm Carb., 12.1gm Fat, 376mg Sodium, 66mg Chol., 3gm Fiber

Italian Winter Salad

10 ounces fresh or frozen Italian green beans
10 ounces fresh or frozen cauliflower
2 carrots, thinly sliced
1/2 cup small pitted green olives
1 small red onion, thinly sliced in rings

Dressing:
1 large clove of garlic, minced
1/2 teaspoon salt
3 tablespoons red wine vinegar
2 tablespoons olive oil
1/4 teaspoon black pepper, ground

Steam Italian green beans, cauliflower and carrots for 5-10 minutes or until just tender. In the bottom of a salad bowl, mash garlic and salt to a paste with the back of a spoon. Stir in vinegar, oil and pepper. Add vegetables, olives, and onion rings to the dressing. Toss gently to coat thoroughly.

Serves: 4 - 6

Great as an accompaniment to Baked Ziti with Spicy Marinara Sauce and Italian bread, this colorful dish can be served at room temperature or slightly warm.

91 Cal., 2gm Protein, 9gm Carb., 6.2gm Fat, 477mg Sodium, 0mg Chol., 3.3gm Fiber

SALADS

Marinated Cauliflower

1	head cauliflower, cut the head into flowerets and cut the stalk into bite-size pieces
1/8	cup olive oil
1/2	cup balsamic vinegar
1/4	teaspoon salt
1/8	teaspoon pepper
1	tablespoon fresh chives, chopped
1	teaspoon fresh thyme, chopped
2	teaspoons fresh dill, chopped
1	clove garlic, minced

Garnish:
    red leaf lettuce
    chopped red bell pepper

Steam the cauliflower until tender but not mushy. Cool. Combine the remaining ingredients, except the red bell pepper and the lettuce. Pour the mixture over the cauliflower and stir to make sure that all of the cauliflower is coated with the marinade. Marinate 8 hours, stirring several times during the marinating process.

    Serve on a bed of red leaf lettuce and sprinkle with red bell pepper.

Serves: 6

Great with Turkey Breast Royale and Garlic Potato Straw Surprise.

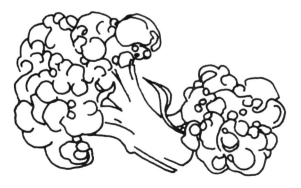

69 Cal., 2gm Protein, 6gm Carb., 4.8gm Fat, 112mg Sodium, 0mg Chol., 2.4gm Fiber

Moroccan Carrot Salad

1 1/2 pounds carrots,
       peeled and sliced
1/2   tablespoon olive oil
1   whole clove garlic, crushed
1 1/2 tablespoon paprika
1 1/2 teaspoon cumin
4   tablespoons white wine vinegar
2   tablespoons tomato paste
2   tablespoons parsley, chopped
2   tablespoons cilantro, chopped
2   tablespoons sugar
1/4   teaspoon salt

Cook carrots, covered in water, over low heat for 5 to 10 minutes or until slightly crisp.

Drain and rinse immediately in cold water. Let cool and mix together with remaining ingredients. Refrigerate.

Serves: 4

127 Cal., 2gm Protein, 27gm Carb., 2.2gm Fat, 203mg Sodium, 0mg Chol., 6.3gm Fiber

Pear Salad with Dijon Vinaigrette

Pear Salad:

    red leaf lettuce

4   ripe red pears, sliced

1   red onion, thinly sliced

Dijon Vinaigrette:

2   teaspoons Dijon mustard

2   tablespoons balsamic vinegar

2   tablespoons olive oil

1/4   cup cold water

1/2   teaspoon sugar

1/4   teaspoon salt

1/8   teaspoon freshly ground black pepper

Pear Salad:

For each portion, place several lettuce leaves on a plate, layer on pear slices, then onion slices. Dress with Dijon Vinaigrette.

Dijon Vinaigrette:

In a small bowl, combine ingredients, whisk until smooth.

Serves: 4

Serve with Scallop Stuffed Sole.

---

172 Cal., 1gm Protein, 28gm Carb., 7.6gm Fat, 174mg Sodium, 0mg Chol., 5.6gm Fiber

Peppy Lima Bean Salad

2	10-ounce packages frozen lima beans, thawed
1	tablespoon salad oil
1	medium green pepper, diced
1	small onion, diced
1	tablespoon pimento, chopped
1/4	cup cider vinegar
2	tablespoons sugar
	salt to taste
	fresh spinach leaves

Garnish:
julienned yellow squash
black pepper, coarsely ground

Place the salad oil in a 12-inch skillet over medium heat. Sauté green pepper and onion until tender (about 4 minutes), stirring occasionally. Add lima beans and cook 4-5 minutes more. Add pimento, vinegar, sugar and salt to skillet, stirring gently and cook 2 minutes longer.

Put skillet ingredients in a glass bowl, cool and refrigerate overnight.

Serve atop fresh spinach leaves on a platter. Garnish with julienned yellow squash placed at each end of the platter. Sprinkle with ground black pepper.

Serves: 8

116 Cal., 6gm Protein, 20gm Carb., 2.1gm Fat, 28mg Sodium, 0mg Chol., 3.4gm Fiber

Piquant Potato Salad

1½	pounds white potatoes
2	large, ripe tomatoes
1	small red onion, peeled
¼	cup pitted green olives, coarsely chopped
¼	cup pitted black olives, coarsely chopped
1	tablespoon capers
2	small garlic cloves, peeled and finely minced
3	tablespoons extra virgin olive oil
¼	cup imported, good quality, red wine vinegar
	salt and freshly ground black pepper to taste

Boil the potatoes in boiling water until tender but firm, about 15 minutes. Drain. Return the potatoes to the pot and toss over high heat to evaporate any remaining moisture. Set aside to cool.

When cool enough to handle, peel and cut into approximately 1-inch cubes, keeping them irregular in size.

Core the tomatoes and cut into chunks about the same size as the potatoes. Cut the red onion into ⅛-inch thick slices.

Combine the potatoes, tomatoes, red onion, olives, capers, and garlic in a large bowl. Add the olive oil, vinegar, salt and pepper. Toss gently to mix. Adjust the seasonings and serve at room temperature.

Serves: 6

Serve with Oven-fried Chicken.

---

181 Cal., 3gm Protein, 27gm Carb., 8gm Fat, 280mg Sodium, 0mg Chol., 3.3gm Fiber

Seafood-stuffed Tomatoes

- ½ cup tomato juice
- ½ cup chili sauce
- 3 ounces low-fat cream cheese
- 2 tablespoons white horseradish
- 1½ teaspoons Worcestershire sauce
- ½ cup nonfat mayonnaise
- ½ cup nonfat sour cream
- 1 green bell pepper, finely diced
- 1 rib celery, finely sliced
- 2 large scallions, finely sliced
- ½ pound baby shrimp
- ½ pound crab meat or imitation crab
- 15 medium to small tomatoes, hollowed out

Heat tomato juice, chili sauce and cream cheese on low heat until cheese melts, set aside to cool.

Place cooled mixture in bowl and add horseradish, Worcestershire, mayonnaise, sour cream, vegetables, shrimp and crab. Lightly toss together.

Fill hollowed-out tomatoes.

Note: Filling may be prepared 24 hours in advance. Tomatoes can be hollowed out and inverted on paper towel-covered plate 24 hours in advance. Fill tomatoes right before serving.

Serves: 15

A wonderful lunch or light supper entree.

96 Cal., 9gm Protein, 11gm Carb., 2.1gm Fat, 313mg Sodium, 46mg Chol., 1.9gm Fiber

SALADS

Shrimp Salad

1½ pounds cooked shrimp,
    coarsely chopped
1   cup celery, coarsely chopped
½   cup leeks, finely chopped
3   tablespoons fresh basil,
    chopped, or
    1½ tablespoons dried basil
1   cup nonfat mayonnaise

Put all the ingredients in a bowl and mix well. Chill for 2 hours.

Serves: 4

Serve as a salad or use the mixture to stuff tomatoes.

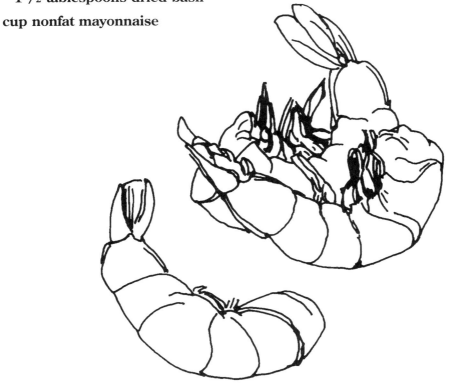

268 Cal., 40gm Protein, 15gm Carb., 3.7gm Fat, 748mg Sodium, 300mg Chol., 1.2gm Fiber

Spicy Chick Pea Relish Salad

Dressing:

2	teaspoons cumin seeds, toasted and ground
1	lemon, juiced
1½	teaspoons salt
½	teaspoon pepper
4	cloves garlic, minced
⅛	teaspoon red pepper, ground
2	teaspoons extra virgin olive oil

Salad:

1	15 or 19-ounce can chick peas, drained
1½	cups English cucumbers, diced
¾	cup celery, diced
¼	cup green onions, chopped
¼	cup toasted walnuts, chopped
1	avocado, diced (optional)

Dressing:
Place cumin seeds in bowl and whisk in lemon juice, salt, pepper, garlic and red pepper. Slowly whisk in oil.

Salad:
Combine the salad ingredients. Toss with dressing and refrigerate.

Serves: 6

Serve with Chicken Arabesque II or as a side dish with grilled fish.

157 Cal., 6gm Protein, 23gm Carb., 5.5gm Fat, 807mg Sodium, 0mg Chol., 4.4gm Fiber

Spicy Corn and Bean Confetti Salad

2	cups of cooked fresh sweet corn or 1 10-ounce package frozen corn, thawed
1	19-ounce can dark red kidney beans, drained
3	green onions, minced
4	teaspoons red wine vinegar
1	lime, juiced
1/2	teaspoon ground coriander
3/4	teaspoon ground cumin
1/2	teaspoon salt
1	tablespoon fresh cilantro, minced
1	tablespoon extra virgin olive oil

In a large serving bowl, combine corn, kidney beans and green onions. Set aside.

In a small mixing bowl, combine vinegar, lime, coriander, cumin, salt and cilantro. Slowly whisk olive oil into mixture and pour mixture over the confetti salad, tossing to coat.

Serves: 4

---

225 Cal., 10gm Protein, 40gm Carb., 4.9gm Fat, 724mg Sodium, 0mg Chol., 7.9gm Fiber

Spinach Salad with Strawberry Vinaigrette

1	pound fresh spinach, washed and patted dry
2	cups fresh strawberries, thinly sliced
½	medium Vidalia onion, shaved (use vegetable peeler)
1	cup fresh mushrooms, sliced
½	cup sliced almonds, lightly toasted
¼	cup strawberry wine vinegar
1	tablespoon walnut oil (optional)

Place spinach, broken into bite-size pieces, in serving bowl.

Toss with next 4 ingredients.

Splash on strawberry vinegar. (Or vinegar mixed with walnut oil, although salad is good without oil.)

Serves: 8

Serve with Pan-seared Spicy Breast of Chicken.

77 Cal., 4gm Protein, 8gm Carb., 4.7gm Fat, 46mg Sodium, 0mg Chol., 3.9gm Fiber

SALADS

Tomato Feta Pasta Salad

1	pound tricolor pasta, cooked
2	large tomatoes, chopped
2	large scallions, thinly sliced
4	ounces feta cheese, crumbled
1/4	cup fresh mint, chopped
1	tablespoon fresh basil, chopped
3	tablespoons fresh dill, chopped, or 1 1/2 tablespoons dried dill
1	tablespoon olive oil
1	lemon, juiced
	freshly ground black pepper

Mix the pasta with the other ingredients. Serve at room temperature.

Serves: 6 - 8

440 Cal., 15gm Protein, 72gm Carb., 10.9gm Fat, 331mg Sodium, 25mg Chol., 4.2gm Fiber

Tunisian Salad with Piquant Dressing

Couscous:

1	tablespoon olive oil
1	small onion, finely chopped
1	stalk celery, finely chopped
1½	cups water
1	cup couscous

Piquant Dressing:

3	tablespoons plain nonfat yogurt
3	tablespoons fresh lime juice
1	tablespoon olive oil
2	teaspoons fresh ginger root, minced
1	clove garlic, crushed
¼	teaspoon cayenne pepper
1	teaspoon ground turmeric
½	teaspoon ground cumin
½	teaspoon ground coriander
½	teaspoon chili powder
	salt and freshly ground black pepper to taste

Couscous:

In a 2-quart saucepan over medium heat, heat oil; add onion and celery; cook 2 to 3 minutes, stirring occasionally until vegetables are softened. Add water; bring to boil, stirring gently. Remove from heat, add couscous and let stand, covered, 30 minutes until cool and liquid is absorbed, uncovering occasionally to fluff with a fork.

Piquant Dressing:

Combine dressing ingredients, beat well to blend. Set aside.

(continued)

Salad:

1/2	cup dried currants or raisins
1/2	cup canned garbanzos, rinsed and drained
1/2	cup yellow bell pepper, chopped
1/2	cup red bell pepper, chopped
1/2	cup cilantro, chopped
2	medium scallions, sliced

Garnish:

lemon wedges

Combine salad ingredients with prepared couscous. Serve accompanied by dressing. Garnish with lemon wedges.

Serves: 4

Piquant Dressing is wonderful over broiled chicken breasts.

235 Cal., 6gm Protein, 39gm Carb., 7.7gm Fat, 592mg Sodium, .2mg Chol., 5.7gm Fiber

Tuna Salad with Fruit

3	6½-ounce cans chunk light albacore tuna, water pack
½	cup red bell pepper, chopped
¼	cup green onions, chopped
2	dill pickles, chopped
1	Granny Smith apple, chopped
2	tablespoons Dijon mustard
1	tablespoon low-fat mayonnaise
¼	teaspoon onion powder
8	ounces plain low-fat yogurt
10	seedless green grapes, cut in half

Drain the water from the tuna, place in medium-sized bowl. Add red pepper, onions, pickles, apple, mustard mayonnaise, onion powder and yogurt, mix well. Add grapes and toss.

Refrigerate until chilled, approximately 2 hours.

Serves: 6

Mound tuna on a platter lined with lettuce leaves and surround with pita bread triangles.

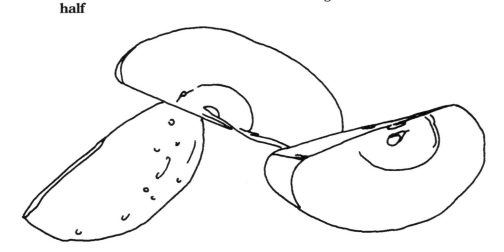

173 Cal., 28gm Protein, 10gm Carb., 1.9gm Fat, 897mg Sodium, 40mg Chol., 1.7gm Fiber

SALADS

White Kidney Bean Salad

1	19-ounce can white kidney beans (cannellini)
1	cup fresh tomatoes, diced
1/2	cup red onion, diced
1/2	cup green pepper, diced
1/4	cup fresh parsley, chopped
2	ounces part-skim mozzarella cheese, diced

Dressing:

1/4	cup lemon juice
1	teaspoon olive oil
1	tablespoon balsamic vinegar
1	clove garlic, minced
2	teaspoons lemon rind, grated
1/2	teaspoon dried tarragon
1/2	teaspoon sugar
1	teaspoon fresh dill, chopped
1/4	teaspoon black pepper, ground

Combine the beans, tomatoes, onion, green pepper, parsley, and mozzarella. Whisk together remaining ingredients to make the dressing. Pour the dressing over the vegetable mixture, toss to mix well. Serve at room temperature or cold.

Serves: 4

Serve with crusty French bread for a light lunch.

125 Cal., 8gm Protein, 16gm Carb., 3.9gm Fat, 293mg Sodium, 8mg Chol., 2.9gm Fiber

PASTA - RICE

Black Beans with Rice

1	pound black beans
2½	quarts water
1	green pepper, chopped
1	medium chopped white onion, divided
¼	cup fresh cilantro, chopped
5	cloves garlic minced or pressed
1	teaspoon dried oregano
1	teaspoon cumin
3	tablespoons vinegar, divided
1	tablespoon olive oil
1	teaspoon salt
3	cups hot cooked rice

Rinse beans. Cover with 6 cups water in a large kettle. Add bell pepper and half of the onion and the cilantro. Soak overnight.

When ready to cook, add 4 cups water and bring to boil. Reduce heat. Cover and simmer until beans are tender, about 2½ hours.

Meanwhile, mash together, using mortar and pestle or food processor, the remaining half onion, garlic, oregano and cumin. Mix in 1 tablespoon vinegar.

In a small frying pan, sauté the onion mixture in 1 tablespoon of olive oil about 5 minutes or until golden.

Stir the remaining 2 tablespoons vinegar into the onion mixture; then add it to the beans. Add salt.

Simmer for about 20 minutes and just before serving, spoon over hot rice.

Serves: 6

241 Cal., 9gm Protein, 45gm Carb., 3gm Fat, 374mg Sodium, 0mg Chol., 9.3gm Fiber

Baked Ziti with Spicy Marinara Sauce

Spicy Marinara Sauce:

1/8	cup extra virgin olive oil
12	cloves garlic, finely chopped
1 1/2	cups red wine
1	teaspoon crushed red pepper
3	28-ounce cans crushed, imported Italian tomatoes
3	pinches of seasoned salt
3	pinches of sugar
6	tablespoons fresh basil, chopped

Spicy Marinara Sauce:

In a heavy saucepan, heat the olive oil over medium heat. Sauté garlic until it begins to color slightly. Pour in wine and cook until a good bit of the liquid evaporates. Add the crushed red pepper, tomatoes, salt and sugar and cook over low heat for 20 minutes, until sauce thickens slightly. Add the basil and cook 5 minutes more.

Yield: 7 1/2 cups

Baked Ziti:

Prepare the marinara.

Prick the sausage with a fork, place it on a broiler rack and bake it in a 400° oven for 20 minutes. When the sausage is done, transfer it to a cutting board, let cool and cut into 1/4-inch slices.

(continued)

Baked Ziti:

1	pound ziti
1	pound turkey sausage
15	ounces low-fat ricotta cheese
1	egg white
1/4	cup fresh parsley, minced
6	cups Spicy Marinara Sauce
1	pound part-skim mozzarella cheese, grated
1 1/2	cups low-fat Romano cheese, grated

Cook the ziti *al dente* and drain thoroughly.

Combine the ricotta, egg white and parsley in a bowl and mix well.

Coat the bottom of a 15 x 10 x 2½-inch baking pan with 2 cups of the Spicy Marinara Sauce. On the sauce, layer half the ziti, half the ricotta mixture, half the sausage, half the mozzarella and half the Romano cheese and cover the mixture with 2 more cups of sauce.

Layer the remaining ziti, ricotta, sausage, and mozzarella. Cover with the last 2 cups of sauce and remaining Romano cheese. Bake in a 375° oven for 45-60 minutes, or until bubbling. Remove from oven, let it stand for 5-10 minutes before serving.

Serves: 10

Freeze the remaining sauce for a quick pasta meal.

---

472 Cal., 39gm Protein, 47gm Carb., 14.1gm Fat, 905mg Sodium, 58mg Chol., 4.7gm Fiber

PASTA - RICE

Capellini with Grilled Chicken and Tarragon Sauce

1	tablespoon olive oil
3	medium shallots, peeled and chopped
1	garlic clove, minced
3	1-pound cans tomatoes
2	tablespoons tomato paste
1	cup chicken broth
½	cup fresh tarragon, chopped, or 3 tablespoons dried
	salt and pepper to taste
2	pounds grilled boneless, skinless chicken breasts cut into 1-inch cubes
1	pound cooked capellini

Heat 1 tablespoon olive oil in heavy 1-quart saucepan. Sauté shallots and garlic until soft (do not brown). Add tomatoes, tomato paste, chicken broth, tarragon, salt and pepper. Bring to a boil; reduce heat to gentle boil and cook until the mixture reaches a sauce consistency (about 35 minutes). Add chicken and heat thoroughly.

Serve over capellini.

Serves: 6

471 Cal., 42gm Protein, 56gm Carb., 8.4gm Fat, 878mg Sodium, 88mg Chol., 5.4gm Fiber

Colorful Linguine Stir Fry

1	pound linguine
1/3	cup pine nuts
1/2	tablespoon sesame oil in spray bottle
	vegetable spray
1	bunch beet greens, washed, cut 2-3 inches from beets and simmered, drained and chopped
1/3	cup Canadian bacon, cut in strips
3/4	cup yellow and red peppers, julienned
3	large garlic cloves, minced
	salt and freshly ground pepper to taste
	Cavender's Greek seasoning

Cook linguine per package instructions.

Lightly cook pine nuts in wok or large skillet sprayed with vegetable spray and sesame oil. Remove pine nuts and add all ingredients but linguine, pine nuts and Cavender's Greek seasoning. Sauté over medium heat and cook until peppers are tender. Pour over linguine, toss lightly while adding Greek seasoning.

Top with pine nuts.

Serves: 4

407 Cal., 17gm Protein, 75gm Carb., 5.5gm Fat, 812mg Sodium, 7mg Chol., 6.8gm Fiber

Faux Fettucine Alfredo

1	pound egg noodles
1	tablespoon butter or margarine
1/4	cup Parmesan Reggiano cheese, freshly grated
1	tablespoon garlic, chopped
1	teaspoon salt
1	teaspoon black pepper, freshly ground
8	ounces plain low-fat yogurt

Cook the noodles per the directions. Drain well and add butter, cheese, garlic, salt and pepper and stir until melted (microwave 1 minute if needed). Stir in the yogurt and serve.

Serves: 4

No cream, but creamy!

491 Cal., 20gm Protein, 80gm Carb., 9.8gm Fat, 758mg Sodium, 114mg Chol., 2.3gm Fiber

Greek Couscous Pilaf

1 1/2	cups chicken broth
1	tablespoon butter
3	tablespoons golden raisins
1	cup couscous
2	tablespoons toasted, slivered almonds
1	tablespoon each minced parsley and scallions
1/4	teaspoon freshly ground coarse black pepper
2	teaspoons melted butter (optional)

Heat chicken broth, butter and raisins in a saucepan to boiling. Add couscous, stir, remove from heat, cover and let sit for 5 minutes. Add toasted almonds, parsley, scallions and black pepper. Drizzle with melted butter and stir.

Serves: 4

Serve with Cajun fish.

159 Cal., 4gm Protein, 24gm Carb., 5.7gm Fat, 540mg Sodium, 8mg Chol., 1.4gm Fiber

Noodle Soufflé

2	tablespoons cornstarch
1	tablespoon water
2	cups skim milk
1¼	teaspoons salt
¼	teaspoon white pepper
¼	teaspoon nutmeg
½	cup plain low-fat yogurt
¾	cup grated light Parmesan cheese
2	egg yolks
½	pound fine noodles (vermicelli), cooked and drained
4	egg whites, stiffly beaten
	vegetable spray

Preheat oven to 375°.

Dilute cornstarch in water. Heat milk in saucepan, add cornstarch and spices and cook over medium heat until thickened, stirring constantly.

Remove from heat, stir in yogurt and Parmesan. Lightly beat 2 egg yolks and add to mixture while stirring. Add cooked noodles and mix well.

Beat egg whites until stiff. Incorporate ⅓ of egg whites to lighten mixture then carefully fold in remaining egg whites. Spray a 3-quart soufflé dish with vegetable spray. Pour in mixture and bake for 40 minutes or until brown on top.

Serves: 4

348 Cal., 22gm Protein, 45gm Carb., 8.6gm Fat, 1,103mg Sodium, 152mg Chol., 1.2gm Fiber

PASTA - RICE

Nutcracker Mart Fruited Rice

1	**cup long grain rice**
1	**tablespoon instant minced onion**
2	**teaspoons curry powder**
2	**beef bouillon cubes**
1/4	**cup mixed dried fruits (apricots, prunes, apples), chopped**
2	**tablespoons golden raisins**
1/4	**cup blanched slivered almonds**
1/2	**tablespoon margarine or butter**
2 1/2	**cups water**

Combine all ingredients and mix with 2 1/2 cups of water. Cover tightly, bring to a boil. Reduce heat and simmer for 20 minutes.

Serves: 4

Package all the dry ingredients and give as a gift with instructions to add margarine and water.

338 Cal., 7gm Protein, 65gm Carb., 6.3gm Fat, 366mg Sodium, 0mg Chol., 2.7gm Fiber

Orecchiette with Tomatoes and Arugula

2	large tomatoes (preferably not too ripe), chopped
2-3	cups arugula, chopped
2	tablespoons olive oil
	salt and pepper to taste
1	pound orecchiette (found at Italian specialty stores)
1	cup salted hard ricotta cheese (found at Italian specialty stores), freshly grated

In a large bowl, combine the chopped tomatoes, half of the arugula, olive oil, salt and pepper and let stand.

Cook the orecchiette in salted boiling water according to instructions. Drain the pasta, combine it with the tomato-arugula mixture. Add the remaining arugula, sprinkle ricotta cheese over it and serve.

Serves: 4

For a change in flavor, substitute fresh basil for arugula.

478 Cal., 18gm Protein, 73gm Carb., 13gm Fat, 538mg Sodium, 19mg Chol., 4.1gm Fiber

Oriental Chicken and Noodles

6	boned, skinless, chicken breast halves, cooked and shredded
4	garlic cloves, minced
2	tablespoons fresh ginger, minced
1/3	cup tahini (sesame seed paste)
6	tablespoons soy sauce (low sodium)
1	tablespoon sugar
3	tablespoons sesame oil
3	tablespoons rice vinegar
3	tablespoons dry vermouth or white wine
1	pound linguine, cooked
5	scallions, sliced into thin rounds
5	tablespoons fresh cilantro, finely chopped

In a large mixing bowl, combine the garlic, ginger, sesame paste, soy sauce, sugar, sesame oil, rice vinegar and wine; mix well.

Add the shredded chicken, linguine, scallions and cilantro. Toss until all is well mixed and serve or refrigerate until serving.

Serves: 6

Serve with a green salad.

581 Cal., 49gm Protein, 50gm Carb., 19.7gm Fat, 602mg Sodium, 99mg Chol., 3gm Fiber

Penne with Green Beans and Arugula Pesto

1 cup Arugula Pesto

1/2 pound green beans, washed and trimmed

1 pound penne

Arugula Pesto:

2 bunches arugula (about 6 packed cups), washed, stems removed and dried

2 tablespoons pine nuts

3/4 cup Parmesan cheese, grated

1-2 garlic cloves

1 tablespoon olive oil

1 teaspoon salt

2 tablespoons water

Put all pesto ingredients except water in food processor and chop. Scrape down sides. With motor running, add water in a stream to make a smooth paste.

Cook the green beans in salted, boiling water until tender but still crisp. Remove with a slotted spoon and keep warm in a large mixing bowl. In the same boiling water, cook the pasta al dente, drain and add to the green beans.

Toss with 1 cup of Arugula Pesto. Add salt and pepper to taste and serve.

Note: Remaining pesto can be kept in refrigerator for 1 week if covered with plastic wrap.

Serves: 4 - 6

317 Cal., 13gm Protein, 48gm Carb., 8.6gm Fat, 570mg Sodium, 8mg Chol., 3.2gm Fiber

Penne with Porcini Mushrooms

1½	cups dry porcini mushrooms
2	shallots, peeled and chopped
1	clove garlic, peeled and chopped
2	teaspoons olive oil
1	28-ounce can peeled plum tomatoes with juice, coarsely chopped
1½	teaspoons Italian seasoning
1	chicken bouillon cube
	salt and pepper to taste
1	pound penne
½	cup fresh parsley, finely chopped
½	cup fresh Parmesan cheese, grated

Soak the mushrooms for at least 2 hours in enough water to cover. Squeeze out and reserve the water and chop the mushrooms. Sauté the chopped shallots and garlic in the oil for 1 minute. Add the chopped tomatoes, Italian seasoning and bouillon cube. Stir well. Add the chopped mushrooms and the reserved water and salt and pepper. Cook for 30 minutes on low heat, stirring occasionally.

While the sauce is cooking, boil 4 quarts of salted water and cook the penne as directed. Drain thoroughly. Add the sauce and toss. Just before serving, add the chopped parsley. Serve with grated Parmesan cheese.

Serves: 4

425 Cal., 17gm Protein, 75gm Carb., 7.2gm Fat, 809mg Sodium, 8mg Chol., 5.7gm Fiber

Risotto with Mushrooms

1	tablespoon butter
2	garlic cloves, minced
2	tablespoons minced leeks or scallions
1	cup Italian Arborio rice
1/4	teaspoon salt
	black pepper to taste
3	cups hot chicken broth, divided
1	teaspoon butter
1/2	cup sliced fresh mushrooms
1/4	teaspoon salt
1/8	teaspoon saffron
1	tablespoon parsley, chopped
1/4	cup Parmesan cheese, freshly grated

Heat 1 tablespoon butter in a heavy saucepan. Sauté garlic and leek or scallions over low heat until soft but not browned. Stir in rice, salt and black pepper and sauté until rice is lightly browned.

Add 1/2 cup hot chicken broth. Simmer over medium heat, stirring often, until broth is absorbed. Continue adding broth, 1/2 cup at a time, cooking until it is absorbed. Total cooking time will be about 20 minutes.

In a small skillet, heat butter and sauté mushrooms. Add salt, saffron and parsley. Add to risotto mixture stirring slowly. Add Parmesan cheese and stir with a fork. Taste for seasoning. Serve immediately.

Serves: 4

274 Cal., 8gm Protein, 43gm Carb., 5.4gm Fat, 1,738mg Sodium, 15mg Chol., .9gm Fiber

PASTA - RICE

Spiced Rice Pilaf

1	tablespoon olive oil
1	cup chopped onion
1/2	cup sliced mushrooms
2	teaspoons fresh ginger, minced
1 1/2	cups long grain rice
3	cups water
1	teaspoon salt
1/4	cup green onions, thinly sliced

Heat oil in large saucepan over medium heat. Add onions and cook 4 minutes. Add mushrooms and cook 3 minutes or until both onions and mushrooms are tender. Stir in ginger, then rice; cook, stirring, 1 minute. Stir in water and salt. Bring to a boil; reduce heat, cover and simmer 20 minutes. Remove from heat and let stand, covered, 5 minutes. Add green onions and fluff with fork.

Serves: 10

Excellent served as an accompaniment to Pork Tenderloin Marco.

199 Cal., 4gm Protein, 40gm Carb., 2.5gm Fat, 372mg Sodium, 0mg Chol., .9gm Fiber

Spinach Ravioli with Shitake Mushroom Sauce

Shitake Mushroom Sauce:

- 1   28-ounce can whole, peeled tomatoes, chopped
- 1/2   cup fresh basil, chopped
- 2   (or more) cloves garlic, pressed
- 1/2   pound Shitake mushrooms, sliced
-     salt and pepper to taste

Spinach Filling:

- 1   cup tomatoes, peeled, seeded and diced
- 1   small onion, chopped
- 1   cup mushrooms, minced
- 2   teaspoons garlic, minced
- 1/2   pound spinach leaves, blanched and chopped
- 1/2   cup nonfat cottage cheese
- 2   tablespoons fresh basil, minced

Shitake Mushroom Sauce:

Place all sauce ingredients in a saucepan and cook over medium heat for 10-15 minutes or until the sauce has reached the desired consistency.

Spinach Filling:

In a large saucepan, combine the tomatoes, onion, mushrooms and garlic. Cook over medium heat until all liquid evaporates. Set aside and cool.

In a large bowl, combine tomato mixture, spinach, cottage cheese and basil. Season to taste with salt and pepper.

(continued)

48   won ton skins

Garnish:
>   **fresh basil**
>   **freshly grated Parmesan cheese
>   (optional)**

To assemble ravioli:

On cutting board, lay a single layer of won ton skins. Using a pastry brush, moisten edges with water. Place 1 tablespoon of mixture in center, cover with second won ton skin and seal edges with fork. Cook the ravioli in boiling water for 3 minutes or until they float.

Serve with Shitake Mushroom Sauce. Garnish with fresh basil and freshly grated Parmesan cheese.

Serves: 4 entrée or 12 appetizer

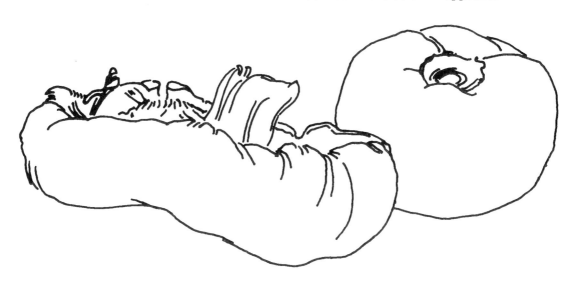

63 Cal., 3.9gm Protein, 12gm Carb., .6gm Fat, 224mg Sodium, .4mg Chol., 2.9gm Fiber

MAIN COURSES

MAIN COURSES

Chicken Arabesque II

6	boneless, skinless chicken breast halves
2	teaspoons cumin seed
1	teaspoon coriander seed
1	teaspoon whole black peppercorns
2	limes, juiced
1	tablespoon cilantro, chopped
1/2	teaspoon red pepper seeds, crushed
1	tablespoon fresh basil, chopped
2	tablespoons extra virgin olive oil
	salt and pepper to taste

Combine cumin, coriander and peppercorns in a mortar and pestle and pulverize. Place mixture in a small skillet and heat on medium until golden in color. Transfer to a small bowl.

To the spice mixture add lime juice, cilantro, crushed red pepper seeds and basil and stir to blend. Slowly add olive oil, stirring continuously. Add salt and pepper to taste. Pour mixture over chicken and marinate at least 4 hours or overnight. Cook on preheated charcoal, grilling for 6 minutes on each side or until cooked thoroughly.

Serves: 6

Serve right off the grill or chill and serve sliced as a cold salad with Spicy Chick Pea Relish Salad. Serve on a bed of mixed greens with radiccio and lime slices.

267 Cal., 33gm Protein, 2gm Carb., 8.6gm Fat, 84mg Sodium, 88mg Chol., .3gm Fiber

MAIN COURSES

Chicken Casserole with Brown Rice and Artichokes

4	chicken breast halves, boned and skinned
2	cloves garlic, minced
1/2	cup onion, finely chopped
2	teaspoons olive oil
1	28-ounce can chopped tomatoes with juice
4	cups chicken broth
1	teaspoon thyme
1	teaspoon oregano
1	teaspoon salt (optional)
1/2	teaspoon black pepper, freshly ground
1	bay leaf
2	cups uncooked long grain brown rice
1	14-ounce can water-pack artichoke hearts, chopped

Cut chicken into bite-size pieces and set aside.

In a large casserole, sauté garlic and onion in olive oil until soft.

Stir in tomatoes and their liquid, chicken broth, thyme, oregano, salt, pepper and bay leaf and bring to a boil.

Add chicken and rice, cover casserole and reduce heat to low.

Cook for 45 minutes or until rice is tender, most liquid is absorbed, and the chicken is cooked through.

Remove bay leaf, stir in artichokes and serve.

Serves: 10

240 Cal., 18gm Protein, 34gm Carb., 4.2gm Fat, 726mg Sodium, 36mg Chol., 3.5gm Fiber

MAIN COURSES

Chicken Loaf

1	whole chicken
2-3	onions, finely chopped
1/2	cup Italian (flat) parsley leaves (more if desired)
1/2	cup fresh cilantro, finely chopped
1	teaspoon dried basil
1	teaspoon salt
1/2	teaspoon pepper
1/2	cup milk or enough to cover
3-4	slices of bread, diced

Preheat oven to 350°.

Skin chicken, reserving skin; remove wings. Bone entire bird.

Using an electric meat grinder, grind chicken alternately adding onions and herbs.

In a separate bowl, soak bread in milk. Mix bread and chicken mixtures. Pour into a loaf pan coated with vegetable spray. Cover with foil or reserved chicken skin and bake in a 350° oven for 45-60 minutes. Remove foil or skin.

Serves: 10

This may be served hot as a main course or chilled and cubed for canapés.

157 Cal., 20gm Protein, 8gm Carb., 4.4gm Fat, 325mg Sodium, 52mg Chol., .7gm Fiber

MAIN COURSES

Chicken Michael

4	large chicken breasts, skinned and boned
1	tablespoon olive oil
1	tablespoon garlic, chopped
1	tablespoon fresh ginger, chopped and divided
2	tablespoons fresh parsley, chopped
1	tablespoon dried oregano
1	tablespoon dried basil
1	teaspoon salt
1	teaspoon black pepper, freshly ground
1	onion cut in $1/2$-inch slices and quartered
1	red bell pepper, cut in $1/2$-inch chunks
3	ripe plum tomatoes, cut into $1/2$-inch chunks
$1/2$	cup white wine
4	cups cooked white rice

In a large covered fry pan, heat olive oil with half of the garlic and ginger, then add chicken with the parsley, oregano, basil, salt and pepper, and sauté over medium heat until brown, about 7 to 10 minutes each side.

Remove the chicken to a covered serving bowl; sauté the onion and pepper until slightly browned, about 5 minutes, add the tomato and the other half of the garlic and ginger and sauté about 5 more minutes. Add the wine to the pan and simmer 5 minutes. Add the chicken for 5 more minutes, turning once. Serve over rice.

Serves: 6

The secret of this chicken is in the fresh ginger.

447 Cal., 48gm Protein, 39gm Carb., 8.6gm Fat, 473mg Sodium, 117mg Chol., 1.6gm Fiber

MAIN COURSES

Chicken Paprikash

1/2	cup unbleached white flour
1	teaspoon salt
1/4	teaspoon black pepper, freshly ground
6	boned and skinned chicken breast halves, cut into bite-sized pieces
1	tablespoon olive oil
1/2	cup onions, chopped
12	ounces fresh mushrooms, sliced
1	tablespoon paprika
1	teaspoon fresh dill
1	teaspoon salt
1/4	teaspoon black pepper, freshly ground
1	13 3/4-ounce can chicken broth
1/4	cup sherry
2	tablespoons fresh lemon juice
1/2	cup plain nonfat yogurt mixed with 1 1/2 tablespoons flour
1	pound cooked yolkless noodles

Place flour, salt and pepper in a plastic bag. Put chicken pieces in bag and toss with flour mixture to coat.

In a large skillet or Dutch oven, sauté chicken pieces in oil until lightly browned. Remove browned chicken from skillet and sauté onion and mushrooms until tender. Sprinkle with paprika, dill, salt and 1/4 teaspoon pepper. Add chicken broth, sherry, and lemon juice. Return chicken to skillet and cook for 15 minutes, covered, on low heat. Add yogurt/flour mixture to thicken sauce. Serve over noodles.

Serves: 6

501 Cal., 43gm Protein, 59gm Carb., 8.2gm Fat, 1,165mg Sodium, 89mg Chol., 3.6gm Fiber

Chicken Roulade with Warm Tarragon Sauce

Chicken Roulade:

3	boneless, skinless chicken breasts, cut in half, tenderloin removed
1	eggplant approximately ½ pound
4	ounces white mushrooms, cleaned and sliced
⅓	cup skim evaporated milk
½	teaspoon salt
	pepper to taste
1	tablespoon butter
4	ounces pork tenderloin, cut in ½-inch pieces
1	tablespoon Madeira
2	tablespoons cognac
1	tablespoon fresh rosemary, chopped
1	tablespoon fresh tarragon, chopped
2	slices stale white bread, toasted and ground into crumbs
2	egg whites
1	cup dry white wine
1	cup chicken broth

Stuffing:

Bake eggplant at 350° for 30 minutes or until soft. Set aside. When cool, cut in half lengthwise and scrape the pulp into a bowl, removing seeds. Place mushrooms in a skillet over medium heat and cook until they begin to render water, add milk, salt and pepper. Simmer for 10-15 minutes or until milk is thick and creamy. Set aside to cool.

Melt butter in skillet and add pork tenderloin, Madeira and cognac. Flame. After flame has subsided and meat is cooked, chop meat, but do not pulverize. Combine eggplant, mushrooms, pork, herbs, toasted bread crumbs and egg whites and stir until evenly mixed.

Pound chicken breast halves in plastic bag to flatten. Divide stuffing into 6 portions and roll 1 chicken breast half around stuffing, secure with toothpicks. Put in 8 x 13-inch baking dish, add wine and broth and bake for 20 minutes at 400° or until meat is no longer pink when cut.

(continued)

Tarragon Sauce:

1	tablespoon butter
1	tablespoon all-purpose flour
1	cup chicken broth
1/4	cup tarragon vinegar
1	teaspoon tarragon, dried
1/4	teaspoon summer savory, dried

Tarragon Sauce:

Melt butter and add flour. Add chicken broth and vinegar, stirring with wire whisk to make a smooth sauce. Add dried tarragon and summer savory. Serve warm.

Serves: 6

339 Cal., 34gm Protein, 17gm Carb., 10.1gm Fat, 826mg Sodium, 92mg Chol., 1.8gm Fiber

MAIN COURSES

Cinnamon Chicken

1/2	cup chicken broth, divided
2	medium onions, chopped
2	cloves garlic, minced
1	pound skinless, boneless chicken thighs
1	tablespoon lemon juice
4	teaspoons ground cinnamon
4	whole cinnamon sticks
2	28-ounce cans chopped tomatoes in purée
	salt and freshly ground black pepper to taste
1	tablespoon Parmesan cheese

Put 1/4 cup chicken broth in skillet. Add onions and garlic and sauté until browned. Move onions and garlic to outside of skillet and add 1/4 cup chicken broth. Add chicken and sauté until browned. Add all remaining ingredients except cheese. Stir very well so that all ingredients are evenly blended. Cover and simmer for 30 minutes. Remove cinnamon sticks, sprinkle with Parmesan cheese and serve.

Serves: 4

Wonderful served over rice.

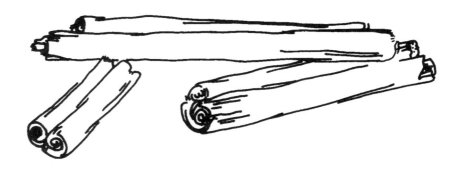

189 Cal., 27gm Protein, 11gm Carb., 4.3gm Fat, 396mg Sodium, 67mg Chol., 2.9gm Fiber

MAIN COURSES

Coq au Vin

1	tablespoon canola oil
6	chicken whole legs (thighs and drumstick attached), skinned, fat removed
3	strips turkey bacon, diced
1	large onion, diced
2	ribs celery, diced
1	large clove garlic, crushed
1/8	cup flour
1	13¾-ounce can chicken broth
1	cup red wine
2	ounces pitted or 5 ounces unpitted Kalamita olives
3	cups cooked white rice

Heat oil in large stove top-to-oven pot. Add the chicken and fry until browned, remove with a slotted spoon and set aside. Add bacon, onion and celery and cook on low heat for 10 minutes, adding water as necessary to prevent burning. Add garlic and flour and cook for one minute. Then add wine and chicken broth. Bring to a boil, add chicken and olives.

Cover and simmer for 5 minutes.
Bake, covered, for 2 hours at 350°.

Serves: 6

Can be cooked in the simmering oven of an AGA for 6 hours.

416 Cal., 42gm Protein, 30gm Carb., 10.3gm Fat, 239mg Sodium, 103mg Chol., 1.2gm Fiber

MAIN COURSES

Cornish Game Hen in Pine Nut Crust with Papaya Relish

Pine Nut Crust:

1½ ounces pine nuts, finely chopped

4 leaves lemon balm, finely chopped, or leaves from 2 sprigs lemon thyme, finely chopped

1½ tablespoons honey

Papaya Relish:

1 papaya, peeled and diced

20 pink or 10 green peppercorns

grated peel and juice of one lime

¼ red bell pepper, diced

dash of paprika

½ bay leaf

4 tablespoons rice vinegar

1-2 tablespoons sugar

1 tablespoon fresh coriander, chopped

1 green onion, sliced into thin rounds

Pine Nut Crust:
   Combine all ingredients in mixing bowl and set aside.

Papaya Relish:
   In a saucepan, put peppercorns, lime peel and juice, red pepper, paprika, bay leaf, rice vinegar and sugar. Bring to a boil, stirring until sugar is dissolved. Remove from heat. Add papaya, coriander and green onion. Mix well and let cool.

(continued)

Cornish Game Hen:

2	**Cornish game hens, breasts divided and skinned, legs separated and skinned, remainder discarded (half a breast and leg per person)**
	salt and pepper
1-2	**tablespoons olive oil**
1	**tablespoon rosemary, crushed**
4	**juniper berries**
2	**tablespoons sherry**
4	**tablespoons chicken broth**

Preheat oven to 375°.

Salt and pepper the Cornish game hen pieces. Heat oil in nonstick frying pan, add rosemary and berries. Brown game hen pieces on all sides. Remove game hen pieces, let cool and pat pine nut mixture on top of each piece. Place in baking pan and add a little broth or water to bottom of pan and bake until done, about 20 minutes.

Meanwhile, drain any remaining oil from frying pan, heat pan and deglaze with sherry and chicken broth. Keep warm.

When game hen pieces are done, arrange each plate with papaya relish on a lettuce leaf, 1/2 breast and one leg and moisten with deglazing liquid.

Serves: 4

Serve Cornish Game Hens with brown rice. Try Papya Relish with Beef Olé!

325 Cal., 36gm Protein, 23gm Carb., 11.1gm Fat, 76mg Sodium, 88mg Chol., 2gm Fiber

MAIN COURSES

Enchiladas Verdes

12	flour tortillas
2	chicken breasts, boned and skinned
1	teaspoon salt, divided
2	garlic cloves, peeled
1	small onion, cut in half
25	tomatillos, chopped
1	jalapeño pepper, seeded and chopped
10	red radishes, finely chopped
$3/4$	cup fresh cilantro, finely chopped

Put chicken in a large pan with water to cover, add $1/2$ teaspoon of the salt, 1 garlic clove and $1/2$ of the onion, cover and simmer 20 minutes or until done. Remove chicken from liquid, reserve 2 cups of the liquid, and cut the chicken breasts into small pieces and keep them warm.

Simmer the tomatillos and jalapeño pepper in a saucepan for 15 minutes, adding water, if necessary.

Put the tomatillo mixture, garlic clove, $1/2$ of the onion, and $1/2$ teaspoon of the salt in a blender and purée very finely.

Return the tomatillo mixture to the saucepan, heat on low gradually adding 2 cups of reserved liquid, stirring continually for about 15 minutes.

Heat the tortillas, spoon a line of chopped chicken down the middle of each, roll up the tortillas, arrange them on a serving plate, cover with sauce and sprinkle chopped radishes and cilantro over all.

Serves: 6

197 Cal., 16gm Protein, 24gm Carb., 4.6gm Fat, 537mg Sodium, 33mg Chol., 4gm Fiber

MAIN COURSES

Grilled Ginger Chicken Patties

2	pounds ground chicken
1/2	cup bread crumbs
1/4	cup fresh gingerroot, shredded
1/4	cup fresh cilantro, chopped
	garlic, salt and pepper to taste

Combine all ingredients. To form patties, place 1/8 of mixture between 2 pieces of waxed paper; patties will be wet to the touch. Spray grill with cooking spray and grill as a hamburger patty. Because this is poultry, make sure the internal temperature of the patty is at least 185°.

Serves: 8

Serve on hamburger buns with lettuce and tomato slices.

---

163 Cal., 26gm Protein, 5gm Carb., 3.6gm Fat, 239mg Sodium, 66mg Chol., .2gm Fiber

MAIN COURSES

Las Enchiladas del Pollo
Gringo Style

1	10-ounce can mild enchilada sauce
1	can low-fat cream of chicken soup
8	ounces nonfat sour cream
1	small can green chilies (or more as desired)
2	cups cooked, shredded chicken breast
4	ounces Monterey Jack cheese (optional)
1	package (10-12) large flour tortillas ($8^{1}/_{2}$-inch diameter)
4	ounces low-fat cheddar cheese, shredded

Combine enchilada sauce with an equal amount of water. Pour a small amount of diluted sauce, just enough to coat the bottom, into a 9 x 13-inch baking dish to prevent the enchiladas from sticking. Combine soup, sour cream and chilies; add chicken. Divide the Monterey Jack cheese into 10-12 strips. Lay one strip at the center of each tortilla. Divide the chicken mixture evenly among the tortillas, placing it on the cheese strips. Roll up each tortilla; place seam down in sauce-coated baking dish. Pour remaining enchilada sauce mixture over the contents of the baking dish. Sprinkle cheddar cheese over all. Bake at 350° about 30 minutes or until lightly browned and bubbling.

Serves: 8

Serve with Black Bean Cakes and Summer Salsa.

286 Cal., 22gm Protein, 36gm Carb., 6.5gm Fat, 586mg Sodium, 39mg Chol., 4.5gm Fiber

MAIN COURSES

Mandarin Chicken

2	pounds chicken drumettes, skin removed
1	teaspoon peanut oil
2	slices fresh ginger root
2	green onions, cut into small pieces
1/4	cup soy sauce
1	tablespoon sugar
1	tablespoon sherry
1	cup water
3	cups cooked white rice

Heat wok with oil. Add ginger root and green onion and cook until golden brown. Add water, if necessary, to prevent burning. Add drumettes and stir fry until they are golden brown. Add soy sauce and sugar and sherry. Add water. Let drumettes gently boil until the juices are absorbed. Turn occasionally. (Sauce should be thick and coat the chicken.) Serve over rice.

Serves: 4

297 Cal., 21gm Protein, 43gm Carb., 3.5gm Fat, 1,071mg Sodium, 44mg Chol., .7gm Fiber

Mexican Chicken and Rice

12	ounces boneless, skinless chicken breasts
2	lemons, juiced
2	limes, juiced
2	tablespoons dark molasses
2	teaspoons chili powder
4	tablespoons teriyaki sauce
3	cups chicken broth, divided
1	cup uncooked rice
1	red bell pepper, diced
1	green bell pepper, diced
1	cup fresh or frozen corn kernels
1	large sweet onion, diced
1	tomato, chopped

To taste:
  chopped chilies
  salt
  black pepper, freshly ground
  fresh cilantro, chopped

Mix together the lemon juice, lime juice, molasses, chili powder and teriyaki. Pour over chicken breasts and allow to marinate for at least one hour.

Bring 2 cups of the chicken broth to a boil, add the rice, reduce heat and cook for 20 minutes.

Place half the marinade in a skillet, add $1/2$ cup chicken broth and boil to reduce to $1/2$ its volume. Cut the chicken into small pieces and stir fry until cooked through and chicken pieces are glazed. Remove from pan.

Place remaining marinade in skillet, add the remaining chicken broth, bell peppers and corn. Lightly sauté vegetables.

Add the cooked rice, chicken and chilies to the sautéed vegetables. Add salt and pepper to taste. Toss in chopped onion, tomato, and cilantro and serve immediately.

Serves: 4

394 Cal., 26gm Protein, 64gm Carb., 4.3gm Fat, 2,128mg Sodium, 50mg Chol., 4.6gm Fiber

MAIN COURSES

Original Chicken Arabesque

3	chicken breasts, skinned, boned and halved
6	strips raw turkey bacon
	coarsely ground black pepper
1 1/2	pints nonfat sour cream
1	can low-fat cream of mushroom soup
1/2	lemon, juiced

Roll each of the half breasts in a strip of bacon and place close together in an ungreased, shallow baking pan. Sprinkle with pepper. Mix together sour cream and soup; pour evenly over the chicken. Again sprinkle with pepper. Cover and bake for 40 minutes at 350°, or until center of chicken breasts are no longer pink. Remove from oven and sprinkle with the lemon juice.

Serves: 6

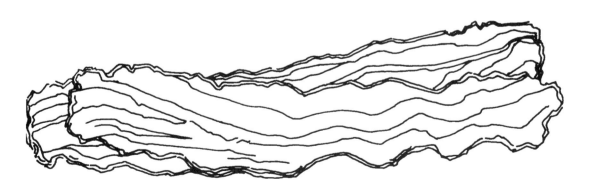

225 Cal., 27gm Protein, 16gm Carb., 4.9gm Fat, 388mg Sodium, 57mg Chol., .1gm Fiber

Orange Chicken

1	pound chicken breasts, skinned and boned
1	orange
¼	cup cornstarch
3	teaspoons sesame oil, divided

Marinade:

1	teaspoon sesame oil
1	teaspoon thin soy sauce
1	tablespoon white wine
½	teaspoon sugar
	salt and pepper to taste
½	egg yolk (optional)

Cut chicken into approximately 2-inch squares and marinate in combined chicken marinade ingredients for at least 1 hour.

Peel ½ the orange and cut peel into ¼-inch strips. Save the other half for garnish.

Combine the orange sauce ingredients in a bowl and stir until the sugar dissolves. Set aside.

Remove the chicken from the marinade and lightly coat the chicken with cornstarch. Heat one teaspoon of the sesame oil in a wok. Stir fry the chicken until it is no longer pink, adding water as necessary to prevent burning. Set aside.

(continued)

Orange Sauce:

2	tablespoons white wine
1	tablespoon hoisin sauce
1	tablespoon oyster sauce
1	tablespoon sesame oil
4	tablespoons orange juice concentrate
1	teaspoon chopped ginger
1	teaspoon chopped scallions
1	teaspoon chopped garlic
1	tablespoon sugar
2	cups cooked white rice

Add two teaspoons of oil to the wok, stir fry the orange peel until crispy. Pour the orange sauce into the wok and stir until the sauce thickens. Add the chicken to the sauce and stir to coat all the chicken.

Serve over rice, adding fresh orange peel as garnish.

Serves: 4

Á La Noodle

410 Cal., 28gm Protein, 46gm Carb., 11gm Fat, 890mg Sodium, 66mg Chol., 1.3gm Fiber

MAIN COURSES

Oven-fried Chicken

1 1/2	cups fat-free saltines, crushed
2/3	cup light Parmesan cheese
1	teaspoon salt
1	teaspoon celery salt
1	teaspoon paprika
1/2	teaspoon onion powder
1/2	teaspoon pepper
24	ounces nonfat plain yogurt
3	pounds chicken pieces, skinned
	vegetable spray

Mix saltines, cheese and spices in one bowl. Put yogurt in another bowl. Dip each chicken piece in yogurt, then into cracker mixture. Place chicken pieces on a baking pan sprayed with vegetable spray. Bake at 450° for 25-30 minutes or just until juices run clear.

Serves: 6

338 Cal., 42gm Protein, 23gm Carb., 7.2gm Fat, 1,217mg Sodium, 97mg Chol., 1gm Fiber

MAIN COURSES

Pan-seared Spicy Breast of Chicken

4	large chicken breasts, boned and skinned
1/4	cup chicken broth
1	tablespoon cilantro, chopped
1 1/2	teaspoons ground turmeric
1	teaspoon ground coriander
1/2	teaspoon allspice
1	teaspoon cumin
1/2	teaspoon cayenne pepper
1/2	teaspoon peppercorns, freshly ground
2	tablespoons paprika
1	lemon, juiced
	zest from one lemon
1	lime, juiced
	zest from one lime
1/2	cup white wine

Mix all ingredients together and pour over chicken in a shallow baking dish. Cover and marinate overnight. Remove chicken and do not rinse off. In heavy, nonstick skillet, sear chicken on both sides, cooking each side about 5 minutes, or until done.

Serves: 6

The Inn at Turner's Mill

212 Cal., 34gm Protein, 4gm Carb., 5gm Fat, 134mg Sodium, 88mg Chol., .8gm Fiber

MAIN COURSES

Poulet Presqu'ile

Filling:

2	tablespoons garlic, minced
1	tablespoon gingerroot, minced
1	teaspoon ground cumin
½	cup shallots, minced
1	cup fresh cilantro, chopped
2	tablespoons Dijon mustard
2	tablespoons sherry

Chicken:

16	chicken breast halves, skinned and boned
16	4-inch strips turkey bacon
	paprika
⅔	cup chicken broth
3	tablespoons wine vinegar
2	tablespoons brown sugar
1	tablespoon soy sauce
2	oranges, juiced
2	lemons, juiced
1	tablespoon cornstarch
2	tablespoons water
3	tablespoons orange zest, grated

Combine filling ingredients and toss well to bind.

Lay a breast half on a bacon strip. Spread about 1 tablespoon filling on the chicken and roll up with bacon. Repeat with remaining ingredients. Place rolls in a shallow roasting pan. Sprinkle with paprika.

Pre-heat oven to 325°.

In a small saucepan, combine broth, vinegar, sugar, soy sauce and juices and bring to a slow boil. In a small bowl, combine cornstarch and water and add mixture to sauce. Simmer until clear and slightly thickened. Pour sauce over chicken rolls.

Bake rolls for 15 minutes or until almost done. Sprinkle with orange zest and place under broiler until bacon is browned, about 3 minutes.

Serves: 8

A good appetizer. Chill rolls completely and slice each into about 10 thin rounds.

388 Cal., 54gm Protein, 10gm Carb., 13.1gm Fat, 607mg Sodium, 142mg Chol., .9gm Fiber

MAIN COURSES

Roast Turkey and Stuffing

1	6-pound skinless, bone-in, turkey breast
5	cups celery, diced
5	cups onion, chopped
8	cups chicken broth
4	tablespoons rubbed sage
	salt and pepper to taste
40	slices whole wheat bread, cubed
	vegetable spray
3	tablespoons cornstarch

Sauté celery and onion in 2 cups of chicken broth until soft. Add the bread and 5 cups of chicken broth and toss. Add $3^1/_2$ tablespoons sage and salt and pepper to taste.

Spray the rack of a broiler pan with vegetable spray. Cover broiler rack with foil. Make holes in the foil to allow juices to drain. Rub the turkey breast with salt, pepper and remaining sage. Place the stuffing on the foil-covered pan in a mound. Place the turkey breast on the mound and cover with foil, piercing vent holes in the foil. Roast at 325° for two hours or for 20 minutes per pound until meat thermometer indicates an internal temperature of 185°. Baste frequently with chicken broth.

Use cornstarch and remaining chicken broth to make gravy from drippings in the broiler pan.

Serves: 12

Serve a crowd or divide into portions and freeze for quick dinners later.

457 Cal., 53gm Protein, 45gm Carb., 7.6gm Fat, 1,536mg Sodium, 104mg Chol., 10.6gm Fiber

Tamale Pie

3	cups chicken broth, divided
3/4	cups yellow cornmeal
1/2	teaspoon salt
1/2	tablespoon safflower or vegetable oil
1	medium onion, chopped
1	garlic clove, minced
1	pound very lean ground turkey
2	cups canned crushed tomatoes, with their juice
1/4	cup tomato paste
1/2	teaspoon chili powder
1	teaspoon oregano

Lightly coat a $2^1/_2$-quart casserole with vegetable spray.

Combine $^3/_4$ cup of the chicken broth with the cornmeal and salt. Bring the remaining $2^1/_4$ cups broth to a boil and stir into the cornmeal. Reduce the heat to low, cover and simmer, stirring occasionally, until the mixture thickens, about 10 minutes.

Heat the oil over medium heat. Add the onion and garlic and cook until soft but not brown, about 5 minutes. Add the ground turkey. Cook until the meat loses its pink color, about 7 minutes.

(continued)

½	teaspoon cumin
¼	teaspoon white pepper
¼	teaspoon cayenne pepper
1	cup fresh, frozen or canned corn kernels
2	tablespoons canned mild chopped green chilies
2	tablespoons grated Parmesan cheese
	vegetable spray

Add the tomatoes with their juice, tomato paste, chili powder, oregano, cumin, white and cayenne peppers to the skillet. Reduce the heat to low, cover and simmer for 15 minutes. Stir in the corn and chilies.

Spoon the cooked cornmeal into the prepared pan, spreading to the edges with a rubber spatula. Evenly ladle the turkey filling over the cornmeal. Sprinkle the cheese over the top. Bake at 375° until the cornmeal layer is firm and the cheese is golden, about 40 minutes.

Serves: 8

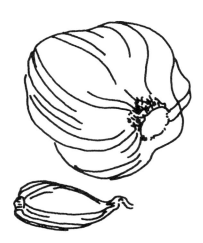

185 Cal., 17gm Protein, 22gm Carb., 3.8gm Fat, 428mg Sodium, 31mg Chol., 3.1gm Fiber

MAIN COURSES

Stir Fry Chicken and Vegetables over Rice

Soy-Ginger Sauce:

1/4	cup low-sodium soy sauce
1/4	cup dry sherry
2	cups chicken broth
3	tablespoons cornstarch
3	tablespoons brown sugar
1	teaspoon fresh ginger, minced

Stir Fry Chicken:

1	pound chicken breasts, skinned and boned and cut into 1/2-inch cubes
1	tablespoon canola oil
1	small red bell pepper, finely chopped
1	small onion, finely chopped
1/2	cup green onions, chopped
2	small firm, ripe tomatoes, finely chopped
1/2	teaspoon black pepper, coarsely ground
3	cups cooked white rice

Soy-Ginger Sauce:
   Combine all ingredients and mix together. Set aside.

Stir Fry Chicken:
   Heat the oil in a wok or large sauté pan. Add chicken and cook, stirring until meat is no longer pink in the center, about 2 - 3 minutes adding water as necessary to prevent burning. Set aside. Add bell pepper, onions, tomatoes and pepper to the pan. Cook, stirring, for 5 minutes. Add the sauce and boil until thickened. Return chicken and juices to the pan. Serve over white rice.

Serves: 4

438 Cal., 30gm Protein, 59gm Carb., 7.4gm Fat, 1,261mg Sodium, 67mg Chol., 1.9gm Fiber

MAIN COURSES

Turkey Breast Royale

- 1/2 turkey breast, skinned and boned (3 - 3 1/2 pounds boned weight)
- 2 tablespoons honey mustard
- 1 1/2 tablespoons beet horseradish
- salt and pepper
- 1 small bunch fresh spinach, cleaned and stems removed
- 6 large fresh basil leaves
- 4 slices low-fat Swiss cheese
- 4 slices low-fat baked or boiled ham
- 1/4 cup dry white wine or hot chicken broth

❊   ❊   ❊

Skin and bone the fresh turkey breast, reserving skin. Make a slice down the middle of the inside of the turkey breast and spread it open butterfly style. Pound the turkey all over with a heavy meat mallet. Spread the cut side of the breast with honey mustard and beet horseradish. Sprinkle with salt and pepper.

Cover entire breast with fresh spinach leaves and fresh basil. Place Swiss cheese and ham covering the breast. Roll up the breast and tie with meat string. Place turkey on a rack in a roasting pan. Cover the meat with its skin and roast uncovered in a preheated 375° oven 1 to 1 1/2 hours depending on the weight of the turkey breast.

When turkey breast is finished roasting, remove it from the oven and discard skin; let turkey rest until it reaches room temperature. Cut and remove the string. Slice turkey into pinwheel slices and arrange decoratively on a serving platter.

Remove all juices from the pan and place in a glass measuring cup. Remove fat as it rises to the top. Return juices to the roasting pan, turn on the burner to medium-high heat and deglaze the pan with either white wine or hot chicken broth. Season with salt and pepper, if desired. Pour over the turkey pinwheel slices.

Serves: 8

381 Cal., 62gm Protein, 4gm Carb., 10.7gm Fat, 620mg Sodium, 144mg Chol., .6gm Fiber

MAIN COURSES

White Chili

1	pound ground chicken or equal parts of white and dark chicken, chopped
1	green chili, roasted, peeled and chopped
1	pound Great Northern beans
6	green peppercorns
6	white peppercorns
6	cups chicken broth
4	medium onions, chopped
4	cloves garlic, minced
1	cup white wine

Garnish:

cilantro, finely chopped

green onion, finely chopped

❋ ❋ ❋

To roast chili:

Place on long fork and rotate over gas flame or red hot electric burner until the surface chars (as if you were toasting a marshmallow). Cool slightly and peel as soon as it can be handled.

Cook the beans according to package directions, rinsing the beans after cooking.

Pulverize the green and white peppercorns in a mortar and pestle. Sauté the spices in a small amount of chicken broth in a saucepan over low to medium heat until they just begin to brown.

Add some chicken broth and the ground or chopped chicken. Sauté the ground chicken breast until browned. Add onion and garlic, a little more broth and brown lightly.

Combine the chicken, remaining chicken broth, beans, roasted chili peppers and white wine and cook for 2 hours. The beans should be soft and the chili thick but not mushy.

Garnish with cilantro and green onions.

Serves: 6

For an extra surprise, pour a generous shot of Tequila into the center of each serving before garnishing.

291 Cal., 26gm Protein, 36gm Carb., 3gm Fat, 1114mg Sodium, 34mg Chol., 5.6gm Fiber

MAIN COURSES

Black Sea Bass Fillet with Citrus Vinaigrette

Vinaigrette:

1	**lime, juiced**
2	**lemons, juiced**
½	**grapefruit, juiced**
1	**orange, juiced**
1	**tablespoon olive oil**
4	**tablespoons sherry vinegar**
½	**teaspoon hot pepper sauce**
1	**teaspoon pink peppercorns, ground**
2	**tablespoon cilantro, chopped**
1	**tablespoon fresh ginger, julienned**
½	**teaspoon cayenne pepper**
4	**5-ounce black sea bass fillets**

Combine all the vinaigrette ingredients. Set aside.

Sear off the sea bass fillets until just cooked through. Serve, pouring ¼ of the vinaigrette over each fillet.

Serves: 4

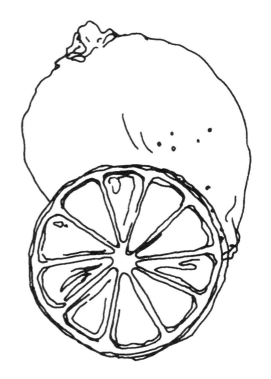

Ritz-Carlton

172 Cal., 25gm Protein, 8gm Carb., 4.3gm Fat, 94mg Sodium, 60mg Chol., .3gm Fiber

MAIN COURSES

Blue Corn Pierogies with Potato and Lobster and Caramelized Onion and Saffron Vinaigrette

Pierogie Dough:

- ¾ cup flour
- ¼ cup blue corn meal
- 1 egg
- 1 tablespoon water
- ½ tablespoon vegetable oil

Potato and Lobster Filling:

- 7½ ounces cooked lobster meat, shredded
- 1 teaspoon vegetable oil
- 1 teaspoon champagne vinegar
- 1 tablespoon fresh herbs, chopped
- 1 large potato, mashed
- salt and pepper to taste

Pierogie Dough:
Combine the flour with cornmeal. Make a well in the center and add the remaining ingredients. Mix together into a dough. Let dough rest 10 minutes. Knead the dough until smooth and let rest another 10 minutes.

Potato and Lobster Filling:
Combine all ingredients and mix well. Set aside.

(continued)

Onion Vinaigrette:

1	**large white onion, thinly sliced**
1	**tablespoon olive oil**
1/2	**teaspoon powdered saffron**
1/2	**cup balsamic vinegar**
1	**clove garlic, minced**
	salt and pepper to taste

Onion Vinaigrette:

   In a large pan, sauté the onion in oil over a low heat until caramelization has occurred, about 15 minutes. Remove from the pan and place in a bowl with the remaining ingredients. Set aside.

To assemble:

   Roll out half of the dough to 1/4-inch thickness. Cut into five equal circles. Place one tenth of the filling in the middle of the dough. Brush edges of the circles with water and fold over into a half circle, sealing well. Repeat with remaining dough until there are 10 pierogies. Cook the pierogies in boiling water for 3 minutes, drain.

To serve:

   Arrange pierogies on a platter and cover with the caramelized onion and saffron vinaigrette.

Yield: 10 pierogies

Café Sausalito

240 Cal., 13gm Protein, 32gm Carb., 6.8gm Fat, 615mg Sodium, 85mg Chol., 2gm Fiber

MAIN COURSES

Broiled Scallops and New Zealand Mussels with Concasse Tomatoes and Minted Lime Vinaigrette

16	sea scallops
8	New Zealand mussels
1/4	cup white wine
1/4	cup lemon juice
2	cups cooked fresh spinach
4	tablespoons Concasse tomatoes
	seasoned salt to taste

Minted Lime Vinaigrette:

1	cup olive oil
1/4	cup fresh lime juice
	zest from 1/2 lime
1	tablespoon chopped fresh mint
1/2	teaspoon Worcestershire sauce
	dash cayenne pepper
1	tablespoon shallots, chopped
1	tablespoon white wine
	salt to taste

Minted Lime Vinaigrette:
Blend well in a blender until all ingredients are incorporated.

To prepare scallops and mussels:
Place scallops and mussels, shell side up, on a broiler pan. Combine the wine and lemon juice. Pour over the shellfish. Place under a broiler. Broil until shellfish open.

To serve:
Arrange 4 scallops and 2 mussels on 1/2 cup spinach on each plate. Drizzle 2 tablespoons vinaigrette over the shellfish and garnish with 1 tablespoon Concasse tomatoes.

Serves: 4

Serve with Cultured Potatoes.

Quail Hollow

368 Cal., 30gm Protein, 12gm Carb., 23.3gm Fat, 771mg Sodium, 62mg Chol., 3.2gm Fiber

MAIN COURSES

Cajun Fish

Cajun Seasoning:
2 teaspoons white pepper
2 teaspoons garlic powder
2 teaspoons onion powder
2 teaspoons ground red pepper
2 teaspoons paprika
2 teaspoons black pepper

4-6 catfish fillets (6-ounces each)
   Cajun seasoning
1 tablespoon olive oil

Garnish:
   fresh limes
   cilantro

Cajun Seasoning:
   In a small mixing bowl stir together white pepper, garlic powder, onion powder, ground red pepper, paprika, and black pepper. Store spice mixture in an airtight container in a cool, dry place. Makes 4 tablespoons Cajun Seasoning.

   Sprinkle Cajun Seasoning liberally on both sides of each fish. Heat a cast-iron skillet over high heat for at least 8-10 minutes. Add olive oil and turn to coat. Cook fish two at a time in hot skillet, turning once, until golden on both sides and fish flakes easily when tested with a fork, 5 to 7 minutes. Remove catfish to platter, keep warm, and repeat with remaining fillets.

Serves: 6

149 Cal., 26gm Protein, 3gm Carb., 3.2gm Fat, 89mg Sodium, 64mg Chol., .4gm Fiber

MAIN COURSES

Creole Baked Shrimp

1	tablespoon Creole or Cajun seasoning
1	tablespoon olive oil
1	tablespoon water
2	tablespoons fresh lemon juice
2	tablespoons fresh parsley, finely chopped
1	tablespoon honey
1 1/2	tablespoons low-sodium soy sauce
1 1/2	pounds shrimp, uncooked, shelled and de-veined

Garnish:

parsley sprigs

lemon slices

1   tablespoon cilantro, chopped

Beat together all ingredients except shrimp in mixing bowl, add shrimp, toss to coat, cover bowl and refrigerate for one hour.

Preheat oven to 450°. Transfer shrimp and marinade to a baking dish and bake about 10 minutes or until shrimp are cooked. Stir once after 5 minutes.

Garnish with parsley sprigs or lemon slices or 1 tablespoon chopped fresh cilantro and serve.

Serves: 4

271 Cal., 39gm Protein, 9gm Carb., 7.3gm Fat, 513mg Sodium, 300mg Chol., .5gm Fiber

MAIN COURSES

Siam Scallops

3/4	cup chicken broth, divided
2	pounds bay scallops
3	garlic cloves, minced
3	shallots, finely chopped
1 1/2	tablespoons fresh ginger, grated
1	onion, chopped
2	cups mushrooms, sliced
2	red peppers, sliced into thin strips
1	green pepper, sliced into thin strips
3/4	cup sherry
1/3	cup low-sodium soy sauce
5	teaspoons Thai curry paste, mild
1/2	cup green onions, sliced

In a large skillet, heat 1/2 cup broth, add scallops, cook 1 minute, add garlic, shallots and ginger, cook 3 minutes. Take scallops out with a slotted spoon and reserve.

Add a little more broth to skillet, heat, add onion, mushrooms, peppers, sherry, soy sauce and curry paste. Stir well, heat to boiling, cook 3 minutes, add scallops cook 1 more minute.

Transfer to serving dish, sprinkle green onion all over. Serve immediately. Serve with rice or linguine.

Serves: 6

191 Cal., 29gm Protein, 13gm Carb., 2.1gm Fat, 932mg Sodium, 61mg Chol., 2.2gm Fiber

Grilled Scallops with Black Bean Salad

Black Bean Salad:

2/3	pound dried black beans
	salt and pepper
1	quart cold water
1	yellow pepper, diced small
1	red pepper, diced small
1	small red onion, diced small
1	lemon, juiced
1	orange, juiced
	salt to taste

Scallops:

1 1/2	pounds sea scallops (use smaller bay scallops, if desired)
2	teaspoons vegetable oil
	salt and pepper, to taste

Black Bean Salad:

Place the beans in a pot and fill with water to 1 inch above top of beans. Bring to a boil. Drain and rinse beans gently with warm water in a colander. Return beans to pot and refill with water to same level as before. Add salt and pepper. Bring to a boil. Reduce heat and simmer for 2 hours, until tender. Drain (without rinsing) and cool.

Combine peppers, onion and juices. Fold all or most of the beans into the pepper mixture, depending on concentration of beans desired. Add salt to taste. Let sit at room temperature at least 1 hour.

Scallops:

Before cooking the scallops make sure they are very dry (pat dry with paper towels). Season with salt and pepper. Heat stovetop grill to very hot and rub with oil. Place scallops on the grill and cook for 2 minutes on each side. (Scallops may also be broiled.)

(continued)

Sauce:

1	teaspoon shallot, minced
1	teaspoon garlic, minced
1	tomato, peeled and seeded, diced
3	tablespoons water
1	cup white wine
	salt and pepper

Sauce:

In a small pan, heat the water with the shallot, garlic and tomato. Add white wine. Bring to a boil and reduce by half. Adjust seasonings and serve.

To serve:

Place bean salad, at room temperature, in center of each plate. Divide scallops into equal portions and place them around the beans. Pour the sauce over the scallops and serve.

Serves: 4 main course or
          8 first course

Piperade

302 Cal., 37gm Protein, 31gm Carb., 4.6gm Fat, 1,307mg Sodium, 68mg Chol., 10.0gm Fiber

Pesce al Cartoccio

Fish:

	parchment paper
2	tablespoons olive oil
4	fresh fish fillets (sole, flounder, or snapper)
	salt and pepper
1	lemon, cut in half
2	scallions, including $1/4$ of green top, finely sliced
2	tablespoons fresh parsley, chopped
2	teaspoons marjoram
2	teaspoons fresh basil, chopped

Preheat oven to 375°.

Cut 4 pieces of parchment paper, approximately 8 inches square, or 1 inch longer than length of fillets. Place one piece of paper on baking sheet. Brush with olive oil. Place one fillet on paper, diagonally. Sprinkle with salt and pepper. Squeeze lemon juice over fish, removing any seeds. Add $1/4$ each of scallions, parsley, marjoram, and basil. Pull two diagonal corners up together over fish and wrap down towards fish, but not too tightly. Roll the other two short ends up toward the ends of the fillet and pinch paper to secure.

(continued)

Salsa Verde:

4	**flat anchovy fillets, chopped**
3	**tablespoons fresh parsley, finely chopped**
1	**tablespoon garlic, minced**
1	**tablespoon capers, drained and chopped**
2	**tablespoons shallots, minced**
3	**tablespons lemon juice**
1/4	**cup olive oil**
1/2	**teaspoon salt**
1/8	**teaspoon freshly ground pepper**

Repeat for each of the other 3 fillets.

Place on center rack of oven and bake for 20 minutes. Baking sheet with prepared fish in parchment paper may be refrigerated for several hours until ready to bake, if desired.

In a mixing bowl, combine anchovy, parsley, garlic, capers, and shallots. Sprinkle lemon juice over them, add oil and mix well. Season with salt and pepper.

To serve, place one fish packet on each plate for guest to open. Serve Salsa Verde on the side. Or, remove fish from parchment, place on plate and top with Salsa Verde.

Serves: 4

Serve with sourdough French bread and Oranges Orientales for dessert.

The Loretta Paganini School of Cooking

290 Cal., 40gm Protein, 4gm Carb., 11.7gm Fat, 737mg Sodium, 98mg Chol., .8gm Fiber

MAIN COURSES

Poached Salmon with Yogurt Sauce

2   large salmon fillets
1   lemon

Yogurt Sauce:
8   ounces nonfat yogurt
3   tablespoons Grey Poupon mustard
½   lemon, juiced
1-2 teaspoons fresh dill, chopped
2   tablespoons capers

Place fillets in glass pan with approximately 1 inch of water. Squeeze the juice of 1 lemon over the fish. Cover with foil and bake for approximately 15-20 minutes at 375° or until fish flakes.

Yogurt Sauce:
   Mix with whisk and serve cold over warm salmon.

Serves: 4 - 6

Serve with Tomato Feta Pasta.

292 Cal., 39gm Protein, 7gm Carb., 11gm Fat, 370mg Sodium, 82mg Chol., .9gm Fiberq

MAIN COURSES

Scallops and Vegetables Over Rice

1	pound bay scallops
1/4	cup unbleached white flour
2	cloves garlic, minced
1	tablespoon olive oil
2	cups snow peas (about 1/2 pound)
2	cups red pepper, sliced
1	cup mushrooms, sliced
3	cups cooked rice

Rinse scallops, dry with a paper towel, and roll scallops in flour.

In a large skillet, sauté scallops and garlic in olive oil until tender (about 5-10 minutes).

Add snow peas, red peppers and mushrooms and cook 5 minutes until heated through and a little soft.

Serve over rice.

Serves: 4

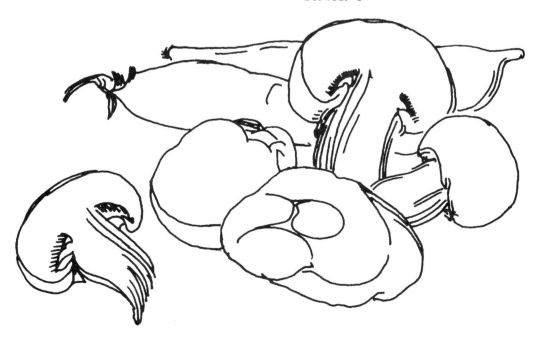

343 Cal., 28gm Protein, 54gm Carb., 2.4gm Fat, 843mg Sodium, 52mg Chol., 3.3gm Fiber

MAIN COURSES

Scallop-stuffed Sole

3/4	pound bay scallops
1	bunch watercress
1	medium carrot, finely grated
1	green onion, minced
1	tablespoon olive oil
1	large egg white
1/4	teaspoon white pepper
1/2	cup dry white wine, divided
	salt

Scallop Stuffing:

Rinse scallops; pat dry. Chop watercress leaves, reserving 1 tablespoon. In 10-inch skillet cook carrot, green onion and remaining watercress over medium heat in 1 tablespoon oil until vegetables are tender. Remove skillet from heat.

In food processor with knife blade attached, blend scallops to a paste. With motor running, blend in egg white, pepper, 1 tablespoon wine, and 1/2 teaspoon salt, then slowly pour in 1/4 cup water and blend just until mixed. Remove blade. Stir in vegetable mixture.

(continued)

Sole:

10	sole fillets (4-6 ounces each)
1	tablespoon butter
2	slices white bread
2	teaspoons margarine
¼	cup bread crumbs
	vegetable spray

Preheat oven to 350°. Spray 13 x 9-inch baking dish with vegetable spray. Arrange 5 sole fillets on bottom, sprinkle with salt. Spread scallop mixture over fillets; top with remaining 5 sole fillets and sprinkle with salt. Pour remaining wine over fillets, dot with 1 tablespoon butter. Bake 15 minutes, basting occasionally with juices in dish.

Meanwhile, tear bread into small pieces. In same skillet over medium heat, in 2 teaspoons margarine, cook bread until lightly browned. Remove skillet from heat, stir in reserved watercress and bread crumbs.

Sprinkle crumb mixture over fillets; bake 5 minutes longer or until fish flakes easily when tested with a fork. Serve stuffed sole with juices in baking dish.

Serves: 5

361Cal., 52gm Protein, 12gm Carb., 8.8gm Fat, 615mg Sodium, 126mg Chol., .9gm Fiber

MAIN COURSES

Pinwheel Tenderloin of Beef with Fresh Tomato Salsa

Tenderloin of Beef:

1	3-pound tenderloin of beef
1½	teaspoons kosher salt
1	teaspoon black pepper, ground
2	tablespoons garlic, minced
6	leaves fresh basil, julienned
¼	cup red onion, diced
8	thin slices lean ham
8	ounces low-fat mozzarella cheese, shredded
½	cup sun-dried tomatoes, softened in warm water and drained
¼	cup pine nuts, toasted
3	whole green onions
1	red bell pepper, julienned
	vegetable spray

Tenderloin of Beef:

Roll the uncut portion away from you and make another 1-inch deep cut and repeat this process until the tenderloin is flat. Cover with plastic wrap and pound to tenderize and flatten evenly.

Remove plastic, season with salt, pepper, garlic and fresh basil. Layer the meat evenly with the diced onion, ham, cheese, sun-dried tomatoes and toasted pine nuts.

Lay the green onion and red pepper along the length of the inside edge and firmly roll up the tenderloin. Tie with cotton string, season with additional salt and pepper, garlic and spray with vegetable oil spray. Wrap in plastic wrap and refrigerate overnight.

Grill or bake in a preheated 350° oven for 25-35 minutes for medium. Remove from oven and let sit for 10 minutes, remove string and slice. Serve with Fresh Tomato Salsa.

(continued)

Fresh Tomato Salsa:

3	medium tomatoes, chopped
3-4	green onions, green parts included, chopped
1-3	teaspoons Cavender's Greek seasoning

Fresh Tomato Salsa:
   Combine and let set at room temperature an hour before serving.

Serves: 12

For best flavor, begin preparation a day in advance. Serve with Garlic Potato Straw Surprise and for dessert, Fruit Trifle.

265 Cal., 36gm Protein, 6gm Carb., 10.6gm Fat, 511mg Sodium, 89mg Chol., 1.8gm Fiber

MAIN COURSES

Stir-fried Beef and Broccoli

1	pound beef, eye of round
1	teaspoon salt
1	teaspoon pepper, freshly ground
1	tablespoon garlic, chopped
1	tablespoon pickled ginger, chopped
1	tablespoon fresh ginger, chopped
1	tablespoon white wine
1	tablespoon soy sauce
1	tablespoon peanut oil
1	bunch broccoli, cut into bite-sized pieces
1	bunch green onion, cut in 1-inch long pieces
1/4	pound snow peas
3	ripe plum tomatoes, cut into 1/2-inch chunks
1	package tofu, cubed
1/4	cup white wine
	Oriental Sauce
2	tablespoons oyster sauce
1	teaspoon toasted sesame oil

Cut the beef into very thin ($1/8$-inch) strips no more than 2 inches long and stir with the salt, pepper, garlic, pickled ginger, fresh ginger, wine and soy sauce; marinate for at least 15 minutes.

In a wok, over high heat, quickly stir fry the beef in the peanut oil and set aside. Stir fry the remaining vegetables and tofu, adding water, if necessary, to prevent burning. Set aside.

Slightly reduce the white wine in the wok and add all the stir-fried ingredients. Stir to heat.

Add the Oriental Sauce and cook a little longer to thicken.

Add the oyster sauce and sesame oil and serve over rice.

Serves: 6

(continued)

Oriental Sauce:

1	**tablespoon corn starch**
1	**tablespoon soy sauce**
1	**tablespoon water**
3	**cups cooked white rice**

Sauce:
    Combine all ingredients and mix well.

Add a little hot sauce if you are adventurous.

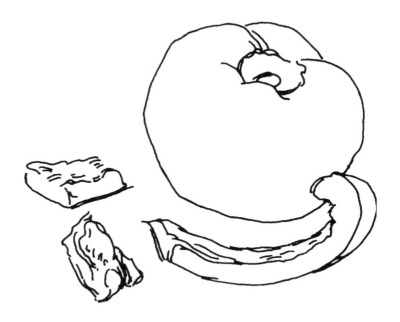

373 Cal., 29gm Protein, 37gm Carb., 12gm Fat, 1,004mg Sodium, 48mg Chol., 4.7gm Fiber

MAIN COURSES

Beef Olé

2	teaspoons whole cumin
1	teaspoon whole coriander
2	teaspoons paprika
1½	teaspoons kosher salt
1	teaspoon black pepper, coarsely ground
¼	teaspoon hot red pepper flakes
1½	pounds top round steak, 1½ inches thick
1	tablespoon garlic, minced

In a small skillet, heat whole cumin and coriander until they reach a toasted brown color. Pulverize cumin, coriander, paprika, kosher salt, ground black pepper and hot pepper flakes in a mortar and pestle. Set aside.

Rub both sides of steak with garlic. Coat all sides evenly with spice mixture. Wrap well and refrigerate overnight.

Heat a cast-iron skillet over medium-high heat until very hot. Add steak and cook 5 to 7 minutes per side for medium rare. Transfer to a carving board and let stand 10 minutes before slicing. Slice thinly against the grain with a diagonal cut.

Serves: 6

Serve with Spicy Corn and Bean Confetti Salad.

184 Cal., 26gm Protein, 2gm Carb., 7.9gm Fat, 598mg Sodium, 72mg Chol., .4gm Fiber

MAIN COURSES

Grilled Indian Lamb

1	boned, butterflied leg of lamb (4 to 5 pounds)
2	medium onions
6	cloves garlic
1	piece (1 1/2 inches) gingerroot, peeled
2	hot chili peppers (leave the seeds in for a hotter taste)
1	tablespoon ground cumin
2	teaspoons ground coriander
1 1/2	teaspoons salt
1/2	teaspoon garam masala (available at Indian specialty stores)
1/2	teaspoon cayenne pepper, or to taste
1/2	teaspoon black pepper, freshly ground
2	cups plain nonfat yogurt

Trim excess fat and membrane from lamb.

Put onions, garlic, ginger and peppers in food processor and chop coarsely. Add spices and yogurt and process until ingredients are finely chopped. (Or finely chop first 4 ingredients by hand, then mix in spices and yogurt.)

Put half of mixture in a non-aluminum dish large enough to hold the lamb. Place lamb in dish and spread remaining mixture over it. Cover and marinate several hours at room temperature or in the refrigerator over night.

Prepare grill. Scrape excess marinade off lamb and grill it about 20 minutes altogether. Remove it when a meat thermometer reaches 120°. Cover it tightly and let it rest 15 to 20 minutes before carving.

Serves: 8 - 10

Serve with Crostini and a fresh green salad.

275 Cal., 41gm Protein, 4gm Carb., 9.7gm Fat, 279mg Sodium, 135mg Chol., .3gm Fiber

Lamb Eggplant Cake

2	pounds long eggplants, ends removed and sliced lengthwise in $1/3$-inch thick slices
	vegetable oil in spray bottle
	salt and pepper to taste
3	onions, finely chopped
2	garlic cloves, minced
$1/2$	cup chicken broth
2	pounds lamb, ground
4-5	slices white bread, crust removed
$1/2$	cup 1% milk
2	eggs
16	black olives, chopped
4	tablespoons parsley, minced
1	cup light Parmesan cheese, grated
$1 1/4$	tablespoons curry powder
	dash of nutmeg

Preheat oven to 350°.

Place sliced eggplants on 2 nonstick cookie sheets which have been sprayed with vegetable oil. Spray eggplant slices, sprinkle with salt and pepper. Bake 10-15 minutes or until soft and lightly browned. Set aside.

In a large nonstick skillet, cook the onions and garlic in the chicken broth until onions are soft. Add lamb to onions and cook, breaking it up with a fork until done. Set aside and let cool.

Soak bread slices in milk.

In a bowl, beat eggs, add olives, parsley, Parmesan cheese, curry powder and nutmeg. Mix well and add to lamb mixture. Squeeze bread slices lightly and add. Mix well (best done with hands). Add salt and pepper to taste.

(continued)

Lightly spray a 2-quart Charlotte mold or soufflé dish with the vegetable oil spray. Line bottom of mold with eggplant slices, press the other slices vertically against the wall, overlapping them a little. Slices should be higher than mold. The entire mold should be covered. Fill in with the meat mixture, pressing down lightly. Smooth the top and fold over the eggplant ends pinwheel fashion. Cover tightly with aluminum foil. Place mold in a roasting pan. Add 3 inches of water to roasting pan and bake 1 hour and 15 minutes.

Let mold cool for 30 minutes, then unmold onto serving platter. Serve warm.

Serves: 6

For dessert, serve Pears in Red Wine.

421 Cal., 42gm Protein, 30gm Carb., 14.7gm Fat, 743mg Sodium, 212mg Chol., 5.3gm Fiber

MAIN COURSES

Hornado's Pork

3	pounds boneless pork loin roast, all visible fat removed, cut into 1-inch cubes
1	tablespoon olive oil
1	large bunch of scallions including green, chopped
4	garlic cloves, crushed
	salt and pepper to taste
1	tablespoon low-sodium soy sauce
2	15 1/2-ounce cans golden hominy, drained
1	red bell pepper, chopped
1	green bell pepper, chopped
1/2	cup fresh cilantro chopped
	hot pepper sauce (optional) to taste
12	cherry tomatoes, cut in half for garnish

Sauté the pork cubes in the olive oil with half of the scallions, garlic and salt and pepper to taste until the meat has browned and cooked through and most of the pan juices have disappeared, about 30 minutes, stirring occasionally. Add the soy sauce and hominy and cook until the hominy is heated through. Add the remaining half of the green onions, red and green bell peppers, cilantro and hot pepper sauce to taste. Stir to combine. Remove from heat and serve immediately; the vegetables should remain crunchy. Garnish with cherry tomatoes.

Serves: 12

An Ecuadorian favorite!

223 Cal., 29gm Protein, 11gm Carb., 7.3gm Fat, 336mg Sodium, 66mg Chol., 1.1gm Fiber

MAIN COURSES

Medallions of Pork with Sauce Charcutière

2¼	pounds pork tenderloin
2	tablespoons butter
1	onion, finely chopped
2	teaspoons flour
¾	cup white wine
2	cups veal stock (or 1 cup chicken broth and 1 cup beef broth)
½	teaspoon Dijon mustard
14	cornichons, finely chopped
2	tablespoons parsley, chopped
2	tablespoons fresh thyme
	salt and pepper to taste

Cut pork into 1½-inch medallions. In nonstick frying pan, melt butter and brown medallions on both sides. Lower heat and cook another 4 to 5 minutes until done. Remove from pan and keep warm.

Add onion to pan with a little of the broth. Cook until translucent. Add flour and mix together. Add wine. Scrape down pan and reduce liquid by half. Add stock or broth. Reduce by one-third. Whisk in mustard. Cook for 1 minute. Strain sauce into bowl. Add cornichons, herbs and season to taste with salt and pepper. Pour sauce over medallions and serve.

Serves: 8

Try with Cultured Potatoes.

244 Cal., 32gm Protein, 3gm Carb., 9.9gm Fat, 752mg Sodium, 82mg Chol., .8gm Fiber

MAIN COURSES

Pork Tenderloin Marco

1/4	**cup soy sauce**
1/4	**cup red wine**
1	**tablespoon light brown sugar**
1	**teaspoon molasses**
1	**tablespoon honey**
1/2	**teaspoon cinnamon**
1	**green onion, minced**
2	**cloves garlic, minced**
2	**pork tenderloins (about 1 1/2 pounds total), trimmed**
2	**teaspoons vegetable oil**

Combine soy sauce, wine, sugar, molasses, honey, cinnamon, green onion and garlic in glass dish for marinade. Add pork, turning to coat. Cover and refrigerate 3 hours or overnight.

Thirty minutes before roasting, remove pork from refrigerator. Preheat oven to 325°. Heat oil in large oven-proof skillet over high heat. Remove pork from marinade; add to skillet and brown on all sides. Transfer skillet to oven and roast 30 minutes or until done. Cool to room temperature and slice thin.

Serves: 6

Serve this great main dish with Spiced Rice Pilaf.

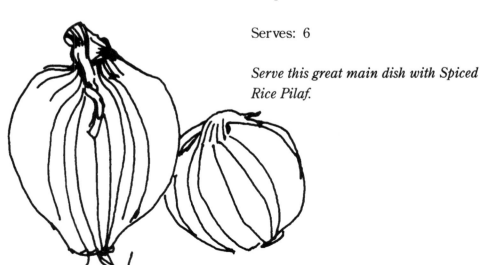

196 Cal., 28gm Protein, 4gm Carb., 7.5gm Fat, 407mg Sodium, 66mg Chol., .1gm Fiber

MAIN COURSES

Rabbit Braised in Red Wine

2	rabbits, cut in serving pieces
1/2	teaspoon salt
1/2	teaspoon pepper
1/2	cup flour
1	tablespoon butter
1	tablespoon vegetable oil
1 1/2	cups chicken broth, divided
3/4	cup onions, finely chopped
1	large garlic clove, minced
1	cup dry red wine
2	tablespoons brandy
1	teaspoon currant jelly
1	bay leaf
1/4	teaspoon dried rosemary
1/4	teaspoon dried thyme
6	turkey bacon strips, cooked and crumbled
2	teaspoons lemon juice

Wash rabbit pieces under cold water, pat dry, season well with salt and pepper, dip in flour.

Heat butter and oil over moderate heat in ovenproof casserole. Brown rabbit pieces a few at a time. When done, set aside on plate.

In same casserole, heat 1/4 cup of chicken broth, add onions and garlic, cook until onions are transparent, scraping down bottom of pan. Pour in red wine and remaining broth, increase heat, add brandy, currant jelly and herbs. Add rabbit pieces and any liquid collected in plate. Sprinkle crumbled turkey bacon over all, cover casserole tightly and simmer over low heat for 1 hour. Test pieces for doneness. Add lemon juice, taste for seasoning (sauce should be peppery); add more if necessary.

Serves: 6

Serve with Fennel Paysanne and for dessert, Champagne Sherbet.

270 Cal., 41gm Protein, 11gm Carb., 12.1gm Fat, 551mg Sodium, 88mg Chol., .5gm Fiber

MAIN COURSES

Grilled Veal Chops with Salad Greens

4	10-ounce veal chops, with bone
2	lemons
3	cloves garlic, thinly sliced
3	sprigs rosemary (about 3 tablespoons leaves), stemmed and lightly crushed
1/2	tablespoon olive oil, divided
	salt and black pepper, freshly ground
1	small radicchio, cored
1	bunch arugula, stemmed
1	small head romaine lettuce

Remove the zest from 1 lemon in broad strips and juice the peeled lemon to obtain 3 to 4 tablespoons juice. Combine the zest, garlic, rosemary, 3/4 teaspoon of the oil, and all but 2 teaspoons of the lemon juice in a small bowl. Stir in plenty of salt and pepper. Rub the veal chops with this mixture and marinate in a shallow pan for 1 hour or longer.

Grill the veal chops over high heat, basting with marinade, for 6 minutes per side, or until cooked.

Slice the greens into 1/4-inch strips. Place in a skillet with the remaining 3/4 teaspoon oil, 2 teaspoons lemon juice and salt and pepper. Quickly heat the greens just until warm but not limp.

Arrange the greens on a plate or plates and top with the veal chops. Garnish with lemon slices or wedges and serve at once.

Serves: 4

Serve with Oven-baked French Fries.

289 Cal., 43gm Protein, 5.8gm Carb., 9.9gm Fat, 362mg Sodium, 119mg Chol., 1.9gm Fiber

MAIN COURSES

Veal Molinari

8	**2-ounce veal slices**
2	**tablespoons flour**
1	**tablespoon olive oil**
1	**teaspoon fresh garlic, minced**
1/2	**cup eggplant, cut in julienne strips**
1/4	**cup roasted red peppers, cut in julienne strips**
2	**tablespoons pitted Kalamata olives**
1/2	**cup dry white wine**
1	**tablespoon fresh basil, chopped**
2	**tablespoons Pecorino Romano cheese**
	salt and pepper to taste

Season veal slices. Sprinkle with flour. Heat olive oil to smoke, add veal. Cook 2 minutes, turn. Add garlic, eggplant, peppers and olives. Cook, stirring continuously, for 3 minutes, add wine and basil. Cook 2 minutes. Divide onto 4 plates. Pour juices over veal. Sprinkle with Romano cheese and serve.

Serves: 4

Serve with Risotto with Mushrooms.

Molinari's

207 Cal., 18gm Protein, 6gm Carb., 9.6gm Fat, 378mg Sodium, 85mg Chol., .9gm Fiber

Veal Birds (Stuffed Veal Scallopini)

Veal Birds:

2	cups broth, half chicken, half beef
6	shallots, finely chopped
3	large garlic cloves, finely chopped
3	tablespoons parsley, finely chopped
2	cups mushrooms, finely chopped
3/4	pound ground veal
3/4	pound ground turkey breast
	salt and pepper to taste
1 1/2	teaspoon thyme
3/4	cup bread crumbs
1	egg
2	egg whites
8	large slices veal scallopini (cut from leg) or 16 small pieces

In a large, nonstick sauté pan heat 1/3 cup broth over low heat. Cook half of the shallots, garlic, parsley and mushrooms until cooked and all liquid is evaporated.

Increase heat to medium, add ground meat, salt and pepper to taste and thyme. Cook until barely done, breaking meat up as small as possible. Taste for seasoning. Transfer mixture to large mixing bowl. Let cool. Add bread crumbs, egg and egg whites. Mix well to make as smooth a mixture as possible.

Depending on the size of scallopine slices, place 1 to 3 tablespoons of meat mixture on one end of each slice and roll up jelly-roll fashion and place sliced end down in a greased baking dish.

(continued)

Sauce:

1		cup white wine
1		28-ounce can crushed tomatoes
2		bay leaves
1		teaspoon ground cumin
		salt and pepper
1		pound broad, flat, yolkless noodles, cooked

Preheat oven to 375°.

In the large, nonstick sauté pan, heat $1/2$ cup of broth over low heat and cook remaining half of shallots, garlic, parsley and mushrooms. Add wine, cook until liquid is reduced by half. Add tomatoes, remaining cup of broth, bay leaves, cumin, salt and pepper. Cook for 5 minutes to reduce a little. Pour over stuffed scallopini. Cover dish with foil and bake for about 30 minutes. Uncover and bake 15 minutes more, basting twice. Serve with noodles.

Serves: 8

336 Cal., 39gm Protein, 16gm Carb., 10.1gm Fat, 831mg Sodium, 178mg Chol., 2.5gm Fiber

Veal with Champagne Sauce

1½	pound veal slices, ¼-inch thick
½	cup flour
¼	teaspoon salt
¼	teaspoon white pepper
¼	teaspoon nutmeg
½	tablespoon butter
½	tablespoon olive oil
½	pound mushrooms, stems removed
2	shallots, chopped
½	cup champagne
½	evaporated skim milk
½	cup light sour cream

Garnish:
    chopped green onion
    lemon slices

Pound the veal slices to a thickness of ⅛-inch and cut into strips across the grain.

Place the flour, salt, pepper and nutmeg in a bag, add the veal and shake to coat.

In a large sauté pan, melt the butter with the oil. Sauté the veal until the strips turn light golden brown. Remove from pan and keep warm. Add the mushroom caps and shallots to the pan and sauté briefly.

Add champagne and evaporated skim milk and reduce the liquid by half over high heat. Lower the heat and stir in the sour cream.

To serve, spoon the sauce over the veal and sprinkle with chopped green onion and lemon slices.

Serves: 6

281 Cal., 27gm Protein, 15gm Carb., 10.6gm Fat, 207mg Sodium, 115mg Chol., 1.3gm Fiber

MAIN COURSES

Veal With Vegetables

3	tablespoons unsalted butter, divided
3	pounds boneless leg of veal cut into 2-inch cubes
1	teaspoon salt
	white pepper, freshly ground
2	cloves garlic, chopped
3/4	cup shallots, finely chopped
3	tablespoons fresh dill, finely chopped, divided
1/4	cup all-purpose flour
1/4	teaspoon nutmeg, freshly grated or ground nutmeg
1 1/4	cups chicken or veal stock
1	cup water
2	carrots, peeled and finely julienned
2	small zucchini, finely julienned
2	leeks, trimmed, washed and finely julienned
1/4	cup heavy cream
1/2	cup evaporated skim milk
1 1/2	pounds wide, yolkless noodles

In a large, flameproof casserole, melt 2 tablespoons of the butter. Add the veal and sprinkle with salt and pepper to taste. Cook over medium heat, stirring occasionally until veal turns white, about 7 minutes. Add the garlic, shallots and 2 tablespoons of the dill. Cook for 4 to 5 minutes.

Sprinkle on the flour and nutmeg. Add the stock and water and bring to a boil over high heat. Reduce heat, cover and simmer very slowly for 45 minutes, stirring once or twice. Do not let liquid evaporate; add more stock, if necessary.

In a large skillet, melt the remaining butter. Add the carrots, zucchini and leeks and toss until wilted, about 5 minutes. Add the wilted vegetables to the veal and stir in the cream and evaporated skim milk. Heat until the stew comes to a simmer; sprinkle remaining dill on top before serving.

Serves: 8 - 10

For dessert serve Tipsy Bananas.

412 Cal., 39gm Protein, 18gm Carb., 19.8gm Fat, 860mg Sodium, 197mg Chol., 2.4gm Fiber

MAIN COURSES

Phyllo Crust

1	package of phyllo
1	egg white
1	tablespoon olive oil
	olive oil spray

Thaw phyllo according to package directions.

Mix egg white with olive oil.

Spray pie plate with olive oil spray.

Working quickly with phyllo, place 1 sheet of phyllo over pie plate allowing sheet to drape over the sides. With hands, press sheet to fit well of pie plate while outer edges drape over sides. Quickly brush some egg mixture over the phyllo only on the inside of the pie plate.

Place another sheet of phyllo over first at right angles to the first sheet and again using a pastry brush, spread with egg mixture.

Repeat until there are 4 layers of phyllo dough.

Take the overlapping edges of phyllo and "scrunching them up," form a pie rim. Dab pie rim or edge with egg mixture.

Fill and bake.

A wonderful crust to be used for Quiche Lorraine and Ski Cheese Pie.

177 Cal., 6gm Protein, 36gm Carb., 2.5gm Fat, 206mg Sodium, 0mg Chol., .6gm Fiber

MAIN COURSES

Ski Cheese Pie

1	phyllo crust
2	cups reduced-fat sharp cheddar cheese, shredded
2	tablespoons flour
1/2	teaspoon salt
1/4	teaspoon dry mustard
1/4	cup onion, chopped
8	slices turkey bacon, diced
1/4	cup skim milk
2	eggs and 2 egg whites beaten together
1	8-ounce can tomato sauce

Preheat oven to 350°.

Toss cheese with flour and seasonings. Set aside.

Cook onion and bacon in skillet for 10 minutes adding cold water in 1/4-cup increments as necessary to prevent burning.

Combine bacon, onions, skim milk, beaten eggs, tomato sauce and mix well. Add cheese mixture; be sure to combine well. Pour into phyllo crust.

Bake at 350° for 40 to 45 minutes.

Note: It may be necessary to cover edges of phyllo crust with foil halfway through baking to prevent burning.

Serves: 8

331 Cal., 22gm Protein, 40gm Carb., 11gm Fat, 922mg Sodium, 96mg Chol., 1.7gm Fiber

MAIN COURSES

Quiche Lorraine

1	phyllo crust
1½	cups white onion, thinly sliced
6	slices turkey bacon, diced
¾	cup low-fat Swiss cheese, shredded
1	cup evaporated skim milk
2	teaspoons cornstarch
⅛	teaspoon sugar
⅛	teaspoon ground nutmeg
⅛	teaspoon ground red pepper
⅛	teaspoon white pepper
2	eggs
2	egg whites

Cook onion and bacon in skillet for 10 minutes adding cold water in ¼-cup increments as necessary to prevent burning.

Spread onion mixture on phyllo crust. Top with cheese.

Mix remaining ingredients with wire whisk until well blended. Pour over cheese.

Bake at 375° for 35 minutes or until a knife inserted 1 inch from center comes out clean.

Note: It may be necessary to cover edges of phyllo crust with foil halfway through baking to prevent burning.

Serves: 8

292 Cal., 17gm Protein, 43gm Carb., 8gm Fat, 286mg Sodium, 82mg Chol., 1gm Fiber

MAIN COURSES

Lavash

1	16-ounce package of soft, white lavash breads (5 rounds)
8	ounces nonfat cream cheese
1	head red leaf lettuce, cleaned, dried and ribs removed
15	slices smoked turkey breast
15	slices low-fat sweet flavored ham
10	hard boiled egg whites, chopped
10	ounces low-fat Muenster cheese, grated
5	medium tomatoes, thinly sliced

On each lavash round layer:
2 tablespoons cream cheese, red leaf lettuce, 3 slices smoked turkey breast, 3 slices ham, chopped egg whites from 2 eggs, 2 ounces Muenster cheese and one thinly sliced tomato. Roll entire sandwich into one long cylinder. Cut into 4 pieces.

Serves: 10

296 Cal., 32gm Protein, 23gm Carb., 8.5gm Fat, 720mg Sodium, 51mg Chol., 1.7gm Fiber

MAIN COURSES

Falafel

2½	cups canned garbanzo beans
2	large cloves garlic, minced
2	tablespoons fresh parsley
1	tablespoon soy sauce (optional)
2	teaspoons coriander
¼	teaspoon turmeric
2	teaspoons cumin
½	teaspoon chili powder
¼	teaspoon cayenne or freshly ground black pepper to taste

Topping:

2	tomatoes, chopped
½	cup onion, minced
3	cups romaine lettuce, chopped
3	whole pita breads

Preheat oven to 400°.

Drain the garbanzo beans well. Combine all the falafel ingredients (including enough cayenne pepper to make this mixture relatively spicy) in a food processor or blender and mix thoroughly into a thick paste.

Lightly spray a baking sheet with vegetable spray. Roll the falafel into small 1-inch balls and place on the sheet. Bake for 15 minutes or until lightly browned.

Combine the chopped tomatoes and minced onions.

To eat, slice a pita bread in half to form two pockets. Fill each pocket with falafel balls, vegetables and Cucumber and/or Yogurt-Tahini Sauce.

Serves: 6

(continued)

Falafel
250 Cal., 10gm Protein, 48gm Carb., 2.2gm Fat, 527mg Sodium, 0mg Chol., 5.8gm Fiber

Cucumber Sauce:

1	English cucumber, shredded
1	scallion, thinly sliced
1	tablespoon lemon juice
1/4	cup plain nonfat yogurt
1/2	teaspoon dried dill weed
1/8	teaspoon garlic powder

Yogurt-Tahini Sauce:

3	tablespoons plain nonfat yogurt
1	tablespoon tahini
1	tablespoon lemon juice
1	small clove garlic, minced
1	teaspoon fresh parsley, minced
	water for thinning (about 1/4 cup)
1/2	teaspoon cayenne pepper or hot pepper sauce to taste
1	tablespoon chili sauce

Cucumber Sauce:
   Combine all ingredients and chill.

Serves: 6

Yogurt-Tahini Sauce:
   Combine all ingredients in a food processor or blender, adding enough water to make a thin sauce and enough cayenne to make it spicy. Refrigerate until ready to use. This sauce thickens as it chills. Thin again with water before serving if necessary.

Serves: 6

Cucumber Sauce
19 Cal., 2gm Protein, 3gm Carb., .1gm Fat, 16mg Sodium, .4mg Chol., .9gm Fiber
Yogurt-Tahini Sauce
24 Cal., 1gm Protein, 2gm Carb., 1.4gm Fat, 40mg Sodium, .2mg Chol., .4gm Fiber

Vegetable Stromboli with Pizza Dough

Pizza Dough:

- 3½ cups unbleached flour
- 1 package rapid-rise, active dry yeast
- 1 cup very warm water (120°-130°)
- 1 tablespoon olive oil
- 2 teaspoons honey
- 1 teaspoon salt

Vegetable Stromboli:

- 1 recipe pizza dough
- 1 tablespoon extra virgin olive oil
- 1 small red onion, sliced
- 1 cup zucchini, sliced ¼-inch thick
- 1 cup yellow squash, sliced ¼-inch thick

In a large bowl, combine 1 cup flour and yeast. Gradually add warm water, oil, honey and salt and mix. Stir in enough additional flour to make a soft dough. Knead on a lightly floured surface until smooth and elastic, about 5-8 minutes. Place dough in a lightly greased bowl, turning dough once to coat. Cover and let rise about 1 hour in a warm place until the dough has doubled in volume.

Punch your fist into the center of the dough. Pull the edges of the dough to the center and turn the dough onto a lightly floured surface. Invert the bowl over the dough on the floured surface and allow the dough to rest another 15 minutes. At this point it can be used for the Vegetable Stromboli recipe.

On a lightly floured surface, roll pizza dough to ¼-inch thickness. Cover with a kitchen towel and let rest.

In a large skillet, heat olive oil on medium-high heat. Sauté red onion, zucchini, yellow squash, red pepper, radicchio and mushrooms for about 5 minutes.

(continued)

1	small red pepper, sliced
1	head radicchio, chopped (optional)
8	ounces fresh mushrooms, sliced
2	cups escarole or spinach or a combination of both, chopped
2	cups skim milk mozzarella cheese, shredded
1	large tomato, chopped
1/4	cup black or green olives, chopped
3	cloves garlic, minced
1/4	cup fresh basil, chopped
	salt and pepper to taste
	garlic powder (optional)
1	egg yolk
1	teaspoon water

Add escarole or spinach and sauté 1 minute longer. Remove from heat, drain in colander, pressing firmly to remove excess moisture, cool.

Cover dough with mozzarella. Spread vegetable mixture on top of cheese. Top with fresh tomato, olives, fresh garlic, basil and salt and pepper to taste. Drizzle with additional extra virgin olive oil, if desired.

Whisk together the egg yolk and the water to make an egg wash.

Roll up the entire sheet of dough and vegetables lengthwise. Tuck each end underneath. Place seam-side down on a lightly greased cookie sheet. Cut slits on surface of dough and brush dough with the egg wash. Sprinkle garlic powder on top, if desired. Place cookie sheet on lowest rack in hot oven. Bake for 15 minutes at 400°. Reduce heat to 350° and bake an additional 25 minutes. Serve immediately.

Serves: 8

332 Cal., 14gm Protein, 47gm Carb., 9.9gm Fat, 648mg Sodium, 50mg Chol., 3.5gm Fiber

Veggie Pizza with Whole Wheat Pizza Dough

Whole Wheat Pizza Dough:

2	tablespoons dry yeast (2 packages)
1 1/2	cups warm water
1	tablespoon honey
1	cup whole wheat flour
3	cups unbleached white flour
4	tablespoons extra virgin olive oil
1	teaspoon salt

Sauce:

2	cups canned, diced tomatoes with juice
1/2	cup tomato paste
2	tablespoons fresh basil, finely chopped
1	tablespoon oregano
2	cloves garlic, minced
1	tablespoon sugar
	salt
10	green peppercorns, ground

In a medium-sized bowl, place yeast, warm water and honey. Let sit 5 minutes. Blend whole wheat flour and 2 1/2 cups unbleached white flour together. When yeast begins to foam, add oil and salt and slowly stir in flours, reserving 1/2 cup white flour for kneading. When 3 1/2 cups flour have been mixed in, turn onto lightly floured board. Knead dough 6 minutes. Wash and lightly oil the bowl and return dough to it. Put in warm spot and cover with damp towel until dough doubles in size (about 1 hour). Then knead dough 3 minutes more. Roll to fit pan 18 x 13-inch pan. Let it rise another 45 minutes, covered.

Proceed with any pizza, calzone or stromboli recipe.

(continued)

Topping:

1	teaspoon olive oil
1	cup each green and red peppers, seeded and sliced
2	cups fresh mushrooms, sliced
1	cup onions, sliced
3	cloves garlic, minced
1/2	cup sun-dried tomatoes, soaked in hot water for 1/2 hour
1	cup skim milk mozzarella cheese, shredded
1/4	cup grated Pecorino Romano cheese
	salt
	black pepper, freshly ground

Preheat oven to 400°.

(If making pizza dough, allow time for all mixing and rising.)

Combine all ingredients for sauce, set aside.

On a lightly floured surface roll out pizza dough to 1/4-inch thickness for an 18 x 13-inch pan. Cover with a kitchen towel and let rest for 45 minutes.

Place 1 teaspoon oil in a large skillet. Add green and red peppers, mushrooms, onions and garlic. Sauté until just beginning to soften. Set aside.

Brush dough lightly with olive oil. Cover dough with sauce. Spread sautéed vegetable mixture on top of sauce. Salt and pepper to taste. Top with dried tomatoes, mozzarella and Pecorino Romano cheese.

Bake at 400° for 25 minutes.

Serves: 12

268 Cal., 10gm Protein, 42gm Carb., 7.9gm Fat, 429mg Sodium, 7mg Chol., 4.8gm Fiber

MAIN COURSES

Synergy Enchiladas Catalina

Enchiladas:

¾	cup onion, finely chopped
4	cups diced cooked vegetables
1	cup vegetable bouillon
1	tablespoon chili powder
10	8-inch flour tortillas
4	cups green chili sauce (recipe below)
1	cup nonfat cottage cheese
1	cup nonfat sour cream
1	cup salsa

Garnish:

shredded lettuce

chopped tomatoes

Green Chili Sauce:

1	8-ounce can chopped green chilies
3	cups vegetable broth
2	tablespoons fresh cilantro
1-2	tablespoons cornstarch

Enchiladas:

Cook the onions in a small amount of the vegetable bouillon until transparent. Drain and add to the cooked vegetables. Season with chili powder. Soften tortillas in vegetable bouillon and spoon a thin layer of green chili sauce over each tortilla. Top with cottage cheese and vegetables, roll up the tortillas. Place in an ovenproof 9 x 12-inch dish. Spoon remaining green chili sauce over the tortillas. Cover with foil and bake at 350° for 20 minutes. Remove foil and dot with sour cream and salsa. Sprinkle with parsley and serve with shredded lettuce and chopped tomatoes.

Green Chili Sauce:

Combine the chilies with the broth and simmer gently for 20 minutes. Add cilantro. Thicken with cornstarch as desired.

Serves: 10

University Hospitals Synergy Culinary School

147 Cal., 9gm Protein, 27gm Carb., 1.4gm Fat, 879mg Sodium, 1mg Chol., 6.1gm Fiber

VEGETABLES

VEGETABLES

Savory Roasted Carrots with Horseradish

12	medium carrots
2	tablespoons margarine, divided
1	medium onion, finely chopped
1	tablespoon horseradish, freshly grated
$1/4$	teaspoon salt
	white pepper, freshly ground
$1/2$	teaspoon fennel seed, ground
2	tablespoons water

Preheat the oven to 350°.

Peel the carrots, halve them lengthwise and cut into $1/4$-inch thick slices. There should be about 3 cups.

Heat 1 tablespoon of the margarine in a large skillet, add onion and sauté over low heat for 2 minutes. Add carrots, increase heat to moderate, add horseradish, salt, pepper to taste, and fennel and stir until well blended.

Place the carrot mixture into a medium baking dish and add water. Dot top with remaining margarine, cover very tightly with foil and bake for 1 hour or until carrots are tender but not overcooked.

Serves: 6

A tasty accompaniment to Veal Birds.

75 Cal., 1gm Protein, 10gm Carb., 3.9gm Fat, 189mg Sodium, 0mg Chol., 2.7gm Fiber

VEGETABLES

Player's Artichokes

2	lemons
4	large artichokes
4	ounces sun-dried tomatoes (loose, dried variety)
4	whole cloves of garlic
¼	cup fresh mint
1	ounce fresh basil
¼	cup olive oil
1	ounce chopped gingerroot
	salt to taste

Use half of one lemon to coat the work surface. Half-fill a large bowl with water. Squeeze remaining lemons and lemon pulp into it. Set aside.

Remove the outer leaves of the artichoke until the yellow leaves are exposed, including those at the bottom. Trim about 1 inch off the tops of the artichokes with a sharp knife. Cut off the stems to leave a flat bottom.

With a teaspoon, remove the inside "choke" of the artichokes. Be sure to remove all of the fuzzy portion inside, firmly scraping the inner sides and bottom of cavity.

Place each artichoke in the bowl of lemon-water as soon as it is prepared, to keep from darkening.

(continued)

Filling:

Boil 4 cups of water in a saucepan. Add sun-dried tomatoes and boil 5 minutes to reconstitute, or until softened. Drain and put tomatoes into a food processor. Process into small pieces. Add remaining ingredients, except salt, and process until mixed.

Assembly:

Drain artichokes and salt the interiors lightly. Spoon the filling into the center of each one. Arrange artichokes in a pot with a lid. Fill with enough water to cover $1/3$ of artichoke. Cover and cook on top of the stove until artichokes are tender, 20-30 minutes. Remove artichokes and reduce the liquid until slightly syrupy. Pour the liquid over the artichokes and serve.

Serves: 4

Serve this with Black Sea Bass Fillets and, for dessert, Orange Sherbet.

183 Cal., 6gm Protein, 29gm Carb., 7.9gm Fat, 381mg Sodium, 0mg Chol., 9gm Fiber

Broccoli with Curry Sauce

2	bunches broccoli (5-6 stalks) separated into small flowerets
2	tablespoons cornstarch
2½	cups 1% milk
1	tablespoon low-sodium soy sauce
2	teaspoons curry powder (or to taste)
	salt and white pepper to taste

In a saucepan, blend cornstarch with the milk and cook over low heat until thickened. Add soy sauce, curry and salt and pepper. Stir to blend and keep sauce warm.

In a vegetable steamer, steam broccoli flowerets until done, but still crisp. Transfer to serving dish and spoon sauce over broccoli.

Serves: 8 - 10

85 Cal., 8gm Protein, 15gm Carb., .9gm Fat, 236mg Sodium, 3mg Chol., 6.1gm Fiber

Red Cabbage in Red Wine

$2^1/_2$	pounds red cabbage, quartered, cored and sliced crosswise into $1/_8$-inch wide strips.
1	cup red wine vinegar
2	tablespoons sugar
2	teaspoons salt
$3/_4$	cup onion, finely chopped
3	cooking apples, cubed
1	onion, pierced with 4 whole cloves
1	bay leaf
4	cups boiling water
1	cup + 4 tablespoons red wine
4	tablespoons red currant jelly

Put shredded cabbage in a large mixing bowl and toss with vinegar, sugar and salt.

In a large casserole, cook chopped onion in a little water until soft. Add apples, cabbage, whole onion, and bay leaf. Add the boiling water and 1 cup of the wine. Stir well, bring to a boil, reduce to very low heat, cover, simmer for $1^1/_2$ to 2 hours until cabbage is tender. Check from time to time to see that cabbage is moist. When done, there should be hardly any liquid left. Before serving, stir in remaining 4 tablespoons red wine and jelly. Taste for seasoning. Remove bay leaf and whole onion.

Serves: 4 - 6

140 Cal., 2gm Protein, 27gm Carb., .5gm Fat, 764mg Sodium, 0mg Chol., 7.2gm Fiber

VEGETABLES

Spicy Cabbage

1/2	Spanish onion, thinly sliced
2	tablespoons vegetable oil
2	large fresh tomatoes or 1 12-ounce can tomatoes
1	Scotch pepper or 1 chili pepper
1	teaspoon salt
1	large cabbage, chopped
1	teaspoon chicken bouillon

In a Dutch oven, sauté onion in oil for 5 minutes. Purée tomatoes and pepper. Add purée to onions. Simmer for 15 minutes. Add salt, cabbage and bouillon. Simmer for 20 minutes or until the cabbage is tender. Serve hot.

Serves: 6

Serve with Scallop-stuffed Sole.

---

98 Cal., 3gm Protein, 13gm Carb., 5gm Fat, 549mg Sodium, 0mg Chol., 6.3gm Fiber

VEGETABLES

Stir Fry Cabbage

1	teaspoon vegetable oil
1/4	cup water
1	small cabbage, chopped into large pieces
1	onion, chopped
1	red pepper, sliced
1	green pepper, sliced
1	bunch green onions, sliced
1	large tomato, cut into wedges
	red pepper flakes (optional)
	salt and pepper to taste

In a large nonstick frying pan, heat oil and water to boiling. Add cabbage, onion and red pepper, cook 4-5 minutes, stirring constantly. Increase heat, add green pepper, green onions and tomato, cook 2 minutes more. Remove from heat, season with red pepper flakes, salt and pepper to taste.

Serves: 6

Serve with steamed rice.

67 Cal., 3gm Protein, 13gm Carb., 1.2gm Fat, 216mg Sodium, 0mg Chol., 6.9gm Fiber

Corn Pancakes with Vegetable Topping

Topping:

½	cup chicken broth
1	onion, chopped
1	garlic clove, finely chopped
1	teaspoon paprika
3	heads broccoli, separated into very small flowerets
8	carrots, diced
3	tablespoons red wine
3	sage leaves, finely chopped
2-3	tablespoons parsley, finely chopped
	salt and pepper to taste
1	cup low-fat sour cream
⅓	cup Parmesan cheese, grated parsley sprigs

Topping:

In a large saucepan heat chicken broth with onions and garlic and cook over low heat until onions are transparent. Add paprika, vegetables and wine. Cook until vegetables are done. Remove from heat, add sage, parsley and salt and pepper. Keep warm.

(continued)

Pancakes:

6	ounces yellow cornmeal
1	egg
$1/2$	cup water
6	sage leaves, finely chopped
$1/2$	teaspoon dried red chili pepper flakes
	salt and pepper to taste
	dash of sugar

Pancakes:

   Blend the cornmeal, egg and water to make a thick batter. Add seasonings, mix well.

   Spray a large nonstick frying pan with vegetable spray. Over medium heat make about 8 to 10 small pancakes, adding vegetable spray between batches. Cook 2 to 3 minutes on each side.

   Top the pancakes with the vegetable mixture and a dollop of sour cream; sprinkle with Parmesan cheese and decorate with sprigs of parsley.

Serves: 4 - 5

345 Cal., 14gm Protein, 53gm Carb., 8.6gm Fat, 1,002mg Sodium, 74mg Chol., 10gm Fiber

VEGETABLES

Fresh Corn Casserole

1/2	tablespoon margarine
1/2	cup green onions, sliced
2 1/4	cups skim milk
1	tablespoon sugar
1/2	teaspoon salt
1/4	teaspoon red pepper, ground
1/3	cup all-purpose flour
3	egg whites
2	whole eggs
3 1/2	cups corn cut from the cob (about 6 ears)
	vegetable spray

Melt margarine in a saucepan over medium heat. Add green onions; sauté 1 minute. Add milk, sugar, salt and red pepper. Cook 3 minutes or until hot, do not boil. Remove from heat and set aside.

Combine flour, egg whites and eggs in a bowl; beat at medium speed until well blended. Gradually stir in 1/2 cup hot milk mixture. Gradually stir in remaining hot milk mixture. Stir in corn; pour into a shallow 2-quart casserole coated with vegetable spray.

Bake at 350° for 40-60 minutes or until a knife inserted near center comes out clean.

Serves: 8

145 Cal., 8gm Protein, 24gm Carb., 3.3gm Fat, 227mg Sodium, 70mg Chol., 3.6gm Fiber

VEGETABLES

Braised Celery

1	bunch celery, cleaned and cut into 2-inch lengths
1	large onion, cut in half and sliced
3	carrots, sliced into $1/8$-inch rounds
$1^1/_2$	cups chicken broth, divided
1	bay leaf
$1^1/_2$	cups beef broth
1	cup white wine
1	tablespoon parsley, chopped
1	teaspoon dried thyme
	vegetable spray

Preheat oven to 350°.

Bring salted water to boil in large saucepan. Blanch celery for 5 minutes. Drain.

Cook onion and carrots over low heat in $1/2$ cup chicken broth until onions become transparent.

Spray baking dish with vegetable spray. Arrange celery over bottom. On top, arrange onion and carrot mixture. Place bay leaf in center.

Heat remaining chicken broth with beef broth, wine, parsley and thyme. Pour over vegetable mixture. Cover with foil, bake $1^1/_2$ hours. Increase temperature to 400°, uncover dish, bake $1/2$ hour more, basting frequently.

Serves: 6

76 Cal., 2gm Protein, 10gm Carb., .5gm Fat, 765mg Sodium, .5mg Chol., 3.1gm Fiber

VEGETABLES

Dennis Nahat's Stewed Eggplant

2	teaspoons butter
$1/8$	cup pine nuts
2	cloves garlic, minced
2	medium onions, chopped
pinch	cinnamon
pinch	nutmeg
pinch	allspice
pinch	paprika
1	20-ounce can chick peas, rinsed and drained
$1/8$	cup olive oil
$1/2$	cup chicken broth
3	medium zucchini, cubed
1	large or 2 medium eggplants, cubed
1	28-ounce can tomatoes
2	cups cooked white rice
	salt and pepper to taste
1	8-ounce container plain nonfat yogurt

In butter sauté the pine nuts until they are golden brown. Add the garlic, onions and spices. Cook until the onions are translucent, adding water as necessary to prevent burning. Add remaining ingredients except rice, salt and pepper and yogurt, cover and cook over low heat for a minimum of 30 minutes. Add water if necessary to prevent burning. Salt and pepper to taste and serve over rice. Yogurt should be served on the side.

Serves: 6

333 Cal., 12gm Protein, 53gm Carb., 10gm Fat, 628mg Sodium, 3mg Chol., 7.7gm Fiber

VEGETABLES

Eggplant Mozzarella

2	eggplants
2	egg whites
2	tablespoons skim milk
1/4	cup bread crumbs
1/2	teaspoon pepper, freshly ground
1	tablespoon parsley, chopped
1	garlic clove, minced
	olive oil spray
2	cups prepared low-fat marinara sauce
1	cup low-fat mozzarella cheese, shredded

Peel eggplant and slice thinly.

Beat egg whites with 2 tablespoons of skim milk. Dip sliced eggplant into egg white mixture and then into bread crumbs seasoned with pepper, parsley and garlic.

Put on cookie sheet which has been sprayed with olive oil spray. Place under broiler. Broil and turn until both sides are browned.

Layer into baking dish alternating layers of sauce and eggplant until all ingredients are used. Top with mozzarella cheese. Cover with foil, bake for 45 minutes at 350°.

Serves: 4

Serve as an appetizer or side dish.

---

177 Cal., 12gm Protein, 22gm Carb., 5.3gm Fat, 434mg Sodium, 16mg Chol., 3.5gm Fiber

VEGETABLES

Eggplant Stuffing

2-1/2 cups water
2 medium eggplants, peeled and chopped
1 tablespoon vegetable oil
2 medium onions, chopped
1 green pepper, chopped
1 cup celery, chopped
1 teaspoon sage
1/2 teaspoon salt
1/4 teaspoon black pepper
1/4 cup egg substitute to equal 1 egg
1/3 cup bread crumbs, reserve 1 tablespoon for topping

Place the eggplant in a pot, add the water and boil for 10 minutes. Drain the eggplant and mash.

Heat the oil in a large pan. Add the eggplant, onions, green pepper and celery. Sauté the vegetables until tender, adding water, if necessary, to prevent burning. Remove from the heat. Add sage, salt, black pepper, egg substitute and bread crumbs.

Place in a 6 x 9-inch baking dish and bake at 350° for 45 minutes. Sprinkle one tablespoon of bread crumbs on top, bake for another 15 minutes.

Variation: Sauté ground turkey and add to the eggplant mixture before baking.

Serves: 4

Serve with grilled chicken or fish.

115 Cal., 4gm Protein, 16gm Carb., 4.2gm Fat, 398mg Sodium, .4mg Chol., 2.9gm Fiber

VEGETABLES

Tian of Eggplant, Yellow Squash and Yellow Peppers

1	tablespoon olive oil
1/3	cup chicken broth, divided
3	onions, cut in half and very thinly sliced
3	large garlic cloves, finely chopped
3	large eggplants, peeled and thinly sliced into rounds
3	yellow squash, thinly sliced into rounds
3	yellow peppers, cored and thinly sliced into rounds
1	tablespoon dried thyme
	salt and pepper
	vegetable spray

Preheat oven to 325°.

In saucepan, heat olive oil and 2 tablespoons chicken broth over low heat. Add onions and garlic and cook until very soft, about 20 minutes.

Spray large gratin dish with vegetable spray. Put half of onion mixture on bottom, overlap with half of the vegetables, alternating slices of the three vegetables to cover onion mixture. Sprinkle with half the thyme and salt and pepper. Spread second half of onion mixture on top. Repeat vegetable layer and seasonings. Add remaining broth and bake for about 40 to 50 minutes pressing on vegetables a couple of times. Vegetables should be very soft and most of the liquid evaporated. If top layer becomes too dry, cover loosely with foil.

Serves: 6

Excellent with Grilled Indian Lamb.

114 Cal., 4gm Protein, 21gm Carb., 3.2gm Fat, 267mg Sodium, .1mg Chol., 6.5gm Fiber

Fennel Paysanne

3	cups water, salted
3	fennel bulbs, quartered
12	small white onions
4-6	new potatoes, peeled and cubed
1	tablespoon butter
	salt and pepper to taste
1/4	cup chicken broth
1	large garlic clove, minced
2	tablespoons parsley, minced

Boil water, add fennel, cook 5 minutes. Remove with slotted spoon, drain. Add onions and potatoes to water. Cook 5 minutes. Drain.

Heat butter over low heat in nonstick skillet. Sauté potatoes and onions until lightly browned. Season with salt and pepper. Add fennel and 1/4 cup chicken broth and garlic. Cover partially and cook 5 to 6 minutes. Transfer to serving dish, sprinkle with parsley.

Serves: 4 - 6

122 Cal., 3gm Protein, 24gm Carb., 2.2gm Fat, 336mg Sodium, 5mg Chol., 4gm Fiber

VEGETABLES

Buddha's Delight

1/2	**cup carrots, diagonally sliced**
1/2	**cup broccoli flowerets**
1/2	**small box of tofu, extra firm**
3	**teaspoons vegetable oil, divided**
4	**Chinese black mushrooms**
12	**straw mushrooms**
1/4	**cup bean sprouts**
1/2	**cup lettuce, chopped**
2	**teaspoons oyster sauce**
1/2	**teaspoon salt**
1/4	**teaspoon sugar**

Parboil carrots and broccoli in boiling water for 5 minutes. Remove and drain.

Cut the tofu into small, bite-size cubes.

Heat wok until very hot and add 1 teaspoon of the oil. Stir fry tofu until slightly golden. Remove from wok.

Add the remaining 2 teaspoons oil and stir fry all the mushrooms, bean sprouts, lettuce, carrots and broccoli for 5 minutes.

Add the oyster sauce, salt, sugar and tofu and cook 1 minute more. Serve hot.

Serves: 4

Serve with Mandarin Chicken and, for dessert, Oranges Orientales.

Royal Pacific

106 Cal., 7gm Protein, 8gm Carb., 6.3gm Fat, 470mg Sodium, 0mg Chol., 2.9gm Fiber

Herbed Mixed Vegetables

2	tablespoons water
1	cup yellow squash, thinly sliced
1	cup zucchini squash, thinly sliced
1/2	cup green bell pepper, cut into 2-inch strips
1/2	cup celery, cut into 2-inch strips
1/4	cup onion, finely chopped
1	teaspoon caraway seed
1/4	teaspoon garlic powder
	salt and pepper to taste
1	medium tomato, cut into 8 wedges

Heat the water in a large sauté pan. Add the squashes, bell pepper, celery and onion. Cover pan and cook over medium heat until the vegetables are tender-crisp, about 4-5 minutes.

Sprinkle the caraway seed, garlic powder, salt and pepper over the vegetables. Add the tomato wedges and cook over low heat until the tomato wedges are just heated through, about 2 minutes.

Serves: 4

31 Cal., 2gm Protein, 7gm Carb., .4gm Fat, 293mg Sodium, 0mg Chol., .1gm Fiber

VEGETABLES

Mushroom Bread Pudding

1¼	cups chicken broth
½	cup nonfat sour cream
1½	cups 1% milk
½	cup egg substitute to equal 2 eggs
½	teaspoon salt
1	tablespoon butter
¼	cup shallots, minced
3	garlic cloves, minced
1½	teaspoons thyme
4-5	cups mushrooms, preferably a mixture of Shitake, portabello and button mushrooms, stemmed and sliced
	salt and pepper to taste
8	slices of wheat bread, toasted

In a small saucepan, heat broth over medium heat and reduce by half.

In a medium mixing bowl, mix together the nonfat sour cream, milk, egg substitute and salt. Slowly whisk in the reduced broth, set aside.

In a large, nonstick skillet, melt the butter, add shallots, garlic and thyme and sauté until soft, add mushrooms and cook until done, about 10 minutes. Add salt and pepper to taste.

Line a 9 x 13-inch baking dish or gratin pan with the bread slices, top with ½ of the mushroom mixture, repeat with another layer of bread and mushrooms, top with a third layer of bread. Pour the egg mixture evenly over it all. Cover with plastic wrap and refrigerate several hours.

Preheat oven to 350°.

Unwrap the dish, press bread into liquid and bake, covered with foil, for 30 minutes, uncover and bake for another 15 minutes. Serve hot.

Serves: 6 - 8

123 Cal., 7gm Protein, 18gm Carb., 2.9gm Fat, 553mg Sodium, 7mg Chol., 3.7gm Fiber

VEGETABLES

Parsnip and Carrot Gratin

- ¾ pound carrots, peeled and shredded
- ¾ pound parsnips, peeled and shredded
- ½ cup scallions, thinly sliced
- 2 tablespoons parsley, minced
- 3 tablespoons cornstarch, divided
- 2½ cups 1% milk
- 1 egg
- ½ cup nonfat sour cream
- salt and pepper to taste
- ½ cup Parmesan cheese, grated
- ½ tablespoon butter
- vegetable spray

❋   ❋   ❋

Preheat oven to 325°.

Spray a 1½-quart baking or gratin dish with vegetable spray.

In a large mixing bowl, toss together carrots, parsnips, scallions, parsley and 2 tablespoons cornstarch. Spread mixture evenly into gratin dish and press down.

In a small saucepan, dissolve remaining 1 tablespoon cornstarch in ¼ cup of the milk, then add rest of milk, bring to a boil, whisking constantly, reduce heat to low.

In a medium mixing bowl, beat egg and nonfat sour cream, season with salt and pepper.

Add egg mixture to milk mixture in a slow stream, stirring until well combined.

Pour the hot custard over vegetables, sprinkle top with Parmesan cheese and top with small pieces of the butter.

Bake in 325° oven for 35 minutes or until it bubbles through a golden crust.

Let stand 5 minutes before serving.

Serves: 12

You can prepare this dish a day ahead, refrigerate and bake the next day.

99 Cal., 5gm Protein, 14gm Carb., 2.6gm Fat, 216mg Sodium, 29mg Chol., 2.1gm Fiber

VEGETABLES

Lemony Peapods

1	**pound fresh peapods**
½	**tablespoon butter**
½	**lemon, juiced**
	salt

Clean peapods and remove stringy part along the top of the peapod. Blanch in boiling water for 10 seconds. Drain.

In a medium-sized skillet, melt butter on medium-high heat, add peapods, lemon juice and salt and stir fry for 2-3 minutes.

Serves: 6

Serve with Sweet Potato Fries and Chicken Loaf.

29 Cal., 1gm Protein, 5gm Carb., 1.1gm Fat, 21mg Sodium, 3mg Chol., 1.8gm Fiber

Cultured Potatoes

16	small (2-inch) redskin potatoes
1	tablespoon butter or margarine
1/2	cup freshly grated Reggiano Parmesan cheese
1	tablespoon garlic, chopped
1	teaspoon salt
1	teaspoon black pepper, freshly ground
8	ounces nonfat plain yogurt

Garnish:
   chopped parsley

Boil the potatoes, covered, for 20 minutes (test with fork). Drain well and cut the potatoes into bite-size pieces, add butter, cheese, garlic, salt and pepper and stir until melted (microwave for 1 minute, if needed). Stir in the yogurt and garnish with parsley before serving.

Serves: 6

The secret is in the cheese. The culture is in the yogurt. Try any leftovers cold as a potato salad.

509 Cal., 14gm Protein, 106gm Carb., 4.3gm Fat, 570mg Sodium, 11mg Chol., 8.2gm Fiber

VEGETABLES

Easy Au Gratin Potatoes

2	pounds nonfat packaged hash browns, thawed if frozen
1	can low-fat cream of potato soup
1	can low-fat cream of chicken soup
1	cup nonfat sour cream
1	12-ounce package nonfat cheddar cheese, shredded
1	medium onion, minced
2½	teaspoons cumin (optional)

Mix all ingredients together and put into a 9 x 13 x 2-inch casserole. Bake covered, at 350° for 1 hour, then uncover and continue to bake for 30 more minutes.

Serves: 12

126 Cal., 12gm Protein, 19gm Carb., .4gm Fat, 360mg Sodium, 6mg Chol., 1.7gm Fiber

VEGETABLES

Garlic Potato Straw Surprise

2	**pounds baking potatoes, peeled and coarsely shredded, divided**
1	**tablespoon vegetable oil**
10	**garlic cloves, peeled**
1	**tablespoon fresh parsley, chopped**
1/2	**teaspoon salt**
1	**tablespoon butter**

Preheat oven to 400°.

Squeeze any excess liquid from shredded potatoes. Heat oil in a large cast iron skillet on medium-high heat. Add half of the potatoes, tossing to coat. Push the garlic cloves into the potato and sprinkle with parsley and salt.

In a separate skillet, heat butter on medium heat and toss remaining potatoes in the melted butter. Immediately layer potatoes on top of the potato/garlic mixture, spreading evenly over the first layer.

Bake in 400° oven for 45 minutes or until potatoes are golden brown and crisp.

Serves: 4

241 Cal., 4gm Protein, 48gm Carb., 4.1gm Fat, 318mg Sodium, 8mg Chol., 4.7gm Fiber

VEGETABLES

Oven Baked French Fries

4	baking potatoes, peeled and cut into large French fry pieces
	salt and pepper
1	teaspoon garlic powder (optional)
	vegetable spray

Preheat oven to 425°.

Distribute potato pieces onto nonstick baking sheet, sprinkle evenly with salt, pepper and garlic powder. Spray with vegetable spray over all and bake for 35 - 40 minutes or until browned. Turn a couple of times during baking.

Serves: 4

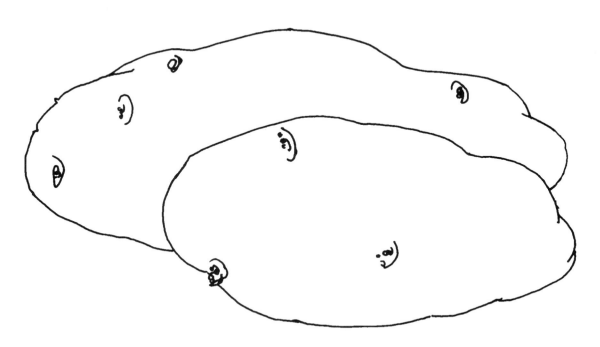

132 Cal., 3gm Protein, 30gm Carb., .4gm Fat, 283mg Sodium, 0mg Chol., 3gm Fiber

VEGETABLES

Potato Cakes with Leeks and Gruyère

2¼	pounds potatoes, peeled, cooked until still firm, chilled, then grated
1	egg, beaten
	salt and pepper
¼	cup chicken broth
2	leeks, white part only, cleaned and cut in half lengthwise and thinly sliced
½	cup low-fat sour cream
1	teaspoon lemon juice
2	teaspoons Dijon mustard
1½	cups low-fat Gruyère cheese or similar cheese, grated
3	tablespoons fresh parsley, minced
1	teaspoon fresh tarragon, minced, or ¼ teaspoon dried tarragon
	salt and pepper to taste
1	tablespoon butter
1	tablespoon vegetable oil

Combine the grated potatoes with the egg and mix well. Season with salt and pepper and set aside.

In a saucepan, heat chicken broth and the leeks and cook until leeks are wilted. Remove from heat.

Add the remaining ingredients, except the butter and oil, to the leeks. Mix well. Taste for seasoning.

With the potato mixture, form pancakes about 3 inches across and ⅓ inch thick.

On top of one pancake, put about 2 tablespoons of leek mixture, flattened well. Cover this with another potato pancake. Set aside. Continue until ingredients are used.

In a nonstick skillet, heat butter and oil over moderate heat. Carefully add pancakes, do not crowd, brown on one side; carefully turn over, using two spatulas, and brown on other side. Pancakes are fragile. The smaller they are, the easier to handle.

Serves: 8 - 10

125 Cal., 3gm Protein, 20gm Carb., 4gm Fat, 192mg Sodium, 30mg Chol., 1.9gm Fiber

VEGETABLES

Baked Sweet Potatoes and Apricots

6	**fresh medium sweet potatoes or 2 large cans of sweet potatoes, drained**
1	**17-ounce can apricot halves in light syrup, cut into thirds**
1½	**tablespoons brown sugar**
1	**tablespoon cornstarch**
¼	**teaspoon salt**
½	**teaspoon cinnamon**
⅓	**cup golden raisins**
¼	**cup dry sherry**
1	**teaspoon grated orange peel**

Cook fresh sweet potatoes in boiling water until tender, 30-35 minutes. Peel and halve potatoes lengthwise. Place in 9 x 13 x 2-inch baking dish.

Drain apricots, reserving syrup; add water to syrup, if necessary, to equal 1 cup of liquid and set aside. Arrange apricots over potatoes.

In saucepan, combine brown sugar, cornstarch, salt and cinnamon. Stir in apricot syrup and raisins. Cook and stir over high heat until mixture comes to a boil. Stir in sherry and orange peel. Pour mixture over potatoes and fruit.

Bake, uncovered, in a 350° oven, basting occasionally for 20 minutes or until well glazed.

Serves: 6

Anyone with a "sweet tooth" will love this dish!

248 Cal., 3gm Protein, 59gm Carb., .2gm Fat, 108mg Sodium, 0mg Chol., 4.7gm Fiber

VEGETABLES

Sweet Potato and Lemon Purée

4	pounds sweet potatoes, cooked and mashed
4	tablespoons lemon juice
1	tablespoon butter
2	egg yolks
	salt and pepper to taste
¹/₈	teaspoon nutmeg
1	lemon, thinly sliced
	vegetable spray

Preheat oven to 325°.

Coat a 3-quart soufflé dish with vegetable spray.

In a large mixing bowl, combine the mashed sweet potatoes, lemon juice, butter, egg yolks, salt and pepper and nutmeg. Mix well until the mixture is smooth. Pour into soufflé dish, top with lemon slices and bake for 40 minutes.

Note: For a lighter version, beat two egg whites until stiff and incorporate into mixture after it is smooth.

Serves: 8

265 Cal., 5gm Protein, 56gm Carb., 3.1gm Fat, 178mg Sodium, 72mg Chol., 5.7gm Fiber

VEGETABLES

Sweet Potato Fries

2	**medium sweet potatoes**
	vegetable spray

Wash and scrub potatoes. Cut potatoes into French fry strips.

Place potatoes in steamer basket and steam over boiling water for 8 minutes.

Spread potatoes on a cookie sheet sprayed with vegetable spray.

Bake potatoes at 350° until ends begin to brown, approximately 25 minutes.

Serves: 4

64 Cal., 1gm Protein, 14gm Carb., .6gm Fat, 6mg Sodium, 0mg Chol., 1.4gm Fiber

VEGETABLES

Yams with Dried Fruit

8	**yams**
1	**cup mixed dried fruits (apricots, apples, raisins)**
1/2	**cup unsweetened frozen apple juice concentrate**
1/4	**teaspoon salt**
1/2	**cup chopped pecans**
2	**tablespoons margarine**

Bake scrubbed yams at 325° for 1 to 2 hours. Yams should release their natural sugar syrup by this time, have toasted skins, and be very soft and aromatic.

While yams bake, chop fruits and combine with 1 cup of boiling water. Cover and allow water to absorb. When completely cool, drain and reserve liquid. Combine thawed apple juice concentrate with 1/4 cup reserved liquid; mix in hydrated dried fruits and salt.

Allow yams to cool. Peel carefully, leaving as much of the candied natural syrup with the flesh. (Or leave the skin on for a stronger toasted flavor.) Slice yams into rounds about 1/2-inch thick. Arrange one layer in a 9 x 13-inch baking dish. Sprinkle with half the fruit mixture. Repeat layers and top with chopped pecans. Dot with margarine.

Bake at 325° for an hour or until juices are absorbed.

Serves: 8

251 Cal., 3gm Protein, 46gm Carb., 7.4gm Fat, 112mg Sodium, 0mg Chol., 4.6gm Fiber

VEGETABLES

Crustless Spinach Pie

2	teaspoons canola oil
1	medium onion, finely chopped
1½	cup chopped spinach, cooked and drained
1	12-ounce carton 1% cottage cheese
1	whole egg
1	egg white
¼	teaspoon salt
½	teaspoon thyme
1	tablespoon cornstarch
½	cup low-fat sharp cheddar cheese, grated
	vegetable spray

Topping:

½	cup nonfat plain yogurt
1	tablespoon cornstarch
½	cup low-fat sharp cheddar cheese, grated (optional)

Preheat oven to 375°. Spray 9-inch pie plate with vegetable spray.

In a sauté pan, heat the oil and sauté the onion until translucent.

In a bowl, combine the onion, cooked spinach, cottage cheese, eggs, seasonings, cornstarch and cheese. Mix well and spoon into the pie plate.

Combine the topping ingredients and spread evenly over the spinach mixture. Sprinkle a little grated cheddar over the top, if desired.

Bake until set, about 40 minutes. Let stand 15 minutes for easier slicing.

Serves: 4 - 6

Serve with Shrimp Salad.

---

136 Cal., 14gm Protein, 9gm Carb., 4.8gm Fat, 470mg Sodium, 55mg Chol., 1.7gm Fiber

VEGETABLES

Oriental Spinach

1	pound washed spinach, stems removed
1	tablespoon sesame seeds, lightly toasted
1	tablespoon soy sauce
3	tablespoons rice vinegar

In a large saucepan, bring 3 quarts of water to a boil, add spinach, turn off heat, and let stand until spinach is just wilted. Rinse spinach in cold water, squeeze water out in small handfuls and put in a bowl in the refrigerator to chill (30-60 minutes). Crush the sesame seeds and sprinkle them on top of the spinach. Add the soy sauce and vinegar and toss. Serve.

Serves: 4

Serve this cold vegetable with broiled chicken or fish.

---

42 Cal., 4gm Protein, 5gm Carb., 1.5gm Fat, 347mg Sodium, 0mg Chol., 4.8gm Fiber

VEGETABLES

Sautéed Greens

1	pound washed spinach, stems removed
1	tablespoon olive oil
1/2	tablespoon chopped garlic
1/2	teaspoon salt
1/2	teaspoon black pepper, freshly ground

In a large frying pan, heat the oil and sauté the spinach over medium heat with the other ingredients until wilted. Serve warm.

Serves: 4

Serve this with Oven Baked Chicken and Garlic Potato Straw Surprise.
For a stronger flavor, use watercress or chicory in place of the spinach!

41 Cal., 3gm Protein, 5gm Carb., 2.1gm Fat, 364mg Sodium, 0mg Chol., 4.6gm Fiber

VEGETABLES

Spinach and Rice

1	cup onions, minced
3	slices turkey bacon, diced
2	tablespoons broth
1	pound spinach, stems removed, washed with water left on leaves
3	cups rice, cooked
1	cup low-fat cottage cheese
1/4	cup low-fat cheddar cheese, shredded
1/4	cup egg substitute to equal one egg
3	tablespoons fresh parsley, minced
1 1/2	teaspoons dried dill
	vegetable spray

In a large, nonstick frying pan, cook the onions and the turkey bacon in the broth until the onions are soft. Add the spinach and cook over low heat, stirring constantly, until wilted. Cook until all liquid has evaporated.

In a large bowl, combine the rice, cottage cheese, cheddar, egg substitute, parsley and dill. Fold in the spinach mixture.

Coat a 1 1/2-quart casserole with vegetable spray. Add the rice mixture. Bake at 375° for 20-25 minutes, or until heated through and light brown on top.

Serves: 4

189 Cal., 18gm Protein, 22gm Carb., 3.9gm Fat, 555mg Sodium, 13mg Chol., 5gm Fiber

VEGETABLES

Spinach Stew

1	pound fresh spinach, chopped coarsely plus ½ cup water, OR
2	10-ounce packages of frozen spinach, thawed, with no water added
1	small onion, thinly sliced
2	medium tomatoes, coarsely chopped
2	tablespoons cooking oil
1	teaspoon salt
1	teaspoon ground red pepper
½	cup melon seed (Equsi) plus ½ cup of water
1	cup of mushrooms

Heat the oil in a Dutch oven. Sauté onions. Add tomatoes, salt and pepper. Simmer for 15 minutes. Grind melon seeds in food processor and add ½ cup of water. Simmer for 10 minutes. Add spinach and ½ cup of water. Cook for 25 minutes. Add mushrooms, cook on low for 5 minutes.

Serves: 6

Equsi can be found in Hispanic or Middle East markets. Serve with Turkey and Stuffing.

79 Cal., 5gm Protein, 11gm Carb., 3gm Fat, 299mg Sodium, 0mg Chol., 5.9gm Fiber

VEGETABLES

Tomatoes Provençales

5	medium, ripe tomatoes, cut in half horizontally, seeds removed
4	tablespoons parsley, finely chopped
4	garlic cloves, minced
3	shallots, minced
	salt and pepper
2	teaspoons olive oil
1	cube beef bouillon

Preheat oven to 350°.

Place tomato halves into baking dish. Mix parsley, garlic and shallots together and with small spoon distribute mixture equally into tomato cavities.

Sprinkle with salt and pepper and olive oil. Crush beef bouillon cube in a little hot water, add to bottom of baking dish and add enough water to cover bottom of dish. Bake for 30-40 minutes, basting tomatoes with liquid, adding more water if necessary.

Serves: 5

Serve with grilled fish or meat.

51 Cal., 2gm Protein, 8gm Carb., 2.1gm Fat, 647mg Sodium, .3mg Chol., 2.1gm Fiber

VEGETABLES

Tomatoes Stuffed with Rice and Vegetables

2 2/3 cups water
1 cup brown rice
1 tablespoon fresh basil, chopped
1 tablespoon oregano
6 large, firm tomatoes
1/3 pound green beans, cut into 1/2-inch pieces
1 medium zucchini, cut into 1/8-inch thick slices; then cut slices in half
    salt and pepper
4 tablespoons Romano cheese, grated
2 tablespoons parsley, minced
1 tablespoon mint, minced

Garnish:
4 large mint leaves

❋   ❋   ❋

Bring water to a rolling boil, stir in rice, basil and oregano. Cover and simmer over low heat for 40 minutes or until rice is tender and liquid is absorbed.

While rice is cooking, cut a slice 1/4-inch thick from the stem end of each tomato.

Hollow tomatoes, seed and strain. Dice pulp and reserve. Sprinkle inside of tomato shells with salt and pepper.

Fill the bottom of a steamer with water and bring to a boil. Steam the green beans and zucchini until just tender. Green beans may take a little longer.

In a large bowl, combine rice, tomato pulp, zucchini, beans, parsley, mint and 2 tablespoons Romano cheese. Season with salt and pepper to taste.

Fill tomatoes with rice mixture and sprinkle with remaining Romano cheese.

Place tomatoes in an ovenproof dish and heat in a 325° oven until heated through, about 10 minutes. Serve, garnished with mint sprigs.

Serves: 6

95 Cal., 4gm Protein, 18gm Carb., 1.9gm Fat, 191mg Sodium, 3mg Chol., 4gm Fiber

VEGETABLES

Baked Zucchini and Rice

1	tablespoon olive oil
1	medium onion, chopped
2	pounds small zucchini, sliced into 1/4-inch rounds
2	cloves garlic, minced
	freshly ground black pepper
1	28-ounce can crushed Italian plum tomatoes
1	cup uncooked long grain rice
2	tablespoons parsley, chopped
1/4	cup Parmesan cheese, grated
1/4	cup bread crumbs

Heat oven to 425°.

Heat oil in large skillet; add onion and cook until lightly browned. Add zucchini and garlic; stir fry for about 3 minutes until zucchini is partially cooked. Season to taste with black pepper.

Add tomatoes and simmer gently, uncovered, about 4 minutes. Stir in rice, parsley and 1/8 cup Parmesan cheese. Spoon into buttered baking dish and sprinkle top with crumbs and remaining cheese.

Bake at 425° for 30-35 minutes, or until top is golden.

Serves: 6

214 Cal., 6gm Protein, 39gm Carb., 4.1gm Fat, 326mg Sodium, 3mg Chol., 3.8gm Fiber

VEGETABLES

Zucchini Luis

1	onion, chopped
1	garlic clove, minced
1	tablespoon vegetable oil
6	zucchini, cubed
5	tomatoes, cubed
1/2	tablespoon salt
1/2	tablespoon black pepper
1/4	teaspoon red pepper flakes

In nonstick skillet heat oil, add onion and garlic, cook until onion is soft. Add zucchini, cover pan and cook 5 minutes. Uncover, add tomatoes, salt and pepper. Cook over low heat 10 minutes. Add red pepper flakes, stir well, cook 2 more minutes. Serve.

Serves: 6

Serve with Enchiladas Verdes.

46 Cal., 2gm Protein, 10gm Carb., .8gm Fat, 560mg Sodium, 0mg Chol., 3.3gm Fiber

VEGETABLES

Zucchini Soufflé

2	pounds zucchini, peeled, cut in half lengthwise and into 1-inch thick pieces
	salt and pepper to taste
1/4	teaspoon nutmeg
1	tablespoon cornstarch
1/2	cup grated Parmesan cheese
1	egg yolk
1	cup low-fat sour cream
4	egg whites
	vegetable spray

Preheat oven to 375°.

Steam zucchini until tender and purée in a food processor. In a nonstick skillet heat purée over low heat until most moisture has evaporated. Add salt and pepper, nutmeg and cornstarch. Mix well with wire whisk and cook 5 minutes, stirring, watching that purée does not brown or begin to stick to pan.

In a large mixing bowl, combine Parmesan, egg yolk and sour cream. Add the zucchini mixture. Set aside.

Beat the egg whites until stiff but still shiny and carefully fold into purée.

Spray a 2-quart soufflé mold with vegetable spray. Pour mixture into it and bake for 30 to 40 minutes. Soufflé is ready when it puffs up and edges are lightly browned. Serve immediately.

Note: Soufflé can be made a couple of hours ahead up to the point of beating and incorporating egg whites.

Serves: 6

Serve with Original Chicken Arabesque.

94 Cal., 5gm Protein, 10gm Carb., 3.8gm Fat, 239mg Sodium, 36mg Chol., 2gm Fiber

SAUCES

SAUCES

Dill Sauce

1	cup watercress leaves
1/2	cup scallions, sliced
4	tablespoons fresh dill, chopped
2	cloves garlic
2	cups nonfat mayonnaise
4	tablespoons lemon juice
2	tablespoons Cognac
1	teaspoon salt
1/2	teaspoon pepper
1	tablespoon corn oil
1/2	cup 1% cottage cheese
1/2	cup nonfat sour cream

Combine all of the ingredients except the sour cream in a blender and mix well.
   Remove from the blender, adjust seasonings, add sour cream and mix well.
   Chill before serving.

Yield: 4 cups
        1/4 cup per serving

A wonderful sauce for any seafood. It can be stored in the refrigerator for one week.

42 Cal., 1gm Protein, 6gm Carb., 1gm Fat, 379mg Sodium, .3mg Chol., .1gm Fiber

Fresh Tomato Sauce

2	tablespoons extra virgin olive oil
2	tablespoons low-fat butter substitute
1	shallot, minced
3	garlic cloves, minced
8	Roma tomatoes, chopped
1/4	cup fresh basil, chopped
1	tablespoon fresh parsley, minced
	salt and pepper to taste
1	teaspoon sugar

Heat oil and butter substitute in a medium saucepan on low heat. Add shallots and garlic and sauté 2 minutes. Add tomatoes and cook for 10 minutes, stirring. Add basil, parsley, salt and pepper, and sugar. Remove from heat.

Serves: 6

Serve over a pound of your favorite pasta.

87 Cal., 3gm Protein, 13gm Carb., 4gm Fat, 296mg Sodium, 0mg Chol., 4.1gm Fiber

SAUCES

Green Peppercorn Sauce

3	**tablespoons butter**
3	**tablespoons flour**
3	**beef bouillon cubes, crushed**
1	**teaspoon mixed dried herbs**
1/2	**teaspoon salt**
1/2	**teaspoon pepper**
1	**cup red wine**
2	**cups water**
1	**tablespoon tomato paste**
2	**tablespoons balsamic vinegar**
1/2	**lemon, juiced**
1/2	**tablespoon sugar**
40	**green peppercorns**

In a skillet, heat butter to bubbling, add flour, bouillon cubes, herbs, salt and pepper. Sauté, stirring continuously, until ingredients turn a rich brown color. Add red wine, stir for 30 seconds; add water, stir well for 2 minutes. Add tomato paste, vinegar, lemon juice, sugar and peppercorns. Continue to cook for 10 minutes, stirring 2-3 times. Remove to 3-quart sauce pan, adjust seasoning and simmer for 30 minutes.

<u>Variation</u>: Use capers instead of peppercorns.

<u>Note</u>: Sauce can be made up to 2 days in advance and stored covered in refrigerator. If reheating, adjust viscosity by adding water.

Yield: 3 cups
     1/4 cup per serving

Excellent on grilled, skinless duck breasts or grilled tenderloin. For dessert, try Grape Sherbet.

58 Cal., 1gm Protein, 4gm Carb., 3.1gm Fat, 295mg Sodium, 6mg Chol., .4gm Fiber

SAUCES

Mango Chutney

6	green mangoes
2	teaspoons salt
3	red chiles, seeded and chopped or 2 teaspoons chili powder
1	cup malt vinegar
2	cups sugar
1½	ounces fresh green ginger, peeled and chopped
3	cloves garlic, crushed
1/2	cup seedless raisins

Peel and chop the mangoes, sprinkle with salt and set aside for 20 minutes. Grind the chilis or powder with a little vinegar to form a paste. Place the remaining vinegar in a saucepan with the sugar and simmer gently until the sugar dissolves. Pour off all the juice from the mango flesh and add the flesh to the pan. Simmer for about 10-15 minutes. Add the ginger, garlic, raisins and chili paste and stir well. Cook for a further 10-12 minutes. Cool and bottle in sterilized jars.

Serves: 24

Serve with Grilled Veal Chops, Oven Baked French Fries and a green salad.

98 Cal., .3gm Protein, 26gm Carb., .2gm Fat, 187mg Sodium, 0mg Chol., 1.1gm Fiber

SAUCES

Mediterranean Sauce

12	large brine-cured black olives or Kalamata olives, pitted
3	garlic cloves
1	tablespoon Dijon mustard
3	tablespoons balsamic vinegar
2	tablespoons fresh thyme leaves or 1 tablespoon dried
3	tablespoons olive oil
5	plum tomatoes, fresh or canned, seeded
2	tablespoon water

Place all ingredients in a blender or food processor and process until smooth.

Serves: 6

This versatile sauce can be used on boiled potatoes and chicken or pasta.

103 Cal., 1gm Protein, 4gm Carb., 10.2gm Fat, 154mg Sodium, 0mg Chol., 1.7gm Fiber

SAUCES

Mock Crème Fraîche

1 1/2 cups low-fat cottage cheese
1/2 cup plain low-fat yogurt
1/4 cup low-fat ricotta cheese

Put all ingredients into food processor and run until everything is perfectly blended and smooth, no more than 7-8 seconds. Transfer mixture to bowl and, using a wire whisk, beat well to add as much air as possible, until mixture is fluffy and light. It should increase to about 2 1/2 cups in 3-4 minutes.

Pour mixture into jars and set in warm place or on hot plate of yogurt maker to stay at a steady 75° so that it will begin to ferment. This should take about 2 hours. Mixture will thicken and take on a subtle sour flavor.

Makes about 2 1/2 cups, which can be stored in refrigerator up to 2 weeks for use in many recipes.

Serves: 6

Great as a topping for fresh berries, this is the best low-fat replacement for Crème Fraîche we have found!

Recipe courtesy of: <u>The Love Your Heart Mediterranean (Low Cholesterol) Cookbook</u>. Carole Kruppa, Published by Surrey Books, Chicago, Illinois. Copyright 1992.

67 Cal., 9gm Protein, 3gm Carb., 1.7gm Fat, 256mg Sodium, 7mg Chol., 0gm Fiber

SAUCES

Roasted Garlic Lemon Sauce

3	large whole heads of garlic
1	tablespoon vegetable oil
2	tablespoons lemon juice
2	tablespoons white wine vinegar
1½	tablespoons low-sodium soy sauce
⅛	teaspoon pepper
⅛	teaspoon salt

Preheat oven to 400°.

Remove white skin of garlic head - do not separate the cloves.

Brush each head with oil and wrap separately in foil.

Bake for 45 minutes or until heads are soft to the touch. Let cool. Separate cloves and squeeze garlic pulp into a blender or food processor. Add remaining ingredients and blend until smooth.

Yield: About ½ cup
       1 tablespoon per serving

Excellent with steamed fish and vegetables or grilled meats.

29 Cal., 1gm Protein, 4gm Carb., 1.7gm Fat, 136mg Sodium, 0mg Chol., .2gm Fiber

BREADS

Banana Raisin Bread

2	cups all purpose flour
1 1/2	tablespoons baking powder
1/2	teaspoon salt
1/2	teaspoon nutmeg, freshly grated
1	tablespoon butter, softened
1	tablespoon canola oil
1	egg
1/2	cup unsweetened applesauce
1/2	cup brown sugar
3	medium bananas (about one pound)
1	teaspoon vanilla extract
2/3	cup raisins
1/4	cup pecans, chopped
	vegetable spray

Prepare an 8 1/2 x 4 x 2-inch loaf pan. Spray the pan with vegetable spray, line the bottom with waxed paper cut to fit and spray again.

Sift together flour, baking powder, salt and nutmeg. Set aside.

Combine butter, oil, egg, applesauce and sugar in a mixing bowl and beat until well combined.

Mash the bananas and add the vanilla extract.

Add the sifted ingredients and the banana alternately to the applesauce mixture and mix until everything is thoroughly blended. Add the raisins and pecans.

Bake at 350° for 45 minutes or until a wooden pick inserted in the center comes out clean.

Serves: 10 - 12

Serve as toast topped with low-fat cream cheese.

207 Cal., 3gm Protein, 40gm Carb., 4.5gm Fat, 260mg Sodium, 25mg Chol., 2gm Fiber

Cornbread Muffins

1 1/4	cups white cornmeal
1	8 1/2 ounce can cream-style corn
1/2	cup buttermilk
1 1/4	cups flour
1/3	cup sugar
1	tablespoon baking powder
1/2	tablespoon baking soda
1/4	teaspoon salt
1/4	cup egg substitute to equal 1 egg
1/4	cup light corn syrup
1	cup fresh corn off the cob or 1 8 1/2-ounce can whole kernel corn, drained
	vegetable spray

Combine cornmeal and cream-style corn with buttermilk in a bowl. Set aside. In a separate bowl, combine flour, sugar, baking power, baking soda and salt. In another bowl, combine the egg substitute, corn syrup and corn off the cob. Stir the egg mixture into the flour mixture. Stir in the cornmeal mixture until just combined.

Spray 12 muffin cups with vegetable spray. Spoon mixture into muffin cups and bake at 375° 15 - 20 minutes.

Yield: 12 muffins

For a flavor change, try adding 1/2 cup of chopped cranberries or 1/2 cup of diced green chilies.

161 Cal., 4gm Protein, 36gm Carb., .6gm Fat, 416mg Sodium, .4mg Chol., 2.6gm Fiber

Cottage Cheese Pancakes

1	**cup low-fat cottage cheese**
2	**egg whites**
1/2	**cup cake flour**
1	**tablespoon sugar**
1/4	**teaspoon ground cinnamon**
1/4	**teaspoon baking soda**
	vegetable spray
	warm maple syrup

Combine cottage cheese, egg whites, cake flour, sugar, cinnamon and baking soda in food processor or blender and process until smooth.

Spray griddle with vegetable spray. Heat until hot. Spoon batter onto griddle, allowing 2 tablespoons batter per 3-inch pancake, leaving 2 inches between each. Cook over medium heat until bubbly on top, then turn and brown other side, cooking 4 minutes total.

Keep cooked pancakes warm in 200° oven while remaining pancakes are cooked. Spray with additional cooking spray as needed. Serve with warm maple syrup.

Serves: 4

116 Cal., 10gm Protein, 16gm Carb., 1gm Fat, 325mg Sodium, 3mg Chol., .4gm Fiber

BREADS

Crostini

2	packages active, dry yeast
$2^2/_3$	cups water at 85°
8	cups flour
2	tablespoons salt
$1/_4$	cup olive oil
$1/_4$	cup light Parmesan cheese
2	tablespoons dry oregano
2	tablespoons black pepper, freshly ground
2	tablespoons fresh thyme, finely chopped
2	tablespoons fennel seeds
	vegetable spray

Combine yeast and water and let stand for 3 minutes. Add remaining ingredients, except vegetable spray, mix well and knead until smooth, about 10 minutes.

Place into a bowl sprayed with vegetable spray and let rise in a warm place for 30 minutes.

Roll into 24 balls and let stand 5 minutes. Roll out balls on a floured surface into 8-inch disks.

Grill on a char-broiler or griddle. Flip to the other side.

Serve immediately or wrap tightly in plastic wrap to avoid drying out.

Yield: 24

Fabulous Feasts

166 Cal., 4gm Protein, 30gm Carb., 2.9gm Fat, 561mg Sodium, .5mg Chol., 1.1gm Fiber

BREADS

Fruited Pumpkin Bread

3	egg whites
1/2	cup granulated sugar
1/2	cup brown sugar
1	teaspoon vanilla
1	cup canned solid-pack pumpkin
1/3	cup salad oil
1/2	cup orange juice, freshly squeezed
2	cups all-purpose flour
1	teaspoon baking soda
1/2	teaspoon baking powder
1/2	teaspoon ground cinnamon
1/2	teaspoon ground nutmeg
1/2	teaspoon ground ginger
1/2	cup chopped dates
1/2	cup chopped dried apricots
	vegetable spray

In a large bowl, beat together egg whites, sugars, vanilla, pumpkin, oil and orange juice.

In another bowl, sift together flour, baking soda, baking powder, cinnamon, nutmeg, and ginger. Add to egg mixture and beat to blend. Stir in dates and apricots. Pour into a 5 x 9-inch loaf pan that has been sprayed with vegetable spray.

Bake in a 350° oven for about 40 minutes or until a wooden pick inserted in center of loaf comes out clean. Let cool for 15 minutes, turn onto a rack. Serve warm or cooled. Makes 1 loaf.

Serves: 10 - 12

Studded with chopped dates and apricots, this spicy pumpkin bread is a special treat.

229 Cal., 3gm Protein, 41gm Carb., 6.3gm Fat, 127mg Sodium, 0mg Chol., 1.7gm Fiber

Fougasse - Provençal Country Bread

1	tablespoon dry yeast
3	cups warm water (110°)
4	cups all-purpose flour, unbleached
1	tablespoon salt, dissolved in 1 tablespoon warm water
2	cups whole wheat flour

In a large bowl sprinkle yeast over warm water, let stand 5 minutes, stir to blend.

One cup at a time, mix in the all-purpose flour. Beat well. Add dissolved salt, mix well, add whole wheat flour one cup at a time, mixing in between. Turn dough onto well-floured surface and knead adding a little more all purpose flour if necessary. Dough should be firm and smooth, but still slightly sticky. Form dough into ball. Put into floured bowl, cover with towel and let rise in a warm, draft-free place until doubled in size, about 1 to $1^1/_2$ hours.

Flour baking sheets. Punch dough down, put on floured surface, divide in half. Roll each piece into a 9 x 13 x $^1/_3$-inch rectangle. Transfer to baking sheet. Cut 6 slits into dough in a spoke pattern, pulling the slits about 2 inches apart. Cover with towel, let rise to about 1 inch thick, approximately 1 hour.

Preheat oven to 375°. Bake 40 - 45 minutes until bread is golden and crisp. Serve warm.

Yield: 2 loaves

(continued)

Fougasse - Provençal Country Bread
139 Cal., 5gm Protein, 29gm Carb., .5gm Fat, 367mg Sodium, 0mg Chol., 2.4gm Fiber

Variations for Fougasse-

Olive Filling:

1	8-ounce can black olives
4	garlic cloves
³/₄	tablespoon mixed dried herbs
1	tablespoon olive oil
³/₄	cup chicken broth
2	anchovy fillets (optional)

Tomato Filling:

³/₄	cup tomato, finely chopped
2	tablespoons sweet onion, finely chopped
1	tablespoon parsley, minced
1	tablespoon tomato paste
¹/₂	tablespoon olive oil

Olive Filling:
Place first four ingredients in a food processor and while motor is running, add the chicken broth in a stream until a smooth, thick consistency is achieved. Add anchovy fillets, if desired, and process again.

Tomato Filling:
Combine all the ingredients and mix well.

To prepare Tomato or Olive Fougasse:
Roll dough slightly thinner. Spread thinly with filling, fold in half, transfer to baking sheet and roll evenly making sure sides are even and closed. Proceed as in original, cutting 6 slits into dough.

As is or with the variations, this dense bread is a Provençal treat!

Fougasse with Tomato Filling:
146 Cal., 5gm Protein, 30gm Carb., .9gm Fat, 384mg Sodium, 0mg Chol., 2.6gm Fiber

Fougasse with Olive Filling:
185 Cal., 5gm Protein, 30gm Carb., 5.6gm Fat, 579mg Sodium, 0mg Chol., 3.3gm Fiber

Harvest Muffins

- ¾ cup oat bran
- ½ cup whole wheat flour
- ½ cup whole bran cereal
- ¼ cup brown sugar, packed
- 2½ teaspoons baking powder
- 1 teaspoon ground cinnamon
- ¼ teaspoon salt
- 1 egg, beaten
- ¾ cup skim milk
- 3 tablespoons applesauce
- 1 small apple, finely chopped (about ½ cup)
- ½ cup raisins
- 1 tablespoon granulated sugar
- 1 tablespoon brown sugar
- 1 tablespoon all-purpose flour
- 1 teaspoon margarine, melted
- ¼ teaspoon ground cinnamon
- vegetable spray

In a large mixing bowl, stir together oat bran, ½ cup whole wheat flour, cereal, brown sugar, baking powder, 1 teaspoon cinnamon and salt. Make a well in the center.

In a small bowl, combine egg, milk and applesauce. Add to flour mixture and stir. Batter should remain lumpy. Fold in chopped apple and raisins.

Spray muffin cups and fill ⅔ full. Combine granulated sugar, brown sugar, 1 tablespoon flour, margarine and ¼ teaspoon cinnamon. Sprinkle over batter.

Bake in a 400° oven for 12-15 minutes or until done.

Yield: 12 muffins

120 Cal., 4gm Protein, 25gm Carb., 1.6gm Fat, 162mg Sodium, 23mg Chol., 2.5gm Fiber

BREADS

Hearty Blueberry Muffins

1¼ cups flour
1 cup old-fashioned oats
¾ cup brown sugar
¼ teaspoon salt
1 tablespoon baking powder
1 teaspoon cinnamon
1 cup nonfat milk
1 teaspoon vanilla
3 tablespoons vegetable oil
¼ cup egg substitute to equal 1 egg
1 cup blueberries
  vegetable spray

Topping:
1 tablespoon sugar
1 teaspoon cinnamon

Preheat oven to 425°.

Combine topping ingredients and set aside.

Combine flour, oats, sugar, salt, baking powder and cinnamon in a large bowl. Make a well in the center and add the milk, vanilla, oil and egg substitute. Mix to blend but do not over mix. Gently fold in the blueberries.

Pour the batter into a muffin tin that has been sprayed with vegetable spray. Sprinkle with the topping mixture. Bake at 425° for 15-20 minutes until golden brown.

Yield: 12 muffins

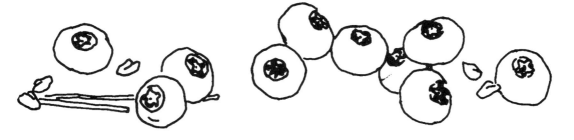

176 Cal., 4gm Protein, 32gm Carb., 4gm Fat, 171mg Sodium, .3mg Chol., 1.1gm Fiber

Rugelachs

- ½ cup whole wheat pastry flour
- ½ cup unbleached white flour
- ¼ teaspoon salt
- ½ teaspoon baking powder
- 2 tablespoons unsalted butter, softened
- 1 tablespoon mild-flavored honey
- 4-6 tablespoons cold water
- ½ cup granulated sugar
- 2 tablespoons cinnamon

vegetable spray

Mix dry ingredients together, cut in butter with food processor or by rubbing between hands. Add honey to processor or bowl and mix in processor or with a wooden spoon. Add water very slowly and mix until mixture forms a ball. Put ball in plastic wrap and refrigerate for at least 2 hours.

Combine the sugar and cinnamon. Roll out half the dough into a 9-inch circle and cut into 8 triangles. Sprinkle with 2 tablespoons of the sugar and cinnamon mixture. Starting at the wider end of the triangle, roll rugelachs to the point and place on cookie sheet which has been sprayed with vegetable spray. Form rugelachs into crescents. Repeat with other half of dough.

Bake at 350° for 8-10 minutes.

Yield: 16

A treat with tea or coffee.

45 Cal., 1gm Protein, 9gm Carb., 1gm Fat, 32mg Sodium, 2mg Chol., .5gm Fiber

Raspberry Bran Muffins

2½	cups flour
2	teaspoons baking powder
½	teaspoon baking soda
½	teaspoon salt
1¾	cups sugar
2	cups buttermilk
½	cup egg substitute to equal 2 eggs
½	cup corn oil
8	cups bran cereal with raisins and nuts
½	cup raspberry jam

Preheat oven to 350°.

Mix all dry ingredients and set aside.

Whisk together buttermilk, egg substitute and corn oil. Stir in dry ingredients and the bran cereal until just combined.

Fill paper-lined muffin tins ⅓ full with batter and dab 1 teaspoon jam in the middle, fill rest of muffin cup with batter. Bake at 350° for 20-25 minutes.

Yield: 24 muffins

---

170 Cal., 3gm Protein, 29gm Carb., 4.9gm Fat, 159mg Sodium, 1mg Chol., .9gm Fiber

Oatmeal Bread with Cinnamon Pear Butter

Oatmeal Bread:

1³/₄	cups low-fat buttermilk
2	cups quick-cooking oats, uncooked
1	cup golden raisins
2	cups unbleached flour
1	tablespoon cocoa powder
1	teaspoon cinnamon
¹/₄	cup sugar
1	tablespoon baking powder
1	teaspoon baking soda
1	teaspoon salt
1	whole egg
2	large egg whites
¹/₃	cup applesauce
1	tablespoon canola oil

Preheat oven to 350°.

Spray a 2-quart soufflé dish with vegetable spray. Set aside.

In a 3-quart saucepan over medium heat, heat buttermilk until very hot but not boiling. Remove from heat, stir in oats and raisins, set aside.

In a large bowl, combine flour, cocoa, cinnamon, sugar, baking powder, baking soda, and salt.

Beat egg and egg whites slightly. Add applesauce and oil to beaten egg mixture.

Stir oatmeal mixture and egg mixture into flour mixture just until flour is moistened (dough will be sticky). Put in sprayed soufflé dish.

Bake bread 1 hour and 25 minutes or until toothpick inserted in center of loaf comes out clean. Cool bread in dish on wire rack 10 minutes. Remove from soufflé dish and finish cooling on wire rack.

Yield: 1 loaf - 20 slices

(continued)

Oatmeal Bread
132 Cal., 4gm Protein, 25gm Carb., 1.9gm Fat, 258mg Sodium, 15mg Chol., 1.8gm Fiber

Cinnamon Pear Butter:

6	large firm ripe pears (about 3 pounds)
1	cup + 2 tablespoons granulated sugar
1	cup + 2 tablespoons packed light brown sugar
2	tablespoons ground cinnamon
1	tablespoon vanilla

Boil unpeeled whole pears in a large pot of water about 30 minutes or until tender. Drain, and set aside until cool enough to handle. Peel and core pears. Cut in chunks and purée in food processor or blender until smooth. There should be about $3^1/_2$ cups purée. Pour into a medium-sized saucepan. Add sugars and cinnamon; mix well. Bring to a simmer over medium heat. Reduce heat to low and cook uncovered, stirring often, about 1 hour and 15 minutes until dark brown, shiny and very thick. Stir in vanilla. Store in refrigerator.

Yield: $2^1/_4$ cups
          20 servings

Spread this heavy, dense bread with Cinnamon Pear Butter and serve for breakfast or brunch.

Cinnamon Pear Butter
132 Cal., .3gm Protein, 34gm Carb., .3gm Fat, 4mg Sodium, 0mg Chol., 2.2gm Fiber

BREADS

Sour Cream Coffe Cake with Pecan and Cinnamon Filling

Pecan and Cinnamon Filling:

1	cup pecans, chopped
¾	cup brown sugar, packed
1	tablespoon cinnamon

Sour Cream Cake:

2	cups unbleached all-purpose flour
1	cup whole wheat pastry flour
1	tablespoon + 1 teaspoon baking powder
1	teaspoon baking soda
½	teaspoon salt
1	cup apple butter
1	tablespoon butter, softened
1	tablespoon canola oil
1	cup sugar
½	cup nonfat yogurt
1	cup nonfat sour cream
1	whole egg plus 3 egg whites
1	teaspoon grated lemon zest
	powdered sugar
	vegetable spray

Filling:
Combine pecans, brown sugar and cinnamon, mix well and set aside.

Preheat oven to 350°. Spray a Bundt pan with vegetable spray and coat with flour.

In a large bowl, sift together the flours, baking powder, baking soda and salt.

In another bowl, place the apple butter, butter, canola oil, sugar, yogurt and sour cream. Mix until creamy. Add egg and egg whites, beating after each addition. Stir in the lemon zest. Add to dry ingredients and beat until smooth.

Spread ⅓ of the batter in the Bundt pan. Spread ½ of the filling over the batter, add another ⅓ of the batter, top with the remaining filling and then the remaining batter.

Bake at 350° for 40-45 minutes or until done. Cool on wire rack for 10 minutes, remove from pan. Dust with powdered sugar.

Serves: 16

246 Cal., 4gm Protein, 42gm Carb., 8gm Fat, 256mg Sodium, 19.2mg Chol., 1.7gm Fiber

DESSERTS

Apple Spice Cake

3	cups all-purpose flour
2	teaspoons baking powder
1/2	teaspoon baking soda
2	teaspoons cinnamon
1/2	teaspoon mace
1/2	teaspoon nutmeg, freshly grated
1/4	teaspoon salt
3/4	cup granulated sugar
1/2	cup brown sugar
1/3	cup canola oil
3	egg whites
1	teaspoon vanilla
1/4	cup lowfat vanilla yogurt
1	cup apple juice
4	cups tart apples, sliced (about 3 medium)
1/4	cup chopped walnuts
	vegetable spray
	powdered sugar

In a large bowl mix flour, baking powder, baking soda, cinnamon, mace, nutmeg and salt. Stir to mix well.

In mixing bowl, beat sugars and oil until combined. Add egg whites, vanilla, vanilla yogurt and apple juice and beat 1 minute. Add flour mixture, using low speed just until mixed. Stir in apple slices and walnuts. Pour into sprayed and floured 10-inch tube pan or 12-cup Bundt pan. Smooth surface and place on center rack of oven.

Bake at 350° for 45 minutes or until wooden pick comes out clean. Cool 10 minutes on rack and gently remove from pan. Dust with powdered sugar pressed through fine sieve.

Serves: 12

306 Cal., 5gm Protein, 55gm Carb., 8gm Fat, 178mg Sodium, .2mg Chol., 1.7gm Fiber

Apple Strudel with Custard Sauce

Custard Sauce:

1	cup skim milk
2	tablespoons sugar
2	teaspoons cornstarch
1	large egg yolk
1	teaspoon vanilla extract

Custard Sauce:

Bring milk to boil in small saucepan. Whisk sugar, cornstarch and egg yolk in small bowl. Gradually whisk in boiling milk. Return mixture to saucepan; cook, stirring, over medium-low heat, until slightly thickened, 1 minute. Remove from heat; stir in vanilla. Transfer to bowl, cover surface and refrigerate.

(continued)

3	Golden Delicious apples, peeled, quartered and thinly sliced
2	tablespoons raisins
1	tablespoon dark rum
1	teaspoon cornstarch
1	teaspoon cinnamon
1/8	teaspoon nutmeg
1	tablespoon granulated sugar
1	tablespoon brown sugar
1	egg white
1	tablespoon vegetable oil
4	sheets phyllo dough
1	tablespoon butter

Garnish:
  fresh raspberries
  mint leaves

Preheat oven to 375°.

Combine apples, raisins and rum. Mix cornstarch, cinnamon and nutmeg and toss with apples, add sugars and toss.

Whisk egg white and 1 tablespoon vegetable oil. Place 1 sheet phyllo on clean towel. Brush lightly with egg white mixture. Layer remaining phyllo on top, lightly brushing each sheet with egg white. Spoon apple mixture along one long side of phyllo. Roll up tightly from long side. Transfer, seam-side down, to jelly roll pan. Fold ends under. Brush with melted butter and sprinkle with additional granulated sugar, if desired.

Bake 30 minutes or until top is slightly brown. Cool on wire rack 30 minutes. Cut into 1 1/2-inch slices. Serve with Custard Sauce and garnish with fresh raspberries and mint leaves.

Serves: 8

157 Cal., 3gm Protein, 28gm Carb., 4gm Fat, 87mg Sodium, 38mg Chol., 1.8gm Fiber

DESSERTS

Autumn Meringues

2	large egg whites, at room temperature
1/8	teaspoon cream of tartar
1/2	cup sugar
1	teaspoon vanilla extract
1/2	teaspoon ground ginger
1/4	teaspoon cinnamon
1/4	teaspoon ground cloves
2	gingersnap cookies, crushed
	coconut (optional)
	vegetable spray

Preheat oven to 250°. Spray a cookie sheet with vegetable spray. Beat egg whites in mixer bowl at medium speed until frothy. Add cream of tartar, beat until stiff, about 1 minute more. Beat in vanilla, ginger, cinnamon and cloves. Gently fold in cookie crumbs. Drop by teaspoonfuls onto prepared cookie sheet. Top with a few flakes of coconut.

Bake 45 minutes or until dry. Turn oven off; let meringues cool in oven, 2 hours.

Yield: 20 cookies

28 Cal., .4gm Protein, 6gm Carb., .3gm Fat, 11mg Sodium, .3mg Chol., .1gm Fiber

Baked Apple and Blackberry Pudding

½	cup flour
½	cup sugar, divided
2	tablespoons butter
½	cup 1% milk
½	cup low-fat sour cream
2	eggs
1¼	pound apples, peeled, cored, sliced ¼-inch thick
3	tablespoons Calvados (optional)
1	tablespoon lemon juice
	vegetable spray
8	ounces blackberries (if using frozen, defrost and drain)

Preheat oven to 375°.

Sift together flour and half of the sugar into a bowl. Melt butter, whisk together with milk, sour cream and eggs. Add mixture to flour and sugar, mix to make a batter.

Toss apples in Calvados and lemon juice and arrange in a shallow 10 or 11-inch gratin or pie dish which has been sprayed with vegetable spray. Pour the batter over it, scatter blackberries on top and sprinkle remaining sugar over all. Bake for 1¼ hours.

Serve hot or at room temperature.

Serves: 8

Apples could be replaced by peaches in this great dessert.

227 Cal., 4gm Protein, 41gm Carb., 5.9gm Fat, 68mg Sodium, 77mg Chol., 3.2gm Fiber

DESSERTS

Baked Fruit

1	1-pound can light pear halves
1	1-pound can light cling peach halves
1	1-pound can pineapple chunks
1	1-pound can apricot halves
1/3	**cup apple butter**
1/3	**cup blanched, slivered almonds**
1/3	**cup sherry**
3/4	**cup light brown sugar**
3	teaspoons cinnamon
3	teaspoons cloves

Drain all fruit. Add sugar and spices to apple butter. Arrange fruits and nuts in casserole; pour apple butter mixture over fruit and add sherry. Bake one hour at 325°. Refrigerate overnight. Reheat at 350° before serving.

Serves: 8

Great served over nonfat frozen yogurt.

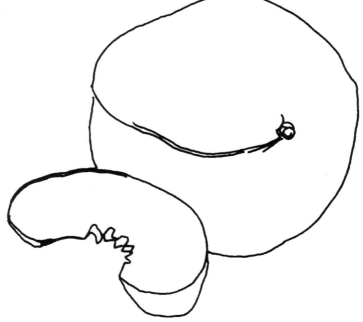

303 Cal., 2gm Protein, 69gm Carb., 3.3gm Fat, 19mg Sodium, 0mg Chol., 4.1gm Fiber

DESSERTS

Carob Cake

3	cups whole wheat pastry flour
3	pinches sea salt
3	teaspoons baking powder
1/2	teaspoon cinnamon
3/4	cup roasted carob powder
3/4	cup corn oil
3/4	cup maple syrup
3/4	cup barley malt
1 1/4	cups apple juice
1	teaspoon vanilla
	vegetable spray

Sift dry ingredients into a large mixing bowl. Combine remaining ingredients in a blender or food processor mixing well. Combine the two well-mixed parts. Pour into two 9-inch round cake pans sprayed with vegetable cooking spray. Bake at 350° for 30 - 35 minutes or until toothpick inserted into center of cake comes out clean.

Serves: 16

An excellent glaze for this cake is apple butter or an all-fruit preserve.

278 Cal., 4gm Protein, 40gm Carb., 10.8gm Fat, 86mg Sodium, 0mg Chol., 3.1gm Fiber

DESSERTS

Carrot Cake with Orange Glaze

1½	cups sifted all-purpose flour
1½	teaspoons baking powder
¾	teaspoon baking soda
¾	teaspoon ground cinnamon
¼	teaspoon ground allspice
¾	cup granulated sugar
¼	cup dark brown sugar
¼	cup walnuts, chopped
¾	cup liquid egg substitute
½	cup canola oil
2	teaspoons orange zest, finely grated
1	teaspoon vanilla extract
1½	cups carrots, finely grated (loosely packed)
¾	cup crushed pineapple with juice
	vegetable spray

Preheat the oven to 350°.

Spray a 9 x 5 x 3-inch loaf pan with vegetable spray. Set aside. Sift flour, baking powder, soda, cinnamon, allspice and granulated sugar into a large mixing bowl. Add the brown sugar and walnuts. Mix the egg substitute with the oil, orange zest, vanilla, carrots and pineapple. Add the egg mixture to the flour mixture and stir enough just to mix. The batter will be thin and lumpy. Put the batter into the prepared pan, spreading it well into the corners and smoothing the top.

Bake for 50 minutes or until the cake is springy to the touch and a toothpick inserted in the center comes out clean. Cool 10 minutes on a wire rack in the upright pan, then invert the cake onto the rack and cool to room temperature.

(continued)

Glaze:

1   **cup sifted confectioner's sugar**

1/2   **teaspoon orange zest, finely grated**

1   **tablespoon lemon juice**

1   **tablespoon orange juice**

Glaze:

Combine all the ingredients in a small bowl and spread over the top of the cooled cake letting the excess run down the sides. Let the glaze harden several hours before cutting the cake.

Serves: 10

Serve this cake after a light lunch of Tuna Salad with Fruit.

Calorie Gallery

336 Cal., 5gm Protein, 52gm Carb., 12.8gm Fat, 189mg Sodium, 0mg Chol., 1.2gm Fiber

Champagne Sherbet

1	cup sugar
1	cup water
1½	cups dry champagne
4	tablespoons lemon juice
2	egg whites
2	tablespoons sugar

Garnish:

½	cup dry champagne
	lemon zest

Combine sugar and water in saucepan. Boil 4 minutes. Chill. Stir in champagne and lemon juice.

Beat whites until foamy, add sugar while beating and continue to beat until whites are stiff but still glossy. Fold into champagne mixture and freeze in ice cream maker according to manufacturer's instructions.

Serve in champagne glasses, spoon 1 tablespoon champagne over each and a sprinkle of lemon zest.

Serves: 8

141 Cal., 1gm Protein, 28gm Carb., 0gm Fat, 17mg Sodium, 0mg Chol., .02gm Fiber

DESSERTS

Chocolate Amaretto Cheesecake

6	chocolate wafers, finely crushed
1 1/2	cups nonfat cream cheese, softened
1	cup sugar
1	cup 1% low-fat cottage cheese
1/4	cup + 2 tablespoons unsweetened cocoa
1/4	cup all-purpose flour
1/4	cup Amaretto
1	teaspoon vanilla extract
1/4	teaspoon salt
1/2	cup egg substitute equal to 2 eggs

Garnish:
white chocolate curls (optional)
fresh raspberries (optional)

Sprinkle chocolate wafer crumbs in the bottom of a 7-inch springform pan. Set aside. In a blender or food processor combine cream cheese, sugar, cottage cheese, cocoa, flour, Amaretto, vanilla, and salt. Process until smooth. Add egg substitute and process just until blended.

Slowly pour mixture over crumbs in pan. Bake at 300° for 65 to 70 minutes or until cheesecake is set. Let cool in pan on wire rack. Cover and chill at least 8 hours. Remove sides of pan and transfer cheesecake to a serving platter. Garnish with chocolate curls or raspberries, if desired.

Serves: 16

Calorie Gallery

111 Cal., 8gm Protein, 19gm Carb., 1gm Fat, 276mg Sodium, 5mg Chol., .2gm Fiber

DESSERTS

Curried Pears

- 3 fresh, firm, unpeeled pears
- 1 8-ounce can crushed pineapple, drained, reserve juice
- ¼ cup brown sugar
- 1 teaspoon curry powder
- ¼ cup juice from canned pineapple
- ¼ cup orange juice

Halve and core pears. Arrange in a single layer in a shallow baking dish, cut side up. Combine pineapple, brown sugar, and curry powder. Spoon into center of each pear. Combine pineapple and orange juice and pour mixture over pears. Bake uncovered at 375° for 20 minutes or until just soft, basting frequently. Cool, basting during the cooling period. Serve warm or cold.

Serves: 6

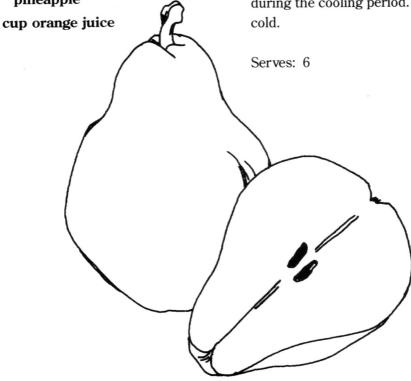

114 Cal., 1gm Protein, 29gm Carb., .4gm Fat, 4mg Sodium, 0mg Chol., 2.8gm Fiber

DESSERTS

Espresso-Chocolate Mousse

3	tablespoons strong coffee
1	tablespoon unflavored gelatin
1	egg
1/4	cup corn syrup
3/4	cup unsweetened Dutch process cocoa powder
1	cup skim milk, divided
2	ounces bittersweet chocolate, chopped
1	teaspoon vanilla extract
3/4	cup sugar
1/3	cup water
4	egg whites
	pinch of salt

❈   ❈   ❈

Pour coffee into small bowl; sprinkle gelatin over it and let stand to soften.

In a medium bowl beat together the egg, corn syrup, cocoa powder and 1/4 cup of the milk until smooth.

In a saucepan heat remaining milk until almost boiling. Slowly whisk hot milk into egg mixture, return to saucepan and cook over low heat until slightly thickened, stirring constantly.

Remove from heat and add gelatin with coffee. Stir until dissolved. Add chocolate and vanilla, stirring until chocolate has melted. Let cool.

In small saucepan, over medium heat, combine sugar with water cooking until syrup reaches 240° on a candy thermometer or the soft-ball stage. Remove from heat.

With an electric mixer beat egg whites until frothy, add salt, continue beating until soft peaks form. Reheat syrup until it boils. Gradually pour hot syrup onto whites while beating, continue beating for about 3 minutes.

Whisk about 1/3 of egg whites into chocolate mixture until well incorporated; gently fold in remaining egg whites.

Pour into serving bowl and refrigerate, covered for 2 hours before serving.

Serves: 8 - 10

For a change in flavor, substitute cognac, Grand Marnier or Kirsh for the coffee.

146 Cal., 5gm Protein, 28gm Carb., 3.8gm Fat, 58mg Sodium, 28mg Chol., .6gm Fiber

DESSERTS

Frosted Fudge Brownies

Brownies:

2/3	cup flour
1 2/3	cups powdered sugar
1/4	cup unsweetened cocoa powder
3/4	teaspoon baking powder
	dash salt
1 1/2	ounces unsweetened chocolate
2 1/2	tablespoons canola oil
1	teaspoon butter
2	tablespoons corn syrup
2	teaspoons vanilla
2	large egg whites

Frosting:

2	cups sifted powdered sugar
1/4	cup unsweetened cocoa
2	tablespoons skim milk
1	teaspoon vanilla

Preheat oven to 350°.

Line an 8-inch square pan with aluminum foil. Spray with vegetable spray.

Sift together flour, powdered sugar, cocoa, baking powder and dash of salt.

In double boiler combine chocolate, oil and butter, cook until melted, stirring frequently. Remove from heat, stir in corn syrup and vanilla. Beat in egg whites. Stir in dry ingredients just until blended. Turn into pan, spreading evenly.

Bake 20-25 minutes until center is firm. Cool 15 minutes before removing from pan. Frost.

Frosting:

Combine all ingredients in a medium bowl stirring until frosting is of spreading consistency. Add warm water to thin, if necessary.

Serves: 12

248 Cal., 2gm Protein, 50gm Carb., 6.1gm Fat, 59mg Sodium, 2mg Chol., .4gm Fiber

DESSERTS

Fruit Baked with Zabaglione

2	slices fresh or canned pineapple, cut in half
1	large banana, peeled and cut in half lengthwise and crosswise
1	small pear, peeled, cored and cut into 8 wedges
4	large strawberries, halved, or 1 kiwi fruit, peeled and sliced

OR

Assorted fruit to equal 4 cups of fruit to fit in the bottom of a shallow casserole dish

2	large egg yolks
2	tablespoons sugar
1/4	cup orange-flavored liqueur

Arrange fruit in a shallow, ovenproof casserole, about 1-quart size. Mix egg yolk, sugar and liqueur in the top of a double boiler. Place over simmering, not boiling, water and beat with a portable mixer or rotary beater for 5-7 minutes until very thick and foamy. Do not overcook or mixture will curdle. Remove from heat and immediately pour over fruit. Broil 5 inches from heat source 15-30 seconds, until lightly browned. Watch carefully - sauce burns easily. Serve immediately.

Serves: 4

194 Cal., 2gm Protein, 35gm Carb., 3.4gm Fat, 7mg Sodium, 136mg Chol., 2.7gm Fiber

DESSERTS

Fruit Trifle

Angel Food Cake:

1	cup + 2 tablespoons cake flour, sifted
1	cup granulated sugar, divided
1¼	cups egg whites at room temperature
¼	teaspoon salt
1¼	teaspoons cream of tartar
1	teaspoon vanilla extract
¼	teaspoon dried lemon peel or ½ teaspoon lemon zest

❋   ❋   ❋

To prepare the yogurt:

Line a colander with 4 layers of cheese cloth. Place all the yogurt in the colander, set it over another bowl and place in the refrigerator and allow the yogurt to drip for one hour before using in the trifle. If this is done early, put the drained yogurt in a plastic container and refrigerate.

Angel Food Cake:
  Preheat oven to 375°.
  Add ¼ cup of sugar to flour and sift mixture 4 times to achieve a fine consistency.
  Combine egg whites, salt, cream of tartar, vanilla and lemon peel and beat at high speed until stiff enough to hold soft peaks.
  Beat in remaining sugar, sprinkling ¼ cup at a time over egg whites.
  Fold ¼ of the flour mixture into egg mixture using 15 fold-over strokes for each addition until all flour is added. Gently fold the batter an additional 10 times.
  Put batter into an ungreased tube pan. Cut through batter once with a spatula without lifting spatula from batter.
  Bake 30-35 minutes or until cake tester inserted in center comes out clean.
  Invert the cake on a bottle or inverted funnel and allow to cool for one hour. Loosen sides with knife, remove from pan and slice cake into thirds, horizontally. Cut sliced cake into cubes.

(continued)

Fruit Trifle:

40	**ounces low-fat vanilla yogurt**
1	**10-ounce package frozen raspberries in light syrup, thawed**
2	**cups frozen blueberries, thawed**
6	**cups fresh strawberries, halved**
3	**tablespoons cream sherry**
4-6	**kiwis**
	fresh mint for garnish

To assemble the trifle:

Purée raspberries in food processor, pour into bowl with thawed blueberries. Place $1/3$ of cake cubes in the bottom of a trifle bowl. Drizzle with 1 tablespoon of cream sherry. Pour $1/3$ of berry mixture over the cake.

Against the inside surface of bowl, begin to alternate a strawberry half with a kiwi slice around the perimeter of the bowl to make a design which can be seen from outside the bowl.

Sprinkle a handful of strawberries on the berry mixture. Cover with $1/3$ of the vanilla yogurt.

Create two more layers and end with yogurt on top.

Over yogurt, place strawberries and kiwi, creating a design. Garnish with fresh mint.

Serves: 12

To save time, use an angel food cake from the bakery.

303 Cal., 9gm Protein, 64gm Carb., 1.8gm Fat, 156mg Sodium, 4mg Chol., 3.9gm Fiber

DESSERTS

Grape Sherbets

Sugar Syrup:

2½ cups water

1¼ cups sugar

Red Grape Sherbet:

½ pound seedless red grapes

1¼ cups sugar syrup

½ cup dry red wine

Green Grape Sherbet:

½ pound seedless green grapes

1¼ cups sugar syrup

½ cup dry white wine

Sugar Syrup:
Cook water and sugar in saucepan over low heat until sugar is dissolved. Simmer 3 minutes. Cool completely.

Red or Green Grape Sherbet:
Purée grapes in food processor. In a non-aluminum bowl, mix together grape purée, syrup and wine. Let stand 4 hours at room temperature. Strain mixture through very fine sieve, discard skins.

Freeze in ice cream maker according to manufacturer's instructions.

Store in freezer.

Serves: 6

These sherbets are pretty if served in champagne glasses and decorated with a couple of sliced fresh grapes.

195 Cal., .3gm Protein, 47gm Carb., .1gm Fat, 3mg Sodium, 0mg Chol., .3gm Fiber

DESSERTS

Layered Fruit Ring with Peach Coulis

Layered Fruit Ring:
1	cup raspberry purée, strained through fine sieve to remove seeds
1	cup blackberry purée, strained through fine sieve to remove seeds
1	cup strawberry purée
3	tablespoons sugar
2	cups apple juice
2	envelopes unflavored gelatin

Peach Coulis:
2	cups peach purée
3	tablespoons sugar
2	tablespoons peach liqueur or Cointreau

Layered Fruit Ring:
  Add one tablespoon sugar to each of purées, stir. Sprinkle gelatin over apple juice, let stand, heat over low heat to dissolve gelatin.
  Add $1/3$ of gelatin mixture to raspberry purée, mix well and pour into chilled ring mold.
  Refrigerate until set. Keeping gelatin mixture liquid, proceed with next 2 purées the same way as with raspberry purée. Chill well until mold is firm. Unmold onto platter and serve with peach coulis.

Peach Coulis:
  Combine all 3 ingredients in saucepan. Cook over medium heat 3 minutes. Chill.

Serves: 8

183 Cal., 3gm Protein, 43gm Carb., .6gm Fat, 9mg Sodium, 0mg Chol., 5.4gm Fiber

DESSERTS

Noodle Kugel

1	3-ounce package nonfat cream cheese, room temperature
1	cup nonfat sour cream
1/2	cup low-fat margarine, melted
1	cup egg substitute to equal 4 eggs
	dash of salt
1	pound yolkless noodles, cooked
1	jar low-sugar apricot preserves

Topping:

1/4	cup low-fat margarine, melted
3	cups corn flakes
1	teaspoon cinnamon
1/2	cup sugar

Day before serving:

Combine the cream cheese, sour cream, butter, egg substitute and salt, blending well.

Place half of the noodles into a 9 x 13-inch pan. Pour half of the cream cheese mixture over the noodles. Cover with half jar of the apricot preserves. Repeat with the remaining noodles, cream cheese mixture and preserves. Cover. Refrigerate overnight.

Topping:

Before baking, combine the butter, corn flakes, cinnamon and sugar. Press evenly onto the top of the kugel.

Bake in a preheated 350° oven for 1 hour. Let rest 10 minutes before serving.

Serves: 12

This dish must be assembled the day before.

284 Cal., 9gm Protein, 45gm Carb., 7.9gm Fat, 194mg Sodium, 1mg Chol., 1.4gm Fiber

DESSERTS

Oatmeal Cranberry Cookies

1/2	cup egg substitute equal to 2 eggs
1/2	cup dark brown sugar, packed
1/2	cup white sugar
2	tablespoons skim milk
1	tablespoon butter, softened
1	teaspoon maple flavoring
1 1/4	cups rolled oats, ground
1	cup all purpose flour
1	teaspoon baking powder
1	teaspoon salt
1/4	cup rolled oats
1	cup dried cranberries or raisins

Combine egg substitute and sugars, milk, butter and maple flavoring and mix to blend well. Combine ground oats with all-purpose flour, baking powder and salt. Stir into sugar-egg mixture. Stir in remaining 1/4 cup rolled oats and cranberries. Drop by tablespoons onto baking sheets lined with parchment paper.

Bake at 375° for 12-15 minutes or until center tests done. Remove from baking sheets while warm to wire rack to cool.

Yield: 3 dozen cookies

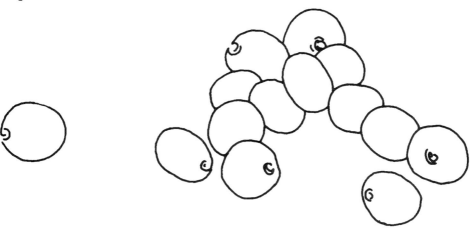

59 Cal., 1gm Protein, 13gm Carb., .5gm Fat, 64mg Sodium, 1mg Chol., .7gm Fiber

Orange Sherbet

2	cups 1% buttermilk
2	cups orange juice, freshly squeezed (4 to 5 large oranges)
2	cups sugar
8	empty orange halves
8	mint sprigs

Combine all ingredients and stir until sugar is dissolved. Freeze in a 1-quart ice cream freezer, following the manufacturer's instructions or place in a bowl in the freezer and whisk every 30 minutes until almost frozen. Freeze empty orange halves.

When sherbet is ready to serve, place $1/8$ of the mixture into each orange half and keep frozen until serving time.

Garnish with mint sprigs.

Serves: 8

Serve in empty orange halves or in a champagne glass garnished with mint.

238 Cal., 3gm Protein, 57gm Carb., .6gm Fat, 65mg Sodium, 2mg Chol., .1gm Fiber

DESSERTS

Orange Tootsies

3	ounces unsweetened chocolate, chopped
1	cup granulated sugar
¾	cup flour
¾	cup 1% low-fat cottage cheese
1	teaspoon vanilla extract
1	teaspoon orange extract
¼	teaspoon salt
	vegetable spray

Orange Glaze:

⅔	cup powdered sugar
1	tablespoon orange juice, preferably freshly squeezed
	zest of one grated orange

Preheat oven to 350°. In the top of a double boiler over very low heat, melt chocolate, cool slightly. In a food processor, purée all ingredients except chocolate until smooth. Add melted chocolate and blend by hand. Pour into a lightly sprayed 8-inch square pan. Bake 20-25 minutes or until just set.

In a small bowl beat powdered sugar together with orange juice until it reaches a glaze consistency. Spread on top of cooled tootsies. Sprinkle with finely grated orange rind. Refrigerate.

Yield: 16 squares

A delicious brownie with a hint of orange flavor.

131 Cal., 2gm Protein, 25gm Carb., 3.2gm Fat, 83mg Sodium, 2mg Chol., .3gm Fiber

DESSERTS

Oranges Orientales

8	large oranges
2/3	cup orange-flavored liquor
3/4	cup sugar
1	orange, juiced
2	black peppercorns
6	juniper berries
1 1/2	cups water

With zester, cut strips of orange skin, avoiding the bitter white part. There should be about 3/4 cup or more.

In a sauce pan, combine zest strips with all the ingredients except oranges and simmer over low heat until liquid is reduced by half, stirring a couple of times. Set aside to cool.

Peel the oranges, cutting away the white membrane. Over a bowl, slice oranges horizontally into 1/3-inch thick slices and arrange on a serving platter.

Add collected orange juice from bowl to zest syrup. Pour the syrup over the orange slices. Serve some juice and zests with slices.

Serves: 6 - 8

223 Cal., 1gm Protein, 46gm Carb., .3gm Fat, 3mg Sodium, 0mg Chol., 3.8gm Fiber

DESSERTS

Peach Slush

1	16-ounce package frozen unsweetened, sliced peaches, partially defrosted
2/3	cup granulated sugar
1	tablespoon lemon juice
2	teaspoons vanilla
3/4	teaspoon almond extract

Garnish:

mint leaves

Put all ingredients in a food processor fitted with a steel blade or use an electric blender and blend half the ingredients at a time. Cover and process 60-80 seconds until almost smooth. Spoon into chilled stemmed glasses and garnish. Serve immediately.

Serves: 4 - 6

179 Cal., 1gm Protein, 45gm Carb., .1gm Fat, 1mg Sodium, 0mg Chol.,1.6gm Fiber

DESSERTS

Peach Kiwi Cheesecake

1	15-ounce container nonfat ricotta cheese
	vegetable spray
32	vanilla wafer cookies
1/4	cup sliced almonds, toasted, if desired (see note)
2	tablespoons margarine or butter, melted
2	tablespoons orange juice
1	envelope unflavored gelatin
1/4	cup cold water
3	ounces nonfat cream cheese
1/3	cup granulated sugar
1	tablespoon fresh lemon juice
1	teaspoon grated lemon peel

Spoon ricotta into strainer set over medium-size bowl; let drain 15 minutes while preparing tart shell.

Spray 9-inch tart pan with removable bottom with vegetable spray.

In food processor, processes vanilla wafers and almonds to fine crumbs. There should be about 1 1/2 cups. Add melted margarine and orange juice; process to mix well. Press crumb mixture firmly and evenly over bottom and up sides of prepared tart pan. Freeze 15 minutes.

Dissolve gelatin in cold water according to package directions, set aside. In clean bowl of food processor combine drained ricotta, cream cheese, sugar, lemon juice and grated lemon peel. With motor running on pulse speed, slowly pour dissolved gelatin through feed tube until just blended.

Pour ricotta mixture into prepared tart pan. Refrigerate at least 30 minutes and up to 4 hours until filling is set.

(continued)

2	large fresh, ripe peaches halved lengthwise, pitted and cut into 1/4-inch slices (about 3 cups)
3	medium-size fresh kiwi, peeled and cut into 1/4-inch crosswise slices (about 1 1/2 cups)
2	tablespoons peach preserves

To serve:

Remove sides of tart pan. Place tart on serving platter and arrange peach and kiwi slices over filling in decorative pattern. Place preserves in small microwave bowl and microwave on high (100% power) 20 to 30 seconds until melted and warm. Brush glaze over fruit on tart.

Note: To toast sliced almonds, heat a skillet over medium heat. Add nuts, cook for 4 to 5 minutes, stirring frequently until golden. Cool before using.

Serves: 10 - 12

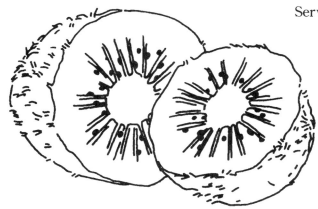

255 Cal., 13gm Protein, 35gm Carb., 8gm Fat, 196mg Sodium, 17mg Chol., 1.8gm Fiber

DESSERTS

Pears in Red Wine

8	whole pears
3	cups red wine
1½	cups sugar (or to taste)
2	3-inch cinnamon sticks
6	cloves
2	2-inch pieces lemon peel

Marinated Orange Peel:

2	oranges
¼	cup Grand Marnier

Peel pears. Leave small pears whole with their stems attached. Larger pears should be cut in half and carefully cored. Put the pears into acidulated water as soon as they are peeled so they won't discolor. Set the pears aside.

Combine remaining ingredients in a non-reactive saucepan and bring to a boil and dissolve the sugar. Remove the pears from the acidulated water, drain them, add them to the wine mixture.

Cook, partially covered, over low heat until tender. Cool pears in wine and then remove to a serving bowl and chill. Garnish with Marinated Orange Peel.

Marinated Orange Peel:

Carefully peel oranges trying not to include any of the white membrane, which is bitter. Cut the peel into thin strips and blanch the strips in boiling water for 10 minutes. Drain strips, cover with Grand Marnier and set aside until needed.

Serves: 8

199 Cal., 1gm Protein, 45gm Carb., .8gm Fat, 2mg Sodium, 0mg Chol., 5.8gm Fiber

DESSERTS

Pineapple Cranberry Bars

1	8-ounce can crushed pineapple in juice, undrained
1	cup cranberries
1/4	cup brown sugar, packed
1/2	tablespoon cornstarch
3/4	cup flour
3/4	cup quick cooking oatmeal
1/3	cup brown sugar, packed
1/2	teaspoon ground ginger
1/2	teaspoon ground cinnamon
1/4	teaspoon ground cloves
3	tablespoons margarine, chilled and cut into small pieces
1	egg white, lightly beaten
2	tablespoons walnuts, finely chopped
	vegetable spray

❋   ❋   ❋

In a saucepan, combine the pineapple, cranberries, 1/4 cup brown sugar and cornstarch. Bring to a boil for one minute. Cover and simmer for 10 minutes until cranberries pop and mixture thickens, stirring occasionally. Set aside to cool.

In a mixing bowl, combine the flour, oatmeal, 1/3 cup brown sugar, ginger, cinnamon and cloves. Cut in the chilled margarine until the mixture resembles coarse meal. Reserve 1/2 cup of the oatmeal mixture. Combine the remaining oatmeal mixture with the egg white. Mix well.

Spray the bottom of an 8-inch square baking pan with vegetable spray. Press the oatmeal-egg white mixture into the pan. Bake at 350° for 10 minutes. Spread the cranberry mixture over the crust. Combine the reserved oatmeal mixture with the walnuts and sprinkle this over the cranberry mixture. Continue baking for 25 to 30 minutes or until lightly browned. Let cool and cut into 2-inch bars.

Serves: 16

103 Cal., 2gm Protein, 18gm Carb., 2.9gm Fat, 30mg Sodium, 0mg Chol.,.8gm Fiber

DESSERTS

Plum Parfait

Plum Sauce:

1	**pound plums** (about 5 medium)
1/3	**cup sugar**
1/2	**cup water**
1	**cinnamon stick**
1	**teaspoon lemon juice**
2	**cups nonfat vanilla yogurt or frozen yogurt**

Slice plums, discarding pits, and place in a bowl. Add sugar and let stand at room temperature for at least 15 minutes. Place plum mixture in a saucepan with water and cinnamon stick. Bring to a gentle simmer and cook 15 minutes, stirring occasionally. Remove from heat, add lemon juice. Let cool, then refrigerate. Remove cinnamon stick. Layer into 4 parfait glasses with yogurt.

Serves: 4

Refreshing - a bit tart. Serve very cold.

166 Cal., 7gm Protein, 35gm Carb., .5gm Fat, 86mg Sodium, 3mg Chol., 1.2gm Fiber

DESSERTS

Pumpkin Pie

4	graham crackers, crushed
16	ounces solid pack canned pumpkin
12	ounces 1% cottage cheese
1	cup brown sugar
1	teaspoon cinnamon
$1/2$	teaspoon ground ginger
$1/4$	teaspoon ground cloves
1	tablespoon flour
$1/4$	teaspoon salt
$1/2$	cup egg substitute equal to 2 eggs

Sprinkle graham cracker crumbs into a 9-inch pie pan or a 9-inch springform pan. In a food processor or blender mix pumpkin and cottage cheese until creamy. Add brown sugar and mix thoroughly. Add all spices, flour and salt. Mix in egg substitute. Blend thoroughly. Pour into pan.

Bake in a 375° oven for 15 minutes, reduce heat to 350° and continue to bake for 40 minutes or until knife inserted in the center of the pie comes out clean.

Serves: 8

184 Cal., 8gm Protein, 37gm Carb., 1gm Fat, 309mg Sodium, 2mg Chol., 1.4gm Fiber

DESSERTS

Spicy Oatmeal Cookies

1/2	**cup brown sugar**
1/2	**cup granulated sugar**
2	**tablespoons molasses**
1	**egg white**
1/2	**cup nonfat vanilla yogurt**
1	**teaspoon vanilla**
1	**cup flour**
2	**cups oatmeal**
1	**teaspoon ground cinnamon**
1/2	**teaspoon allspice**
1/4	**teaspoon ground cloves or ginger**
1/2	**teaspoon baking soda**
1/4	**teaspoon salt**
1/2	**cup raisins, chopped**

Beat together sugars, molasses, egg white, yogurt and vanilla.

Stir together flour, oatmeal, spices, soda and salt and add to yogurt mixture. Add raisins and stir together just until blended. Do not overmix or cookies will be tough.

Drop by tablespoonfuls onto baking sheets lined with waxed or parchment paper.

Bake at 350° 10-12 minutes or until lightly browned. Remove from paper while still warm. Cool on wire racks.

Yield: About 3 dozen

These cookies can be stored, but they are best if eaten right away!

63 Cal., 1gm Protein, 14gm Carb., .3gm Fat, 37mg Sodium, .1mg Chol., .5gm Fiber

DESSERTS

Strawberry Mousse in Meringue Shell

Meringue Shell:

4	egg whites
¼	teaspoon cream of tartar
1	cup sugar

Strawberry Mousse:

2	cups strawberry purée
¼	cup low-fat sour cream
¼	cup sugar
1	envelope unflavored gelatin
¼	cup water
4	egg whites

Meringue Shell:
　　Beat 4 egg whites until stiff, but not dry, adding cream of tartar. Add sugar and beat until glossy. Spread in a 10-inch pie plate, making a deep ring around the edge; bake in a 300° oven for 1 hour.

Strawberry Mousse:
　　Mix together strawberry purée, sour cream and sugar.
　　Sprinkle gelatin over water in small saucepan. Heat over low heat until gelatin is dissolved. Add to purée. Mix well. Beat egg whites until stiff and carefully incorporate into purée. Pour into prepared Meringue Shell and cool to set.

Serves: 8

169 Cal., 5gm Protein, 38gm Carb., .5gm Fat, 52mg Sodium, 0mg Chol., 2.4gm Fiber

DESSERTS

Tipsy Bananas

4	yellow or green-tipped bananas
1/4	cup fresh lemon juice
1/2	cup apple butter
1/2	cup minus 1 tablespoon sugar
1/3	cup cognac
2	cups nonfat vanilla frozen yogurt

Peel bananas and cut in half lengthwise. Pour lemon juice over bananas.

Put apple butter in chafing dish and heat. Add sugar and melt. Add bananas.

Turn the bananas until warmed through.

Add cognac and flame.

Serve over frozen yogurt.

Serves: 4

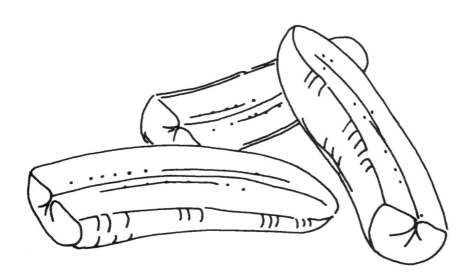

387 Cal., 8gm Protein, 79gm Carb., 1.1gm Fat, 90mg Sodium, 3mg Chol., 2.8gm Fiber

DESSERTS

Vanilla Pudding

1½ cups evaporated skim milk
½   cup skim milk
3   tablespoons cornstarch
⅓   cup granulated sugar
    pinch salt
1½ teaspoons vanilla extract

In a medium saucepan, cook the evaporated milk over medium heat until very hot and bubbles appear around the sides of the pan.

In a small bowl, combine the skim milk with the cornstarch, sugar and salt. Whisk until smooth.

Stir the cornstarch mixture into the hot milk. Bring to a boil, stirring frequently. Cook, whisking until thick and smooth, 2 to 3 minutes. Add the vanilla and stir until blended. Pour the hot pudding into a bowl or individual custard cups. Cover the pudding directly with waxed paper to prevent a skin from forming. Refrigerate until cold, at least 2 hours.

Variation 1:
  Substitute 1 teaspoon orange extract for vanilla and add 1 teaspoon grated orange rind.

Variation 2:
  Add one sliced banana to cooled vanilla pudding and serve with vanilla wafers.

Serves: 4

163 Cal., 7gm Protein, 32gm Carb., .4gm Fat, 165mg Sodium, 4mg Chol., .01gm Fiber

DESSERTS

Tiramisu

Angel Food Cake:

1¼	cup egg whites (10-12 eggs), room temperature
1	cup + 2 tablespoons sifted cake flour
1	cup sifted granulated sugar, divided
¼	teaspoon salt
1¼	teaspoon cream of tartar
1	teaspoon vanilla extract
1	teaspoon espresso

Filling:

¼	cup + 1 tablespoon dry marsala
1	large egg + 1 egg white
¼	cup + 1 tablespoon sugar
3	tablespoons low-fat sour cream
1	8-ounce package low-fat cream cheese
2	tablespoons mascarpone
½	cup espresso
1	tablespoon light rum
¼	cup European unsweetened cocoa

Angel Food Cake:

Preheat oven to 375°. Add 1/4 cup of sugar to flour and sift mixture 4 times to achieve a very fine consistency. Set aside.

Combine egg whites, salt, cream of tartar, vanilla extract and espresso and beat at high speed with electric mixer until stiff enough to hold soft peaks. Beat in ³/₄ cup sugar, sprinkling ¹/₄ cup at a time over egg whites and then beat on high speed until all sugar is blended.

Using a rubber spatula and dividing flour into fourths, add flour to egg whites by using approximately 15 fold-over strokes of the rubber spatula. When all flour is folded in, stroke batter an extra 10 to 20 times gently.

Using at least 4 8-inch cake pans, invert cake pans and spray bottoms with vegetable oil spray. Put one cup of angel food cake mixture on bottom and spread with spatula to cover entire surface.

Bake in 425° oven for 5 minutes or until lightly browned. Let cool. Remove by pressing long sharp knife under angel food cake and against cake pan.

(continued)

Do this under entire surface until loosened. Set aside on wire rack until ready to use. There will be 9 angel food cake layers. Three are needed for one Tiramisu. The other 6 can be individually wrapped, frozen, and used up to one month later.

Filling:

In double boiler combine the dry marsala, eggs and sugar. Using wire whisk, mix until foamy. When pudding-like mixture takes the place of foam, remove from heat and whisk in sour cream. Let cool.

Beat cream cheese and mascarpone. Add cooled marsala mixture in thirds, beating after each addition.

To assemble Tiramisu:

Line 8-inch cake pan with long sheet of extra-wide plastic wrap.

Put $1/2$ cup of espresso and 1 tablespoon of rum into 9-inch cake pan. Dip an angel food cake layer quickly into espresso (do not soak or the cake will fall apart).

Place a soaked angel food cake layer into plastic wrap lined cake pan. Spread with half of filling.

Dip another angel food layer in espresso. Place on filling in pan. Add the remainder of filling, spreading evenly.

Add final espresso-dipped angel food cake layer and cover with plastic wrap which was draped over the sides of the cake pan. Refrigerate overnight.

To serve:

Just before serving, unwrap plastic wrap from top of cake and place serving dish on top of cake pan. Invert cake pan onto serving dish and remove cake pan. Carefully remove plastic wrap. Dust top of Tiramisu with unsweetened European cocoa.

Serves: 14+

This spectacular dessert needs to be made one day in advance.

184 Cal., 6gm Protein, 27gm Carb., 5.3gm Fat, 159mg Sodium, 33mg Chol., .3gm Fiber

TO DIE FOR

Avgolemono Soup
Egg and Lemon Soup

6	**cups chicken stock**
1/3	**cup uncooked rice**
4	**eggs**
6	**tablespoons lemon juice, freshly squeezed**
	dried mint

Bring chicken stock to a boil, add rice, reduce heat and simmer for 20 minutes. Put eggs and lemon juice in a bowl and beat with a wire whisk until the eggs are frothy and very smooth. Return broth to a boil and pour egg-lemon mixture into the broth in a thin stream, stirring constantly. The soup should have a creamy texture. Put soup in bowls and garnish with dried mint.

Serves: 4

Broccolini

1	bunch fresh broccoli
¼	cup extra virgin olive oil
¼	teaspoon red pepper seeds
1-2	cloves garlic, minced
⅓	cup chicken broth
4	tablespoons butter
2	egg yolks
1	cup heavy cream
	salt and pepper to taste
	Parmesan cheese
12	ounces linguine

Clean and pat dry 1-inch long broccoli flowerets. In a large skillet, heat olive oil and add broccoli. Cook, stirring constantly for a few minutes. Add hot red pepper seeds, garlic and chicken broth and stir. Cover and heat 5 minutes on medium-low heat. Add butter, stir to blend and turn off heat.

Prepare linguine according to package directions.

Put 2 egg yolks in a glass measuring cup or bowl and beat slightly with a fork. Add the heavy whipping cream and blend together. Heat broccoli on medium heat, add yolk-cream mixture and stir. Add salt and pepper.

Serve the broccoli-sauce mixture on the linguine and top with fresh grated Parmesan cheese, if desired.

Serves: 4

TO DIE FOR

Decadent Cake

1	cup butter, room temperature
2	cups granulated sugar
4	eggs
1	teaspoon vanilla
1½	cups self-rising flour
2	tablespoons cocoa
2	cups pecans, chopped

Topping:
2	cups miniature marshmallows

Frosting:
1	square unsweetened chocolate, melted
¼	cup butter, melted
2	cups powdered sugar, sifted
¼	cup heavy cream

Cream the butter and sugar until light. Add the eggs and mix well. Add the vanilla. Mix in the flour and cocoa until incorporated. Stir in nuts.

Spread into an ungreased large glass baking pan. Bake in a preheated 325° oven for 45 minutes or until a toothpick comes clean.

Topping:
As soon as the cake is done, sprinkle the marshmallows evenly on the top of the hot cake and return to the oven until marshmallows melt together, about 5 minutes. Remove cake from oven and let cool.

Frosting:
Combine all ingredients and beat until smooth. Adjust frosting if needed for a good spreading consistency.

When cake is cool, spread frosting on top of marshmallows. Let set about 2 hours after frosting. Cut into squares.

Serves: 16

Delice au Chocolat

½ cup raisins
⅓ cup Armagnac or cognac
12 ounces bittersweet chocolate, chopped
1 cup strong coffee
6 eggs + 2 egg whites
3 sticks butter, softened

Garnish:
18 walnut halves

Soak raisins in Armagnac for one hour.

Melt chocolate with coffee in a double boiler.

Separate the eggs.

Pour melted chocolate into a large mixing bowl, add the butter a little at a time, the raisins, Armagnac and egg yolks.

Beat the 8 egg whites until stiff, carefully fold into chocolate mixture.

Line a loaf pan with foil, pour chocolate mixture into it and refrigerate overnight.

Before serving, invert onto serving platter, remove foil, slice and decorate with walnut halves.

Serves: 18

Disappearing Brownies

1	6-ounce package butterscotch morsels
3	tablespoons butter
¾	cup flour
⅓	cup brown sugar, firmly packed
1	teaspoon baking powder
¼	teaspoon salt
½	teaspoon vanilla
1	egg
1	cup miniature marshmallows
1	6-ounce package semi-sweet morsels
¼	cup pecans, chopped

Preheat oven to 350°.

Grease bottom and sides of a 9 x 9-inch baking pan. Melt butterscotch morsels and butter in a large, heavy saucepan over medium-low heat, stirring constantly. Remove mixture from heat and cool until lukewarm.

Combine the flour, sugar, baking powder and salt. Set aside.

Add vanilla and egg to the saucepan and stir. Add the dry ingredients to the saucepan and stir. Fold in marshmallows, semi-sweet morsels and nuts. Spread into the prepared pan. Bake at 350° for 20-25 minutes. Do not overbake - the top of the brownies will have puffed and look wet but will firm upon cooling.

Yield: 16 brownies

Filled Zucchini Flowers

16	zucchini flowers (male only)
5-6	medium zucchini
3/4	cup Crème Fraîche
3	eggs, slightly beaten
	salt and pepper to taste
	pinch of nutmeg
1	sprig fresh thyme
1 1/2	cups chicken broth
1	tablespoon sherry

Preheat oven to 325°.

Remove stems from zucchini flowers; set flowers aside.

Peel zucchini, cut into 1-inch pieces and steam in vegetable steamer until tender. Purée in food processor.

Over low heat, in a nonstick skillet, cook zucchini purée until most moisture has evaporated. Remove from heat, add Crème Fraîche, eggs, salt, pepper and nutmeg. Mix well.

Fill zucchini flowers with mixture (about 1 tablespoon each), depending on size. Place flowers into baking dish to which thyme, chicken broth and sherry has been added. Liquid should come to 1/4 of height of flowers. Bake for 30 minutes. Serve.

Serves: 8

Italian Stuffed Shells

1	cup sautéed mushrooms
2	teaspoons olive oil
16	ounces mozzarella cheese
2	10-ounce packages frozen creamed spinach, thawed
1	15-ounce container ricotta cheese
1	egg
	salt and pepper to taste
1	box large pasta stuffing shells
	spaghetti sauce to cover, preferably homemade
1/2	cup Parmesan cheese

Sauté mushrooms in a small skillet in olive oil. Set aside. In a large mixing bowl grate mozzarella cheese, add creamed spinach, ricotta cheese and egg, salt and pepper to taste.

Prepare shells according to directions and set aside.

Fill shells with stuffing mixture, place them in a large buttered baking pan, cover with sauce and bake in a preheated 325° oven for 40 minutes, covered.

Remove cover, sprinkle additional mozzarella cheese or Parmesan cheese and broil for 5 minutes.

Serves: 8

Lasagna

Pasta:

2½ cups flour

3 eggs

pinch of salt

¼ cup water, approximately

Filling:

1¼ pounds bulk hot Italian sausage

1-2 tablespoons extra virgin olive oil

2 carrots, sliced

1 large rib celery, sliced

1 medium yellow onion, chopped

1 cup fresh mushrooms, sliced

1 tablespoon butter

1 14-ounce can beef broth or homemade beef stock

½ cup dry red wine

Pasta:
   Put the flour into a large mixing bowl. Make a well in the center, add the eggs and salt, beat a bit with a fork, add the water and incorporate the flour into the egg mixture. Knead 5-8 minutes or until dough is smooth and firm. Cover with a bowl or pastry cloth and let rest for one hour at room temperature.
   Cut dough into four equal portions. Roll out one portioned dough ball into a large rectangle to fit a lasagna pan. Cut lengthwise three 2½-inch wide strips. Repeat for the remaining dough balls.
   Drop in boiling salted water and cook about 5 minutes. Drain and lay lasagna strips on a kitchen linen towel.

Filling:
   In a large skillet cook Italian sausage. Remove sausage and discard grease. In the same skillet heat olive oil and sauté carrots, celery and onion until tender. Add mushrooms and heat 5 minutes more. Add butter, beef broth and red wine. Cook until liquid is somewhat reduced but not evaporated.

(continued)

Cheese mixture:

1	28-ounce container small curd cottage cheese or ricotta cheese
16	ounces mozzarella cheese, shredded, divided
2	large eggs

Sauce:

2	tablespoons extra virgin olive oil
3	garlic cloves, minced
1	tablespoon butter
1	28-ounce can tomato purée
	salt and coarsely ground black pepper
¼	teaspoon crushed red pepper
4	leaves fresh basil, chopped
2	tablespoons fresh parsley, minced
1	6-ounce can tomato paste
6	Roma tomatoes, chopped

Cheese mixture:

In a medium mixing bowl, combine cottage cheese or ricotta, 12 ounces of the shredded mozzarella and eggs. Set aside.

Sauce:

In a saucepan heat olive oil, garlic and butter. Add tomato purée, salt, black pepper, crushed red pepper, basil, parsley, tomato paste and tomatoes. Cook ½ hour. Set aside.

To assemble lasagna:

Place three lasagna noodles in the bottom of a rectangular, buttered lasagna pan. Layer with sauce, cheese and filling three times between layers of lasagna. Cover top with final layer of lasagna noodles. Top with sauce and remaining mozzarella cheese and bake 40 minutes in a preheated 350° oven.

Serves: 12

Mexican Queso Dip

8	ounces sharp cheddar cheese, grated
2	4-ounce cans chopped green chilies, drained
2	cups sour cream
8	ounces mild cheddar cheese, grated
8	ounces Monterey Pepper Jack cheese, grated
	tortilla chips

Preheat oven to 375°. In an 8 x 8-inch baking dish layer $1/3$ each of sharp cheddar cheese, chilies, sour cream, mild cheddar cheese and Monterey Pepper Jack cheese. Repeat layering twice. Bake until the cheeses are melted and bubbly, 25-30 minutes. Serve hot with tortilla chips.

Serves: 8

Poached Eggs with Truffle Cream

1	cup Crème Fraîche
½	cup heavy cream
1	whole black truffle, grated
1	tablespoon butter
1	tablespoon flour
½	cup chicken broth
½	cup Madeira
1	cup beef broth, reduced to 4 tablespoons
1	truffle, thinly sliced
6	eggs
3	tablespoons butter
6	slices Bavarian ham
¼	cup white wine
6	slices whole wheat toast

Combine Crème Fraîche with heavy cream and grated truffle. Let stand one hour.

In a saucepan, melt 1 tablespoon butter, add flour and cook, stirring until lightly colored. Add chicken broth and Madeira, blend well. Add cream-truffle mixture and beef broth reduction. Heat through and add truffle slices. Keep warm.

Poach eggs in water to which a little vinegar has been added, remove with slotted spoon. Keep warm.

In a skillet, melt 3 tablespoons butter and quickly heat ham slices on both sides. Keep warm. Deglaze pan with a little white wine, add to sauce. Reheat sauce.

Place one slice of toast on each plate, cover with one slice of ham and put one trimmed poached egg on each. Spoon sauce over each and serve immediately.

Serves: 6

Roasted Spicy Chicken Wings

Sauce:

1	cup hot pepper sauce
4	tablespoons butter
1	tablespoon Dijon mustard
1	cup sesame seeds
1/4	cup coarsely ground slivered almonds
2	pounds chicken wings

Combine hot pepper sauce, butter and mustard. Cook over low heat until blended. Set aside.

Heat sesame seeds in a dry skillet until they begin to pop. Add almonds and heat until brown. Set aside.

Pat chicken wings dry. Roll in sesame-nut mixture. Place on broiler rack. Place rack in 425° oven for 30 minutes. After 30 minutes, remove from oven and dip wings in sauce. Turn wings and replace on broiler pan. Bake another 30 minutes. Serve with sauce for dipping.

Serves: 6

Sinful Salad

4	tablespoons extra virgin olive oil, divided
1	small red onion, cut in half and thinly sliced
1	large red pepper, cut in thin strips
10	sun-dried tomatoes
2	tablespoons pine nuts
2	tablespoons fresh parsley, chopped
1	tablespoon dried oregano
1	tablespoon dried dill
1/2	teaspoon coriander
1	tablespoon garlic, chopped
1/2	teaspoon salt
1	teaspoon black pepper, freshly ground
1	tablespoon balsamic vinegar
1	head red leaf lettuce
2	large, ripe tomatoes, cut in half and thinly sliced
2	ripe avocados, cut in half and thinly sliced
4	ounces Stilton cheese, crumbled

In a large, covered frying pan, sauté at the lowest heat until softened (15-20 minutes, do not brown), 3 tablespoons olive oil, onion, red pepper, dried tomatoes, pine nuts, parsley, oregano, dill, coriander, garlic, salt and ground pepper, stirring occasionally. While this is sautéing, arrange a bed of lettuce on each plate. Place a line of fresh tomato slices on the lettuce and a line of avocado slices on the tomatoes and crumbled Stilton on the avocado. When the vegetables are finished, add 1 tablespoon olive oil and the vinegar, stir and spoon over the salad. Serve warm.

Serves: 6 appetizers or
        4 meal-size salads

The secret of this salad is lightly sautéing the onion and pepper which gives them a more delicate texture and flavors the oil.

Substitution Guide

The following list of substitutions is not intended to be a "one-for-one" chart of equivalents, such as two pints = one quart. These are alternatives and techniques which have proven successful in low-fat cooking, including many of the recipes in this book. Any one of them will work perfectly in some recipes but not as well in others. It ultimately rests with the cook to experiment and find the best possible combination.

High Fat/Calorie/Cholesterol Ingredients	Substitutions/Suggestions/Techniques
Eggs	
- whole eggs	Replace 4 whole eggs with 2 whole eggs + 2 egg whites.
	Substitute each whole egg with 1 egg white + one teaspoon vegetable oil.
	Commercial egg substitute.
- egg yolks	Replace 4 yolks with 2 whole eggs.
	Replace 6 yolks with 3 whole eggs + 3 egg whites.
- chopped hard-boiled eggs	Chopped whites only.
Oils	
- for coating with oil	Put oil in a spritz bottle.
- for sautéing vegetables	Reduce oil; use nonstick skillet or eliminate oil and sauté in water or chicken broth.
- in salad dressings	Reduce oil; use fruit juices, nonfat yogurt, defatted chicken stock, vinegars, fresh herbs.
- in baking	Reduce oils; substitute with fruit purées.
- in stir-frying	Reduce oil; add a little water or broth if food begins to stick.

Butter

- **in pastry crusts**	Low-fat cream cheese + vegetable oil.
- **in graham cracker crusts**	Canola oil.
- **in cookies, brownies, quickbreads, scones**	Reduce butter by $1/2$ and replace remainder with vegetable oil.
	Reduce butter to $1/4$ original and replace remainder with fruit purée.
	Prune or other fruit purées, prune butter, apple butter, applesauce + corn syrup.
	Low-fat/nonfat cottage cheese + vegetable oil.
- **in cream sauces**	Replace butter by blending flour thoroughly in cold milk.
- **in cinnamon rolls**	Pressed nonfat cottage cheese + vegetable oil. Press cottage cheese through a double layer of cheesecloth.
- **in waffles**	Replace butter and milk with low-fat buttermilk.
- **in baking fish**	Poach in white wine or broth.
- **in phyllo**	Brush leaves with 1 large egg white mixed with 1 tablespoon oil. Brush top layer with 1 tablespoon melted butter before baking.

Light or Heavy Creams

- **in cream sauces**	$1 1/2$ cups evaporated skim milk + 2 cups puréed low-fat (1%) cottage cheese.
	$1/3$ cup skim milk + $2/3$ cup evaporated skim milk.
	Cornstarch or flour dissolved in a little cold water or broth.
- **in soups**	Low-fat milk, thickened with cornstarch.
	Evaporated skim milk.
- **in casseroles**	Evaporated skim milk.
- **in ice cream**	$2/3$ cup skim milk + $1/3$ cup marshmallow fluff.

Sour Cream	Low-fat or nonfat sour cream.
	Nonfat yogurt (use cornstarch to thicken, if desired).
	2 cups low-fat cottage cheese + 2 tablespoons lemon juice + $1/3$ cup skim milk, well blended.
	1 cup low-fat cottage cheese + $1/4$ cup nonfat plain yogurt, well blended.
	$3/4$ cup ricotta cheese + $1/4$ cup yogurt or buttermilk, well blended.
	1 cup evaporated skim milk whipped with 1 teaspoon lemon juice.
	Buttermilk (for baked goods).
Mayonnaise	"Light" or nonfat mayonnaise.
	$1/4$ cup plain low-fat yogurt + 1 tablespoon low-calorie mayonnaise.
Nuts	Reduce by $1/2$; toast to enhance flavor.
Almonds/coconut	Substitute prunes and dried apricots.
Chocolate	
- 12 ounces unsweetened	$3/4$ cup unsweetened cocoa powder + 1 ounce unsweetened chocolate.
- 12 ounces semisweet	2 ounces semisweet chocolate + 2 tablespoons instant coffee powder + $3/4$ cup unsweetened cocoa powder.
	3 ounces semisweet chocolate + $1/2$ cup corn syrup + 1 cup sugar + unsweetened cocoa powder + 1 envelope unsweetened gelatin.

Whole Milk	Low-fat/skim milk.
Whipped Cream	Chilled evaporated skim milk, whipped.
	Egg whites, whipped.
	$^1/_2$ cup heavy cream, chilled and beaten until stiff + $1^1/_2$ cups nonfat yogurt, folded in.
	Italian meringue. While beating egg whites, slowly pour cooled sugar syrup into whites.
Crème Fraîche	Low-fat plain yogurt or see recipe for Mock Crème Fraîche included in this book.
Yogurt	Low-fat/nonfat yogurt.
Ricotta	Low-fat ricotta.
Hard and semi-soft cheeses	Reduce amount.
	Low-fat or nonfat versions.
Cream Cheese	Low-fat/nonfat cream cheese.
-in cheesecake	4 cups pressed nonfat cottage cheese + 1 cup low-fat or "light" cream cheese. (Press cottage cheese through a double layer of cheesecloth.)
	Yogurt cheese. (Strain nonfat plain yogurt through colander lined with cheesecloth and cover with plastic wrap overnight in refrigerator. 2 cups yogurt yields 1 cup yogurt cheese.)

Meats

- pork	Lean, boneless loin roast, all fat removed.
	Tenderloin, all fat removed.
- veal	Lean loin chop, all fat removed.
	Lean scallopini.
- beef	Lean top round, all visible fat removed.
	Lean eye of round, all visible fat removed.
	Lean tenderloin, all visible fat removed.
- ground chuck	Lean ground beef or ground turkey breast.
- poultry	Skinned and all visible fat removed.

Cream or Condensed Soups

	Sauté vegetables in minimum amount of oil, sprinkle with small amount of flour, add evaporated milk, yogurt, salt and pepper.
	Canned low-fat soups.
- Cream of chicken	Thicken chicken stock and skim milk with flour, add yogurt (for flavor and consistency).
- Cream of mushroom	Skim milk + peppercorns, bay leaf, nutmeg, fresh onion, fresh garlic, low-fat sour cream, sautéed mushrooms.

Hints

Put oil (canola, olive, etc.) in a regular spritz bottle and use to spray pans.

Choose leaner cuts of meat, trim off excess fat, and remove the skin from poultry.

Place a rack at the bottom of the roasting pan so that fat from the meat or poultry can drip off. For fat-free flavor, baste with tomato juice or broth instead of butter or margarine.

Store canned broth in the refrigerator so fat will rise to the top. When opening the can, remove the entire lid and skim off the solidified fat.

Drain oils and salty liquids from canned salmon, tuna and sardines, then rinse with water and drain again.

Brown meatballs in the broiler rather than in a skillet.

For moist, tender poultry, fish and meat, bake in covered cookware with a little wine, broth or other liquid. This method is particularly good for fish and chicken breasts.

Juicy meat and great stock depend on the temperature of the water. Boiled or poached meat should be started in hot water to seal in the juices and flavor. For tasty stocks, start the meat in cold water so the flavor is absorbed by the liquid.

Deglaze a pan with hard cider instead of vinegar or wine. It will add more zest to the sauce and is great with pork and chicken.

For added taste in steaming vegetables, try sprinkling herbs into the water or use broth instead of water.

In cooking soups, dry herbs go in at the beginning and fresh herbs go in at the end.

To prevent yogurt from separating in sauces, mix one tablespoon of cornstarch with one tablespoon of yogurt, then combine with sauce.

For high-volume egg whites, the whites must be clean and at room temperature. Add a pinch of salt or sugar, too.

Add a drop of lemon juice rather than salt to the water when you cook pasta.

Index

A

Amaretto
   Chocolate Amaretto Cheesecake, 235
Angel Food Cake (Fruit Trifle), 240
Angel Food Cake (Tiramisu), 260
Appetizers
   Black Bean Cakes with Summer Salsa, 24
   Crab Cakes with Sauce Remoulade, 8
   Eggplant Mozzarella, 175
   Gravelax (Cured Salmon), 7
   Grilled Scallops with Black Bean Salad, 126
   Layered Taco Dip, 1
   Los Frijoles Negros Fritos con Salsa de Verano, 24
   Marinated Shrimp with Herb Mayonnaise, 10
   Middle East Chick Pea Dip, 2
   Mussels in Herbed Vegetable Broth, 12
   Onion Tart, 20
   Oven-dried Tomatoes, 23
   Parmesan Artichoke Toast, 21
   Pesto Dip, 3
   Potassium Froth, 27
   Potato Rounds with Tapenade, 26
   Poulet Presqu'ile, 112
   Red Pepper Dip, 4
   Salmon Carpaccio with Frankfurt Green Sauce, 16
   Seafood Dip, 5
   Seafood Strudel, 22
   Smoked Trout with Dill Sauce, 14
   Spicy Pork Tenderloin with Lime Mayonnaise, 30
   Spinach Dip, 6
   Steamed Whole Fish with Lime Mousseline Sauce, 18
   Terrine of Chicken and Herbs, 28
   Tuna Tartare, 15

Apple Spice Cake, 225
Apple Strudel with Custard Sauce, 226
Apples
   Apple Spice Cake, 225
   Apple Strudel with Custard Sauce, 226
   Baked Apple and Blackberry Pudding, 229
Apricots
   Baked Sweet Potatoes and Apricots, 189
Artichokes
   Chicken Casserole with Brown Rice and Artichokes, 92
   Parmesan Artichoke Toast, 21
   Player's Artichokes, 164
Arugula, 86
   Arugula Pesto, 84
   Orecchiette with Tomatoes and Arugula, 82
Arugula Pesto, 84
Asparagus
   Asparagus Soup, 31
Asparagus Soup, 31
Autumn Meringues, 228

B

Baked Apple and Blackberry Pudding, 229
Baked Fruit, 230
Baked Sweet Potatoes and Apricots, 189
Baked Ziti with Spicy Marinara Sauce, 74
Baked Zucchini and Rice, 200
Banana Raisin Bread, 211
Bananas
   Banana Raisin Bread, 211
   Tipsy Bananas, 258
Bar Cookies
   Frosted Fudge Brownies, 238
   Orange Tootsies, 247
   Pineapple Cranberry Bars, 253

INDEX

Basil
    Squash Soup with Lemon and Basil, 46
Batter Breads
    Banana Raisin Bread, 211
    Fruited Pumpkin Bread, 215
    Oatmeal Bread with Cinnamon Pear Butter, 222
Beans, Italian Green
    Italian Winter Salad, 56
Beans, Red Kidney
    Spicy Corn and Bean Confetti Salad, 65
Beans, White Kidney
    White Kidney Bean Salad, 71
Beef
    Beef Olé, 138
    Pinwheel Tenderloin of Beef with Fresh Tomato Sals, 134
    Stir-fried Beef and Broccoli, 136
Beef Olé, 138
Beverages
    Potassium Froth, 27
Black Bean Cakes with Summer Salsa, 24
Black Bean, Corn and Tomato Salad, 49
Black Bean Salad, 126
Black Bean Soup, 42
Black Beans
    Black Bean Cakes with Summer Salsa, 24
    Black Bean, Corn and Tomato Salad, 49
    Black Bean Salad, 126
    Black Bean Soup, 42
    Black Beans with Rice, 73
    Spanish Black Bean Soup, 41
Black Beans with Rice, 73
Black Sea Bass Fillet With Citrus Vinaigrette, 119
Black-eyed Pea Salad, 50
Black-eyed Peas
    Black-eyed Pea Salad, 50
Blackberries
    Baked Apple and Blackberry Pudding, 229
    Blue Corn Pierogies with Potato and Lobster and Carmelized Onion and Saffron Vinaigrette, 120

Braised Celery, 173
Breads
    Banana Raisin Bread, 211
    Cornbread Muffins, 212
    Cottage Cheese Pancakes, 213
    Crostini, 214
    Fougasse - Provençal Country Bread, 216
    Fruited Pumpkin Bread, 215
    Harvest Muffins, 218
    Hearty Blueberry Muffins, 219
    Oatmeal Bread with Cinnamon Pear Butter, 222
    Phyllo Crust, 152
    Pizza Dough, 158
    Provençal Country Bread, 216
    Raspberry Bran Muffins, 221
    Rugelachs, 220
    Whole Wheat Pizza Dough, 160
Broccoli
    Broccoli with Curry Sauce, 166
Broccoli with Curry Sauce, 166
    Broiled Scallops and New Zealand Mussels with Concasse Tomatoes and Minted Lime Vinaigrette, 122
Brownies
    Frosted Fudge Brownies, 238
Buddha's Delight, 179

C

Cabbage
    Golden Raisin Coleslaw, 54
    Spicy Cabbage, 168
    Stir Fry Cabbage, 169
Cabbage, Red
    Red Cabbage in Red Wine, 167
Cajun Fish, 123
Cake
    Angel Food Cake (Fruit Trifle), 240
    Angel Food Cake (Tiramisu), 260
    Apple Spice Cake, 225
    Carob Cake, 231
    Carrot Cake with Orange Glaze, 232

INDEX

Capellini
    Capellini with Grilled Chicken and Tarragon Sauce, 76
Capellini with Grilled Chicken and Tarragon Sauce, 76
Caramelized Onion and Saffron Vinaigrette, 120
Carob
    Carob Cake, 231
Carob Cake, 231
Carrot Cake with Orange Glaze, 232
Carrot Soup, 32
Carrots
    Carrot Cake with Orange Glaze, 232
    Carrot Soup, 32
    Golden Raisin Coleslaw, 54
    Moroccan Carrot Salad, 58
    Parsnip and Carrot Gratin, 182
    Savory Roasted Carrots with Horseradish, 163
Cauliflower
    Italian Winter Salad, 56
    Marinated Cauliflower, 57
Celery
    Braised Celery, 173
Champagne Sauce, 150
Champagne Sherbet, 234
Cheesecake
    Chocolate Amaretto Cheesecake, 235
    Peach Kiwi Cheesecake, 250
Cheeses
    Quiche Lorraine, 154
    Ski Cheese Pie, 153
Chick Peas (Garbanzos)
    Falafel, 156
    Middle East Chick Pea Dip, 2
    Spicy Chick Pea Relish Salad, 64
Chicken
    Capellini with Grilled Chicken and Tarragon Sauce, 76
    Chicken Arabesque II, 91
    Chicken Casserole with Brown Rice and Artichokes, 92
    Chicken Loaf, 93
    Chicken Michael, 94
    Chicken Paprikash, 95
    Chicken Roulade with Warm Tarragon Sauce, 96
    Cinnamon Chicken, 98
    Coq au Vin, 99
    Enchiladas Verdes, 102
    Grilled Ginger Chicken Patties, 103
    Grilled Marinated Chicken on Oriental Salad, 55
    Las Enchiladas del Pollo, 104
    Mandarin Chicken, 105
    Mexican Chicken and Rice, 106
    Orange Chicken, 108
    Oriental Chicken and Noodles, 83
    Original Chicken Arabesque, 107
    Oven-fried Chicken, 110
    Pan-seared Spicy Breast of Chicken, 111
    Poulet Presqu'ile, 112
    Stir Fry Chicken and Vegetables over Rice, 116
    Tamale Pie, 114
    Terrine of Chicken and Herbs, 28
    White Chili, 118
Chicken Arabesque II, 91
Chicken Casserole with Brown Rice and Artichokes, 92
Chicken Loaf, 93
Chicken Michael, 94
Chicken Paprikash, 95
Chicken Roulade with Warm Tarragon Sauce, 96
Chlodnik, 33
Chocolate
    Chocolate Amaretto Cheesecake, 235
    Espresso-Chocolate Mousse, 237
Chocolate Amaretto Cheesecake, 235
Chowder
    Corn Chowder, 34
    Manhattan Clam Chowder, 37
Chutney
    Mango Chutney, 206

INDEX

Cinnamon Chicken, 98
Cinnamon Pear Butter, 222
Citrus Vinaigrette, 119
Clams
    Manhattan Clam Chowder, 37
Coffee Cake
    Sour Cream Coffe Cake with Pecan and Cinnamon Fill, 224
Cold Vegetable and Yogurt Soup, 33
Coleslaw
    Golden Raisin Coleslaw, 54
Colorful Linguine Stir Fry, 77
Cookies
    Autumn Meringues, 228
    Oatmeal Cranberry Cookies, 245
    Spicy Oatmeal Cookies, 256
Coq Au Vin, 99
Corn
    Black Bean, Corn and Tomato Salad, 49
    Corn Chowder, 34
    Corn Pancakes with Vegetable Topping, 170
    Fresh Corn Casserole, 172
    Fresh Corn Salad, 53
    Spicy Corn and Bean Confetti Salad, 65
Corn Chowder, 34
Corn Pancakes with Vegetable Topping, 170
Cornbread Muffins, 212
Cornish Game Hen
    Cornish Game Hen in Pine Nut Crust with Papaya Rel, 100
Cornish Game Hen in Pine Nut Crust with Papaya Rel, 100
Cornmeal
    Cornbread Muffins, 212
Cottage Cheese Pancakes, 213
Couscous
    Greek Couscous Pilaf, 79
    Tunisian Salad with Piquant Dressing, 68
Crab
    Crab Cakes with Sauce Remoulade, 8
    Seafood-stuffed Tomatoes, 62

Crab Cakes with Sauce Remoulade, 8
Cranberries
    Oatmeal Cranberry Cookies, 245
    Pineapple Cranberry Bars, 253
Crème Fraîche
    Mock Crème Fraîche, 208
Creole Baked Shrimp, 124
Crostini, 214
Crustless Spinach Pie, 193
Cucumber Mint Soup, 35
Cucumber Sauce, 157
Cucumber Tomato Salad, 51
Cucumbers
    Cucumber Mint Soup, 35
    Cucumber Tomato Salad, 51
Cultured Potatoes, 184
Curried Pears, 236
Curry
    Curried Pears, 236
    Curry Sauce, 166
Curry Sauce, 166
Custard Sauce, 226

D

Dennis Nahat's Stewed Eggplant, 174
Desserts
    Angel Food Cake (Fruit Trifle), 240
    Angel Food Cake (Tiramisu), 260
    Apple Spice Cake, 225
    Apple Strudel with Custard Sauce, 226
    Autumn Meringues, 228
    Baked Apple and Blackberry Pudding, 229
    Baked Fruit, 230
    Carob Cake, 231
    Carrot Cake with Orange Glaze, 232
    Champagne Sherbet, 234
    Chocolate Amaretto Cheesecake, 235
    Curried Pears, 236
    Espresso-Chocolate Mousse, 237
    Frosted Fudge Brownies, 238
    Fruit Baked with Zabaglione, 239

INDEX

Fruit Trifle, 240
Grape Sherbets, 242
Layered Fruit Ring with Peach Coulis, 243
Meringue Shell, 257
Noodle Kugel, 244
Oatmeal Cranberry Cookies, 245
Orange Sherbet, 246
Orange Tootsies, 247
Oranges Orientales, 248
Peach Kiwi Cheesecake, 250
Peach Slush, 249
Pears in Red Wine, 252
Pineapple Cranberry Bars, 253
Plum Parfait, 254
Pumpkin Pie, 255
Spicy Oatmeal Cookies, 256
Strawberry Mousse in Meringue Shell, 257
Tipsy Bananas, 258
Tiramisu, 260
Vanilla Pudding, 259
Dijon Vinaigrette, 59
Dill Sauce, 14, 203
Dips
    Layered Taco Dip, 1
    Middle East Chick Pea Dip, 2
    Pesto Dip, 3
    Red Pepper Dip, 4
    Seafood Dip, 5
    Spinach Dip, 6
Dressings
    Caramelized Onion and Saffron Vinaigrette, 120
    Citrus Vinaigrette, 119
    Dijon Vinaigrette, 59
    Minted Lime Vinaigrette, 122
    Piquant Dressing, 68
    Strawberry Vinaigrette, 66
Dried Fruit
    Fruited Pumpkin Bread, 215
    Nutcracker Mart Fruited Rice, 81
    Yams with Dried Fruit, 192

E

Eggplant
    Dennis Nahat's Stewed Eggplant, 174
    Eggplant Mozzarella, 175
    Eggplant Stuffing, 176
    Lamb Eggplant Cake, 140
    Tian of Eggplant, Yellow Squash and Yellow Peppers, 177
Eggplant Mozzarella, 175
Eggplant Stuffing, 176
Enchiladas Verdes, 102
Espresso
    Espresso-Chocolate Mousse, 237
Espresso-Chocolate Mousse, 237

F

Falafel, 156
Fattoosh, 52
Faux Fettucine Alfredo, 78
Fennel
    Fennel Paysanne, 178
Fennel Paysanne, 178
Feta
    Tomato Feta Pasta Salad, 67
Fettucine
    Faux Fettucine Alfredo, 78
Fish
    Black Sea Bass Fillet With Citrus Vinaigrette, 119
    Cajun Fish, 123
    Gravelax (Cured Salmon), 7
    Pesce al Cartoccio, 128
    Salmon Carpaccio with Frankfurt Green Sauce, 16
    Scallop-stuffed Sole, 132
    Smoked Trout with Dill Sauce, 14
    Steamed Whole Fish with Lime Mousseline Sauce, 18
    Tuna Salad with Fruit, 70
    Tuna Tartare, 15

INDEX

Fougasse - Provençal Country Bread, 216
Frankfurt Green Sauce, 16
Fresh Corn Casserole, 172
Fresh Corn Salad, 53
Fresh Tomato Salsa, 134
Fresh Tomato Sauce, 204
Frosted Fudge Brownies, 238
Frostings
    Frosting (Frosted Fudge Brownies), 238
Fruit
    Baked Fruit, 230
    Curried Pears, 236
    Fruit Baked with Zabaglione, 239
    Fruit Trifle, 240
    Grape Sherbets, 242
    Layered Fruit Ring with Peach Coulis, 243
    Orange Sherbet, 246
    Orange Tootsies, 247
    Oranges Orientales, 248
    Peach Kiwi Cheesecake, 250
    Peach Slush, 249
    Pear Salad with Dijon Vinaigrette, 59
    Pears in Red Wine, 252
    Plum Parfait, 254
    Strawberry Mousse in Meringue Shell, 257
    Summer Fruit Soup, 47
    Tipsy Bananas, 258
Fruit Baked with Zabaglione, 239
Fruit Trifle, 240
Fruited Pumpkin Bread, 215

G

Garbanzos (Chick Peas)
    Falafel, 156
    Middle East Chick Pea Dip, 2
    Spicy Chick Pea Relish Salad, 64
Garlic
    Garlic Potato Straw Surprise, 186
    Roasted Garlic Lemon Sauce, 209

Garlic Potato Straw Surprise, 186
Garnishes
    Marinated Orange Peel, 252
Ginger
    Grilled Ginger Chicken Patties, 103
Glazes
    Orange Glaze, 232
Golden Raisin Coleslaw, 54
Grape Sherbets, 242
Gravelax (Cured Salmon), 7
Greek Couscous Pilaf, 79
Green Beans
    Penne with Green Beans and Arugula Pesto, 84
Green Beans, Italian
    Italian Winter Salad, 56
Green Peppercorn Sauce, 205
Grilled Ginger Chicken Patties, 103
Grilled Indian Lamb, 139
Grilled Marinated Chicken on Oriental Salad, 55
Grilled Scallops with Black Bean Salad, 126
Grilled Veal Chops with Salad Greens, 146
Gruyère
    Potato Cakes with Leeks and Gruyère, 188

H

Harvest Muffins, 218
Hearty Blueberry Muffins, 219
Herb Mayonnaise, 10
Herbed Mixed Vegetables, 180
Herbed Vegetable Broth, 12
Hints, 281
Hominy
    Hornado's Pork, 142
Hornado's Pork, 142
Horseradish
    Savory Roasted Carrots with Horseradish, 163

INDEX

Hot Pepper Oil, 44

I

Italian Bread Soup, 36
Italian Winter Salad, 56

K

Kiwi
    Peach Kiwi Cheesecake, 250

L

Lamb
    Grilled Indian Lamb, 139
    Lamb Eggplant Cake, 140
Lamb Eggplant Cake, 140
Las Enchiladas del Pollo, 104
Lavash, 155
Layered Fruit Ring with Peach Coulis, 243
Layered Taco Dip, 1
Leeks
    Potato Cakes with Leeks and Gruyère, 188
Lemon
    Squash Soup with Lemon and Basil, 46
Lemons
    Lemony Peapods, 183
    Roasted Garlic Lemon Sauce, 209
    Sweet Potato and Lemon Purée, 190
Lemony Peapods, 183
Lima Beans
    Peppy Lima Bean Salad, 60
Lime Mayonnaise, 30
Lime Mousseline Sauce, 18
Linguine
    Colorful Linguine Stir Fry, 77
Los Frijoles Negros Fritos con Salsa de Verano, 24

M

Main Courses
    Beef Olé, 138
    Black Sea Bass Fillet With Citrus Vinaigrette, 119
    Blue Corn Pierogies with Potato and Lobster and Carmelized Onion and Saffron Vinaigrette, 120
    Broiled Scallops and New Zealand Mussels with Concasse Tomatoes and Minted Lime Vinaigrette, 122
    Cajun Fish, 123
    Chicken Arabesque II, 91
    Chicken Casserole with Brown Rice and Artichokes, 92
    Chicken Loaf, 93
    Chicken Michael, 94
    Chicken Paprikash, 95
    Chicken Roulade with Warm Tarragon Sauce, 96
    Cinnamon Chicken, 98
    Coq au Vin, 99
    Cornish Game Hen in Pine Nut Crust with Papaya Rel, 100
    Creole Baked Shrimp, 124
    Enchiladas Verdes, 102
    Falafel, 156
    Grilled Ginger Chicken Patties, 103
    Grilled Indian Lamb, 139
    Grilled Scallops with Black Bean Salad, 126
    Grilled Veal Chops with Salad Greens, 146
    Hornado's Pork, 142
    Lamb Eggplant Cake, 140
    Las Enchiladas del Pollo, 104
    Lavash, 155
    Mandarin Chicken, 105
    Medallions of Pork with Sauce Charcutière, 143
    Mexican Chicken and Rice, 106
    Orange Chicken, 108
    Original Chicken Arabesque, 107
    Oven-fried Chicken, 110
    Pan-seared Spicy Breast of Chicken, 111
    Pesce al Cartoccio, 128
    Phyllo Crust, 152
    Pinwheel Tenderloin of Beef with Fresh Tomato Sals, 134
    Poached Salmon with Yogurt Sauce, 130
    Pork Tenderloin Marco, 144

INDEX

Poulet Presqu'ile, 112
Quiche Lorraine, 154
Rabbit Braised in Red Wine, 145
Roast Turkey and Stuffing, 113
Scallop-stuffed Sole, 132
Scallops and Vegetables Over Rice, 131
Siam Scallops, 125
Ski Cheese Pie, 153
Spinach Ravioli with Shitake Mushroom Sauce, 88
Stir Fry Chicken and Vegetables over Rice, 116
Stir-fried Beef and Broccoli, 136
Synergy Enchiladas Catalina, 162
Tamale Pie, 114
Turkey Breast Royale, 117
Veal Birds (Stuffed Veal Scallopini), 148
Veal Molinari, 147
Veal with Champagne Sauce, 150
Veal With Vegetables, 151
Vegetable Stromboli with Pizza Dough, 158
Veggie Pizza with Whole Wheat Pizza Dough, 160
White Chili, 118
Mandarin Chicken, 105
Mango Chutney, 206
Manhattan Clam Chowder, 37
Marinated Cauliflower, 57
Marinated Orange Peel, 252
Marinated Shrimp with Herb Mayonnaise, 10
Medallions of Pork with Sauce Charcutière, 143
Mediterranean Sauce, 207
Meringue
   Autumn Meringues, 228
   Meringue Shell, 257
Meringue Shell, 257
Mexican Chicken and Rice, 106
Middle East Chick Pea Dip, 2
Mint
   Cucumber Mint Soup, 35
   Minted Lime Vinaigrette, 122

Minted Lime Vinaigrette, 122
Mock Crème Fraîche, 208
Moroccan Carrot Salad, 58
Mousse
   Espresso-Chocolate Mousse, 237
   Strawberry Mousse in Meringue Shell, 257
Muffins
   Cornbread Muffins, 212
   Harvest Muffins, 218
   Hearty Blueberry Muffins, 219
   Raspberry Bran Muffins, 221
Mushroom Bread Pudding, 181
Mushroom Soup, 38
Mushrooms
   Mushroom Bread Pudding, 181
   Mushroom Soup, 38
   Parsnip Mushroom Soup, 39
   Risotto with Mushrooms, 86
Mushrooms, Porcini
   Penne with Porcini Mushrooms, 85
Mushrooms, Shitake
   Shitake Mushroom Sauce, 88
Mussels
   Broiled Scallops and New Zealand Mussels with Concasse Tomatoes and Minted Lime Vinaigrette, 122
   Mussels in Herbed Vegetable Broth, 12
Mussels in Herbed Vegetable Broth, 12

N

Noodle Kugel, 244
Noodle Soufflé, 80
Noodles
   Noodle Kugel, 244
   Noodle Soufflé, 80
   Oriental Chicken and Noodles, 83
Nutcracker Mart Fruited Rice, 81

O

Oatmeal
   Oatmeal Cranberry Cookies, 245

INDEX

Spicy Oatmeal Cookies, 256
Oatmeal Bread with Cinnamon Pear Butter, 222
Oatmeal Cranberry Cookies, 245
Oils, Hot Pepper
    Hot Pepper Oil, 44
Onion Tart, 20
Onions
    Onion Tart, 20
Orange Chicken, 108
Orange Glaze, 232
Orange Sherbet, 246
Orange Tootsies, 247
Oranges
    Marinated Orange Peel, 252
    Orange Glaze, 232
    Orange Sherbet, 246
    Orange Tootsies, 247
    Oranges Orientales, 248
Oranges Orientales, 248
Orecchiette
    Orecchiette with Tomatoes and Arugula, 82
Orecchiette with Tomatoes and Arugula, 82
Oriental
    Oriental Salad, 55
Oriental Chicken and Noodles, 83
Oriental Spinach, 194
Original Chicken Arabesque, 107
Oven Baked French Fries, 187
Oven-dried Tomatoes, 23
Oven-fried Chicken, 110

P

Pan-seared Spicy Breast of Chicken, 111
Pancakes
    Corn Pancakes with Vegetable Topping, 170
    Cottage Cheese Pancakes, 213
Papaya Relish, 100
Parfaits
    Plum Parfait, 254

Parmesan Artichoke Toast, 21
Parsnip and Carrot Gratin, 182
Parsnip Mushroom Soup, 39
Parsnips
    Parsnip and Carrot Gratin, 182
    Parsnip Mushroom Soup, 39
Pasta
    Tomato Feta Pasta Salad, 67
Pasta - Rice
    Baked Ziti with Spicy Marinara Sauce, 74
    Black Beans with Rice, 73
    Capellini with Grilled Chicken and Tarragon Sauce, 76
    Colorful Linguine Stir Fry, 77
    Faux Fettucine Alfredo, 78
    Greek Couscous Pilaf, 79
    Noodle Soufflé, 80
    Nutcracker Mart Fruited Rice, 81
    Orecchiette with Tomatoes and Arugula, 82
    Oriental Chicken and Noodles, 83
    Penne with Green Beans and Arugula Pesto, 84
    Penne with Porcini Mushrooms, 85
    Risotto with Mushrooms, 86
    Spiced Rice Pilaf, 87
    Spinach Ravioli with Shitake Mushroom Sauce, 88
Peach Coulis, 243
Peach Kiwi Cheesecake, 250
Peach Slush, 249
Peaches
    Peach Coulis, 243
    Peach Kiwi Cheesecake, 250
    Peach Slush, 249
Peapods
    Lemony Peapods, 183
Pear Salad with Dijon Vinaigrette, 59
Pears
    Curried Pears, 236
    Pear Salad with Dijon Vinaigrette, 59
    Pears in Red Wine, 252

INDEX

Pears in Red Wine, 252
Penne
    Penne with Green Beans and Arugula Pesto, 84
    Penne with Porcini Mushrooms, 85
Penne with Green Beans and Arugula Pesto, 84
Penne with Porcini Mushrooms, 85
Peppercorns
    Green Peppercorn Sauce, 205
Peppers, Red
    Red Pepper Soup, 40
Peppy Lima Bean Salad, 60
Pesce al Cartoccio, 128
Pesto
    Arugula Pesto, 84
    Pesto Dip, 3
Pesto Dip, 3
Phyllo
    Apple Strudel with Custard Sauce, 226
    Phyllo Crust, 152
    Quiche Lorraine, 154
    Seafood Strudel, 22
    Ski Cheese Pie, 153
Phyllo Crust, 152
Pies
    Pumpkin Pie, 255
Pilaf
    Greek Couscous Pilaf, 79
    Spiced Rice Pilaf, 87
Pineapple
    Pineapple Cranberry Bars, 253
Pineapple Cranberry Bars, 253
Pinwheel Tenderloin of Beef with Fresh Tomato Sals, 134
Piquant Dressing, 68
Piquant Potato Salad, 61
Pizza Dough, 158
    Pizza Dough, 158
    Whole Wheat Pizza Dough, 160

Player's Artichokes, 164
Plum Parfait, 254
Plums
    Plum Parfait, 254
Poached Salmon with Yogurt Sauce, 130
Pork
    Hornado's Pork, 142
    Medallions of Pork with Sauce Charcutière, 143
    Pork Tenderloin Marco, 144
    Spicy Pork Tenderloin with Lime Mayonnaise, 30
Pork Tenderloin Marco, 144
Potassium Froth, 27
Potato Cakes with Leeks and Gruyère, 188
Potato Rounds with Tapenade, 26
Potatoes
    Cultured Potatoes, 184
    Easy Au Gratin Potatoes, 185
    Garlic Potato Straw Surprise, 186
    Oven Baked French Fries, 187
    Piquant Potato Salad, 61
    Potato Cakes with Leeks and Gruyère, 188
    Potato Rounds with Tapenade, 26
Poulet Presqu'ile, 112
Poultry
    Capellini with Grilled Chicken and Tarragon Sauce, 76
    Chicken Arabesque II, 91
    Chicken Casserole with Brown Rice and Artichokes, 92
    Chicken Loaf, 93
    Chicken Michael, 94
    Chicken Paprikash, 95
    Chicken Roulade with Warm Tarragon Sauce, 96
    Cinnamon Chicken, 98
    Coq au Vin, 99
    Cornish Game Hen in Pine Nut Crust with Papaya Rel, 100
    Enchiladas Verdes, 102
    Grilled Ginger Chicken Patties, 103
    Grilled Marinated Chicken on Oriental Salad, 55
    Las Enchiladas del Pollo, 104

INDEX

Mandarin Chicken, 105
Mexican Chicken and Rice, 106
Orange Chicken, 108
Oriental Chicken and Noodles, 83
Original Chicken Arabesque, 107
Oven-fried Chicken, 110
Pan-seared Spicy Breast of Chicken, 111
Poulet Presqu'ile, 112
Roast Turkey and Stuffing, 113
Stir Fry Chicken and Vegetables over Rice, 116
Tamale Pie, 114
Terrine of Chicken and Herbs, 28
Turkey Breast Royale, 117
White Chili, 118
Provençal Country Bread, 216
Pudding
    Baked Apple and Blackberry Pudding, 229
    Vanilla Pudding, 259
Pumpkin
    Fruited Pumpkin Bread, 215
    Pumpkin Pie, 255
Pumpkin Pie, 255

Q

Quiche
    Quiche Lorraine, 154
Quiche Lorraine, 154

R

Rabbit
    Rabbit Braised in Red Wine, 145
Rabbit Braised in Red Wine, 145
Raisins
    Banana Raisin Bread, 211
Raisins, Golden
    Golden Raisin Coleslaw, 54
Raspberry Bran Muffins, 221
Ravioli
    Spinach Ravioli with Shitake Mushroom Sauce, 88
Red Cabbage
    Red Cabbage in Red Wine, 167

Red Cabbage in Red Wine, 167
Red Pepper Dip, 4
Red Pepper Soup, 40
Rice
    Baked Zucchini and Rice, 200
    Black Beans with Rice, 73
    Nutcracker Mart Fruited Rice, 81
    Spiced Rice Pilaf, 87
    Spinach and Rice, 196
    Tomatoes Stuffed with Rice and Vegetables, 199
Rice, Brown
    Chicken Casserole with Brown Rice and Artichokes, 92
Risotto
    Risotto with Mushrooms, 86
Risotto with Mushrooms, 86
Roast Turkey and Stuffing, 113
Roasted Garlic Lemon Sauce, 209
Rugelachs, 220

S

Salads
    Black Bean, Corn and Tomato Salad, 49
    Black Bean Salad, 126
    Black-eyed Pea Salad, 50
    Cucumber Tomato Salad, 51
    Fattoosh, 52
    Fresh Corn Salad, 53
    Golden Raisin Coleslaw, 54
    Grilled Marinated Chicken on Oriental Salad, 55
    Italian Winter Salad, 56
    Marinated Cauliflower, 57
    Moroccan Carrot Salad, 58
    Oriental Salad, 55
    Pear Salad with Dijon Vinaigrette, 59
    Peppy Lima Bean Salad, 60
    Piquant Potato Salad, 61
    Seafood-stuffed Tomatoes, 62
    Shrimp Salad, 63
    Spicy Chick Pea Relish Salad, 64
    Spicy Corn and Bean Confetti Salad, 65

INDEX

Spinach Salad with Strawberry Vinaigrette, 66
Tomato Feta Pasta Salad, 67
Tuna Salad with Fruit, 70
Tunisian Salad with Piquant Dressing, 68
White Kidney Bean Salad, 71
Salmon
    Gravelax (Cured Salmon), 7
    Poached Salmon with Yogurt Sauce, 130
    Salmon Carpaccio with Frankfurt Green Sauce, 16
Salmon Carpaccio with Frankfurt Green Sauce, 16
Salsa
    Fresh Tomato Salsa, 134
Salsa de Verano, 24
Salsas
    Salsa de Verano, 24
    Salsa Verde, 129
    Summer Salsa, 24
Sauce Charcutière, 143
Sauce Remoulade, 8
Sauces
    Arugula Pesto, 84
    Caramelized Onion and Saffron Vinaigrette, 120
    Champagne Sauce, 150
    Citrus Vinaigrette, 119
    Cucumber Sauce, 157
    Curry Sauce, 166
    Custard Sauce, 226
    Dill Sauce, 14, 203
    Frankfurt Green Sauce, 16
    Fresh Tomato Salsa, 134
    Fresh Tomato Sauce, 204
    Green Peppercorn Sauce, 205
    Herb Mayonnaise, 10
    Herbed Vegetable Broth, 12
    Lime Mayonnaise, 30
    Lime Mousseline Sauce, 18
    Mango Chutney, 206
    Mediterranean Sauce, 207
    Minted Lime Vinaigrette, 122
    Mock Crème Fraîche, 208
    Papaya Relish, 100
    Peach Coulis, 243
    Piquant Dressing, 68
    Roasted Garlic Lemon Sauce, 209
    Salsa de Verano, 24
    Salsa Verde, 129
    Sauce Charcutière, 143
    Sauce Remoulade, 8
    Shitake Mushroom Sauce, 88
    Spicy Marinara Sauce, 74
    Summer Salsa, 24
    Tapenade, 26
    Tarragon Sauce, 76
    Warm Tarragon Sauce, 96
    Yogurt Sauce, 130
    Yogurt-Tahini Sauce, 157
Sautéed Greens, 195
Savory Roasted Carrots with Horseradish, 163
Scallop-stuffed Sole, 132
Scallops
    Broiled Scallops and New Zealand Mussels with Concasse Tomatoes and Minted Lime Vinaigrette, 122
    Grilled Scallops with Black Bean Salad, 126
    Scallop-stuffed Sole, 132
    Scallops and Vegetables Over Rice, 131
    Siam Scallops, 125
Scallops and Vegetables Over Rice, 131
Seafood
    Black Sea Bass Filet With Citrus Vinaigrette, 119
    Blue Corn Pierogies with Potato and Lobster and Carmelized Onion and Saffron Vinaigrette, 120
    Broiled Scallops and New Zealand Mussels with Concasse Tomatoes and Minted Lime Vinaigrette, 122
    Cajun Fish, 123
    Crab Cakes with Sauce Remoulade, 8
    Creole Baked Shrimp, 124
    Gravelax (Cured Salmon), 7
    Grilled Scallops with Black Bean Salad, 126
    Manhattan Clam Chowder, 37
    Marinated Shrimp with Herb Mayonnaise, 10

INDEX

Mussels in Herbed Vegetable Broth, 12
Pesce al Cartoccio, 128
Poached Salmon with Yogurt Sauce, 130
Salmon Carpaccio with Frankfurt Green Sauce, 16
Scallop-stuffed Sole, 132
Scallops and Vegetables Over Rice, 131
Seafood Dip, 5
Seafood Strudel, 22
Seafood-stuffed Tomatoes, 62
Shrimp Salad, 63
Siam Scallops, 125
Smoked Trout with Dill Sauce, 14
Steamed Whole Fish with Lime Mousseline Sauce, 18
Tuna Salad with Fruit, 70
Tuna Tartare, 15
Seafood Dip, 5
Seafood Strudel, 22
Seafood-stuffed Tomatoes, 62
Sherbets
    Champagne Sherbet, 234
    Grape Sherbets, 242
    Orange Sherbet, 246
Shitake Mushroom Sauce, 88
Shrimp
    Creole Baked Shrimp, 124
    Marinated Shrimp with Herb Mayonnaise, 10
    Seafood-stuffed Tomatoes, 62
    Shrimp Salad, 63
Shrimp Salad, 63
Siam Scallops, 125
Ski Cheese Pie, 153
Smoked Trout with Dill Sauce, 14
Sopa De Frijoles Negro, 42
Soufflé
    Zucchini Soufflé, 202
Soup au Pistou, 43
Soups
    Asparagus Soup, 31
    Black Bean Soup, 42
    Carrot Soup, 32

Chlodnik, 33
Cold Vegetable and Yogurt Soup, 33
Corn Chowder, 34
Cucumber Mint Soup, 35
Italian Bread Soup, 36
Manhattan Clam Chowder, 37
Mushroom Soup, 38
Parsnip Mushroom Soup, 39
Red Pepper Soup, 40
Sopa De Frijoles Negro, 42
Soup au Pistou, 43
Spanish Black Bean Soup, 41
Spicy Gazpacho with Hot Pepper Oil, 44
Squash Soup with Lemon and Basil, 46
Summer Fruit Soup, 47
Winter Vegetable Soup, 48
Spanish Black Bean Soup, 41
Spiced Rice Pilaf, 87
Spicy Cabbage, 168
Spicy Chick Pea Relish Salad, 64
Spicy Corn and Bean Confetti Salad, 65
Spicy Gazpacho with Hot Pepper Oil, 44
Spicy Marinara Sauce, 74
Spicy Oatmeal Cookies, 256
Spicy Pork Tenderloin with Lime Mayonnaise, 30
Spinach
    Crustless Spinach Pie, 193
    Oriental Spinach, 194
    Sautéed Greens, 195
    Spinach and Rice, 196
    Spinach Dip, 6
    Spinach Ravioli with Shitake Mushroom Sauce, 88
    Spinach Salad with Strawberry Vinaigrette, 66
    Spinach Stew, 197
Spinach and Rice, 196
Spinach Dip, 6
Spinach Ravioli with Shitake Mushroom Sauce, 88
Spinach Salad with Strawberry Vinaigrette, 66
Spinach Stew, 197
Squash
    Squash Soup with Lemon and Basil, 46

INDEX

Squash Soup with Lemon and Basil, 46
Steamed Whole Fish with Lime Mousseline Sauce, 18
Stir Fry Cabbage, 169
Stir Fry Chicken and Vegetables over Rice, 116
Stir-fried Beef and Broccoli, 136
Strawberries
    Strawberry Mousse in Meringue Shell, 257
Strawberry Mousse in Meringue Shell, 257
Strawberry Vinaigrette, 66
Strudel
    Apple Strudel with Custard Sauce, 226
    Seafood Strudel, 22
Substitution Guide, 276
Summer Fruit Soup, 47
Summer Salsa, 24
Sweet Potato and Lemon Purée, 190
Sweet Potato Fries, 191
Sweet Potatoes
    Baked Sweet Potatoes and Apricots, 189
    Sweet Potato and Lemon Purée, 190
    Sweet Potato Fries, 191
Synergy Enchiladas Catalina, 162

T

Tahini
    Oriental Chicken and Noodles, 83
    Yogurt-Tahini Sauce, 157
Tamale Pie, 114
Tapenade, 26
Tarragon
    Warm Tarragon Sauce, 96
Terrine of Chicken and Herbs, 28
Tian of Eggplant, Yellow Squash and Yellow Peppers, 177
Tipsy Bananas, 258
Tiramisu, 260
To Die For
    Avgolemono Soup, 263
    Broccolini, 264
    Decadent Cake, 265
    Delice au Chocolat, 266

Disappearing Brownies, 267
Filled Zucchini Flowers, 268
Italian Stuffed Shells, 269
Lasagna, 270
Mexican Queso Dip, 272
Poached Eggs with Truffle Cream, 273
Roasted Spicy Chicken Wings, 274
Sinful Salad, 275
Tomato Feta Pasta Salad, 67
Tomatoes
    Black Bean, Corn and Tomato Salad, 49
    Cucumber Tomato Salad, 51
    Fresh Tomato Sauce, 204
    Orecchiette with Tomatoes and Arugula, 82
    Oven-dried Tomatoes, 23
    Seafood-stuffed Tomatoes, 62
    Tomato Feta Pasta Salad, 67
    Tomatoes Provençales, 198
    Tomatoes Stuffed with Rice and Vegetables, 199
Tomatoes Provençales, 198
Tomatoes Stuffed with Rice and Vegetables, 199
Toppings
    Vegetable Topping, 170
Trifle
    Fruit Trifle, 240
Trout
    Smoked Trout with Dill Sauce, 14
Tuna
    Tuna Salad with Fruit, 70
    Tuna Tartare, 15
Tuna Salad with Fruit, 70
Tuna Tartare, 15
Tunisian Salad with Piquant Dressing, 68
Turkey
    Roast Turkey and Stuffing, 113
    Turkey Breast Royale, 117

INDEX

Turkey Breast Royale, 117

V

Vanilla Pudding, 259
Veal, 151
    Grilled Veal Chops with Salad Greens, 146
    Veal Birds (Stuffed Veal Scallopini), 148
    Veal Molinari, 147
    Veal with Champagne Sauce, 150
    Veal With Vegetables, 151
Veal Birds (Stuffed Veal Scallopini), 148
Veal Molinari, 147
Veal Scallopini
    Veal Birds (Stuffed Veal Scallopini), 148
Veal with Champagne Sauce, 150
Veal With Vegetables, 151
Vegetable Stromboli with Pizza Dough, 158
Vegetables
    Baked Sweet Potatoes and Apricots, 189
    Baked Zucchini and Rice, 200
    Braised Celery, 173
    Broccoli with Curry Sauce, 166
    Buddha's Delight, 179
    Corn Pancakes with Vegetable Topping, 170
    Crustless Spinach Pie, 193
    Cultured Potatoes, 184
    Dennis Nahat's Stewed Eggplant, 174
    Easy Au Gratin Potatoes, 185
    Eggplant Mozzarella, 175
    Eggplant Stuffing, 176
    Fennel Paysanne, 178
    Fresh Corn Casserole, 172
    Garlic Potato Straw Surprise, 186
    Herbed Mixed Vegetables, 180
    Lemony Peapods, 183
    Mushroom Bread Pudding, 181
    Oriental Spinach, 194
    Oven Baked French Fries, 187
    Parsnip and Carrot Gratin, 182
    Player's Artichokes, 164
    Potato Cakes with Leeks and Gruyère, 188
    Red Cabbage in Red Wine, 167
    Sautéed Greens, 195
    Savory Roasted Carrots with Horseradish, 163
    Spicy Cabbage, 168
    Spinach and Rice, 196
    Spinach Stew, 197
    Stir Fry Cabbage, 169
    Sweet Potato and Lemon Purée, 190
    Sweet Potato Fries, 191
    Tian of Eggplant, Yellow Squash and Yellow Peppers, 177
    Tomatoes Provençales, 198
    Tomatoes Stuffed with Rice and Vegetables, 199
    Yams with Dried Fruit, 192
    Zucchini Luis, 201
    Zucchini Soufflé, 202
Veggie Pizza with Whole Wheat Pizza Dough, 160
Vinaigrettes
    Caramelized Onion and Saffron Vinaigrette, 120
    Citrus Vinaigrette, 119
    Dijon Vinaigrette, 59
    Minted Lime Vinaigrette, 122
    Strawberry Vinaigrette, 66

W

Warm Tarragon Sauce, 96
White Chili, 118
White Kidney Bean Salad, 71
Whole Wheat Pizza Dough, 160
Winter Vegetable Soup, 48

Y

Yams
    Yams with Dried Fruit, 192
Yams with Dried Fruit, 192
Yeast Breads
    Crostini, 214
    Fougasse - Provençal Country Bread, 216

Yogurt Sauce, 130
Yogurt-Tahini Sauce, 157

Z

Zabaglione
    Fruit Baked with Zabaglione, 239
Ziti
    Baked Ziti with Spicy Marinara Sauce, 74
Zucchini
    Baked Zucchini and Rice, 200
    Zucchini Luis, 201
    Zucchini Soufflé, 202
Zucchini Luis, 201
Zucchini Soufflé, 202

Supporters

Aladdin's Baking Company
1301 Carnegie Avenue
Cleveland, Ohio 44115
(216) 861-0317
Located near Gateway, the Committee use Aladdin Pita made on our premises for their falafel recipe and our lavash bread for their lavash sandwiches. We also carry sumac used in the fattoosh recipe.

Á La Noodle
20123 Van Aken Boulevard
Shaker Heights, Ohio 44122
(216) 283-1800
A contemporary noodle house featuring a wide variety of pastas. Chicken dishes, salads and wines by the glass are available.

Cleveland Tile and Cabinet Company
19560 Center Ridge Road
Rocky River, Ohio 44116
(216) 331-2088
For over 60 years, one of Cleveland's oldest and most respected kitchen and bathroom remodelers.

Fruit Baskets by Maury
3212 West 25th Street
Cleveland, Ohio 44109
(216) 741-5117
Aidells turkey and chicken sausages are available from Fruit Baskets by Maury.

Gallucci's Italian Foods
6610 Euclid Avenue
Cleveland, Ohio 44103
(216) 881-0045
Specialty foods, olive oils, balsamic vinegars, pastas and wines; the perfect place to find all your gourmet needs.

Great Lakes Lithograph Company
4005 Clark Avenue
Cleveland, Ohio 44109
(216) 651-1500

Impiria Foods
234 St. Nicholas Avenue
South Plainfield, New Jersey 07080
(908) 756-7333
The Committee endorses the use of our Lite Parmesan Cheese in their Oven-fried Chicken and our Lite Romano Cheese in their Baked Ziti with Spicy Marinara Sauce.

KCJ Vanilla Co.
c/o Cleveland Ballet Council
One Playhouse Square, Suite 330
1375 Euclid Avenue
Cleveland, Ohio 44115
KCJ's double strength, 100% pure vanilla. "Fabulous Unique Vanillas" - Food and Wine, 5/94. Order Vanilla Sampler - 2 oz. each of: Tahitian 2x, Mexican 2x and Bourbon 2x. Send check for $15.50 plus $4.00 shipping and handling made payable to KCJ Vanilla Co.

Mario's International Spa & Hotel
35 East Garfield Road
Aurora, Ohio 44202
(216) 656-2439
Close to home and work–but far from stress. Mario's International voted "Top 10 U. S. Spas" in 1993.

Miceli Dairy Products Company
2721 East 90th Street
Cleveland, Ohio 44104
(216) 791-6222
Manufacturers of fine Italian cheese: Ricotta, Mozzarella, Provolone and Bocconcini.

Player's on Larchmere
13114 Larchmere Boulevard
Cleveland, Ohio 44120
(216) 283-7529
Cleveland's premier trattoria.

Player's on Madison
14523 Madison Avenue
Lakewood, Ohio 44107
(216) 226-5200

Quail Hollow Resort & Country Club
11080 Concord-Hambden Road
Concord, Ohio 44077
(216) 352-6201
Luxury in the country...for conventions of 400 or a weekend for two, Quail Hollow is Ohio's finest resort.

**The Restaurant
at the Ritz-Carlton, Cleveland**
1515 West Third Street
Cleveland, Ohio 44113
(216) 623-1300
Contemporary continental cuisine combined with casual elegance for breakfast, lunch and dinner. The Lobby Lounge serves afternoon tea, cocktails and desserts.

Royal Pacific
13215 Shaker Square
Cleveland, Ohio 44120
(216) 751-1550
Pacific Rim, Chinese and Japanese cuisine. Sushi bar, daily entertainment, weekend jazz and Sunday brunch in an exciting contemporary setting.

Somrak Kitchens, Inc.
26201 Richmond Road
Bedford Heights, Ohio 44146
(216) 464-6500
Custom Cabinet Design Center. Visit our showroom.

Sweetwater's Café Sausalito
The Galleria at Erieview
Cleveland, Ohio 44114
(216) 696-2233
The showplace of fun dining.

The Thomas Brick Company
27750 Chagrin Boulevard
Cleveland, Ohio 44122
(216) 831-9116
A complete selection of architectural brick and unique tiles. Handmade and custom painted tiles of superb craftsmanship produced both domestically and abroad.

Acknowledgments

Debbie Abdalian-Thompson
Sandra Abookire
Dr. Mariella Alfidi
Toby Alfred
Dee Altig
Frank Andorka
Diane Andrica
Frances Andrica
John Andrica
Diana Armstrong
Judith E. Auletta
Judy Bailey-Archer
Cathy Baluch
Chuck Bednar
Linda L. Bradley
Barbara Brennen
Gerald J. Breen
Kathy Breen
Carolyn Brinkley
Rita Buchanan
Elisa Budoff
Margaret E. Burgess
E. John Busser
Lonnie Butts
Café Brio
Calorie Gallery
Barbara Campbell
Loretta Campbell
Karen Caponi
Patricia Cornacchione
Linda Tuley Carpenter
Dottie Clark
Classics
Mary Colarik
Kathy Coleman
Halle Conner
Melanie Corcoran
Karen Doll
Embassy Suites Hotel
Gwen Emery
En Provence
Anne Everson
Fabulous Feasts
Fandango
Fern F. Felice
Ida Felice
Tootsie Felice
Candy Fiero
Marilyn Finkel
Lynda Fisco
Kathy G. Fleegler
Helen Foley
Margaret Furry
Rebecca B. Gelfman
Norma Glazer
Mariann Grdina
Fran Golden
Grace Gordon
Bettyann S. Gorman
Barbara Gracey
Donna Washington Gracon
Great Lakes Lithograph
Evelyn Greene
Ned Grieg
Gretchen Hamann
Susan Hannebrink
Chavanne B. Hanson
Iris Harvie
Kathleen M. Hazelton
Elizabeth Heller
Jane Herget
Jim Hoffman
Nancy Hoffman
Joanne Hughes
Johnny's Downtown
Ruth Kanner
Kathryn Karlovitch
Irene Kazura
Christine de Kergariou
Susan Krajewski
Universe Krist
Jean Krizman
Carol LaMalfa
Nancy LaMantia
Pamela LaMantia
Debbie Latson
Donna Ledin
Diane Lewis
Donna Lipson
Mary Anne Lucas
Barbara Maikut
Tracy Maroon-Kelly
Janis L. McLaughlin
Mildred McLaughlin
William McLaughlin
Joan McVeen
Marina Melnik
Paulette E. Mentler
Linda Meyer
Bonnie Miller
Molinari's
Cesar Munoz
Dennis Nahat
Nate's Deli & Restaurant
Luis Negrete
Chrys Newell
Nina O'Hern
Ako Okushima
Ann Olszewski
Agnes T. Orringer, M.D.
Madeleine Parker
Patrick Parker
Madame Peri
Donna Pestotnik
Pat Peters
Teresa Phillips
Piperade
Florence Pollack
Carol Provan
Barbara Pugel
Anah Pytte
Rochelle Reeves
JoAnn Remington
Rose Marie Rosalina
Dede Rose
Michael Salkind
Joann Schenkelberg
Janie Sexton
Sheraton City Center Grill
Elaine Sodowski
Stancato's
Kathleen Stenson
Lee Anne S. Stueber
Jean Rothgery Sullivan
Jean Sustar
The Inn at Brandywine Falls
The Inn at Turner's Mill
The Loretta Paganini School of Cooking
Thomson & Thomson
Jean L. Triner
Tanya Tuffuor
University Synergy
Gale Vazquez
The Watermark
Marlene Wedren
Janet Weimann
Mrs. Harry Weiner
Barbara Wheeler
Ruth Wylie
Victoria Windle
Sheila Wyse
Deborah Yeager
Bob Yun

Order Forms

Please send me Cleveland Ballet Council's *Light Kitchen Choreography: A Collection of Lower-fat Recipes to Benefit Cleveland Ballet.*

NAME _____

ADDRESS _____

CITY _____

STATE, ZIP _____

DAY PHONE (_____) _____

Price: $19.95. In Ohio, add 7% sales tax. Please add a shipping and handling fee of $3.00 for each book. (Special postage and handling rates apply to quantities over 25 units. Call Cleveland Ballet Council at 216-621-2260 to inquire.)

QUANTITY _____ x $19.95 EACH =	
(IN OHIO) 7% SALES TAX	
$3 SHIPPING AND HANDLING PER BOOK	
TOTAL	

Method of Payment

☐ Check ☐ Visa ☐ MasterCard

CARD# _____

EXPIRATION DATE _____

SIGNATURE _____

Make checks payable to *Cleveland Ballet Council.*

Mail this order form and your check to:
Cleveland Ballet Council
One Playhouse Square, Suite 330
1375 Euclid Avenue
Cleveland, Ohio 44115

Proceeds benefit Cleveland Ballet.
Please allow 3-4 weeks for delivery.

Please send me Cleveland Ballet Council's *Light Kitchen Choreography: A Collection of Lower-fat Recipes to Benefit Cleveland Ballet.*

NAME _____

ADDRESS _____

CITY _____

STATE, ZIP _____

DAY PHONE (_____) _____

Price: $19.95. In Ohio, add 7% sales tax. Please add a shipping and handling fee of $3.00 for each book. (Special postage and handling rates apply to quantities over 25 units. Call Cleveland Ballet Council at 216-621-2260 to inquire.)

QUANTITY _____ x $19.95 EACH =	
(IN OHIO) 7% SALES TAX	
$3 SHIPPING AND HANDLING PER BOOK	
TOTAL	

Method of Payment

☐ Check ☐ Visa ☐ MasterCard

CARD# _____

EXPIRATION DATE _____

SIGNATURE _____

Make checks payable to *Cleveland Ballet Council.*

Mail this order form and your check to:
Cleveland Ballet Council
One Playhouse Square, Suite 330
1375 Euclid Avenue
Cleveland, Ohio 44115

Proceeds benefit Cleveland Ballet.
Please allow 3-4 weeks for delivery.